ON THE EDGE: (AUTO)BIOGRAPHY AND PEDAGOG
RELIGIOUS EDUCATION

On the Edge: (Auto)biography and Pedagogical Theories on Religious Education

Edited by

Ina ter Avest
Vrije Universiteit, Amsterdam, The Netherlands

SENSE PUBLISHERS
ROTTERDAM / BOSTON / TAIPEI

A C.I.P. record for this book is available from the Library of Congress.

ISBN 978-94-6209-173-3 (paperback)
ISBN 978-94-6209-174-0 (hardback)
ISBN 978-94-6209-175-7 (e-book)

Published by: Sense Publishers,
P.O. Box 21858, 3001 AW Rotterdam, The Netherlands
https://www.sensepublishers.com/

Printed on acid-free paper

TABLE OF CONTENTS

JOHN HULL

FOREWORD

*I do not like large comfortable armchairs
because the front edge of the seat is soft
and it is difficult to perch there.
I prefer a hard, upright chair
so I can squat on the very edge*

Members of my family sometimes tease me about a curious habit I seem to have developed. I like to sit on the very edge of my chair. I do not like large comfortable armchairs because the front edge of the seat is soft and it is difficult to perch there. I prefer a hard, upright chair so I can squat on the very edge. My family say "Why don't you sit back, and just relax? Aren't you uncomfortable?" But I prefer to be on the edge.

As I read your publications, I realise that you are a bit like this yourself. Your work over several decades includes contributions to the psychology of religion, the sociology of religious belonging, the history and development of religious education, pedagogical and curriculum studies from various points of view, and above all your interest in the lives of your students and colleagues. When I consider this achievement in the light of religious education in Europe as a whole, I see that you are very much a frontier thinker, and always on the edge.

In paying tribute to your work, it is not surprising to find that your colleagues have decided to write about the close connection between their own biographies and their professional work. They deal with this from many perspectives, some emphasising the significance of their own childhood and upbringing, often in religious family life, while others concentrate upon the academic influences which have shaped their thinking. But I will not anticipate here in any detail what they have to say.

As I introduce this volume, it seems appropriate that I also should follow the lead given by most of the contributors, and say something about the development of my own work, as a religious educator and more recently a theological educator. The institution in which I now work has honoured me with the title 'Professor of Practical Theology' and as I look back upon my life and work, it strikes me that I have never worked in anything else but practical theology. As I understand it, practical theology is concerned with the frontier between the Church and the world, between Christian faith and society. Education as a whole, including religious education, forms a significant aspect of this. My major concern has always been to link contemporary developments in religious education with Christian faith. The urgency and challenge of this task have arisen from the process of development that religious education in England, and indeed in north-western Europe as a whole, has been passing through during the past 50 or 60 years.

My first experience of teaching religion was in secondary schools in Melbourne even before I had trained as a teacher. Religious education in state schools was provided by teams of voluntary instructors, since the regular teachers were not allowed to deal with it. The classes I took usually lasted for about half an hour, either at the beginning or the ending of the school day, so as not to interrupt the official curriculum. Armed with a piano accordion and a repertoire of exciting Bible stories, I conducted these classes as evangelistic meetings, doing my best to interest the sceptical teenagers, who viewed me with a mixture of hilarity, fascination and awe, but on the whole more hilarity than awe. I had not distinguished the school classroom from the mission on the beach. To me, the school was just one more opportunity to proclaim the Gospel.

I came to England in 1959 to study theology, and after three years, finding to my dismay that the collapse of my evangelical faith prevented me from returning to Australia to enter the Methodist ministry, I resumed my work teaching religious education. I soon discovered that the subject was still in the tradition of Christian piety, although on a much more professional basis, and without the piano accordion. The content, however, was basically stories from the Old Testament in the first year, the life of Jesus in the second year, the journeys of Paul and some missionary heroes in the third year, and so on. Although still seeking to nurture the faith of the students, religious education was already passing from the pietistic strand of the European Enlightenment into a more critical approach to religion. World religions and ethical problems were soon introduced and over the next 30 or 40 years the subject moved from the context of a decaying Christendom through modernity to post-modernity.

At every stage this threefold development was greeted with controversy. Whether it was about educational norms replacing Christian nurture or the later full impact of pluralism, lifestyles and changing social attitudes, religious education seemed always to be on the edge. Was it sacred or secular? Was it education or indoctrination? Was it to be related to Church or state?

In the sixties the controversies in England surrounded the question of life themes versus Bible teaching, in the seventies the problems of phenomenology took centre stage, and in the eighties the huge conservative reaction required a militant defence of religious education as a critical, descriptive religious discipline making a valuable contribution to student values while remaining faithful to religion itself. From the early 1990s until the present time, the focus of attention has been more upon pedagogy although the task of explaining and defending the distinctions between religious education and religious nurture seems never-ending. The question of the relationship between religion and this kind of pluralistic religious education has been further complicated by the naturalisation of Islam as a European faith.

The religious educators of north-western Europe have created something of cultural significance and social value. We have shown how the religions of the world can become a resource to enrich the growing lives of children and young people, challenging their values, and preparing them for intelligent citizenship in the modern world. No other subject does this with such intimate care for children's lives, such careful handling of the spiritual traditions and such relevance to community reconciliation. The most significant aspect of my own contribution has been the attempt to show that a self-critical Christian faith can support these trends, enriching them whilst also being enriched. Teachers committed to Christian faith discovered that they could teach world religions not in spite of their faith but because of it. Theology of education can take its place alongside the other aspects of the study of education, dealing not only with the teaching of religion but with the wider questions about educational aims and the values involved in the teaching of other school subjects.

I am conscious of the fact that my life has been lived on frontiers in more senses than those related to professional education. Brought up in Australia but spending most of my working life in England, I have always been slightly removed from the social class ethos of these two countries. More significant has been the fact that well into adult life I was a sighted person and for the past 30 years have been totally blind. The problem of being on the frontier between sight and blindness, having been in both states, has been for me the most problematic encounter of my life. Although I have some idea of how this has affected my personal Christian faith, I find it more difficult to say how it has affected my work in education. Of course, the impact upon relationships, particularly with younger children, was immediate and profound. Not being able to see the faces of children when they are listening to a story is a loss that no ingenuity can overcome.

In a more general sense, I think that becoming a member of the disabled community, and especially immersed in the curious ambiguities of the blind condition, has sensitised me to the problems of all minority groups and given me a feeling of solidarity with all categories of marginalised people. Perhaps this has made me more sharply aware of the problems of justice, dialogue and inclusion in schools, and it has also made me realise more deeply the close connection between the personal life of the teacher and the content and style of teaching.

This brings us back to the purpose and context of this set of essays. Much of the vitality of religious education in Europe springs from the fact that many of its leading figures have experienced personally the challenges of faith in the midst of secular pluralism, and the threat to humanitarian values of a world dominated by money. Reading these pages one is impressed by the transforming impact of contact with poverty, the scarring impact of tension within one's own community of faith, and the stimulating effect of always having to explain and defend one's work to sceptical colleagues.

It only remains for me to thank you, Siebren, for your own personal kindness to me and to thank you on behalf of all the contributors to this volume for your own inspirational leadership, helping us to cross many of these boundaries and to remain on the edge without losing our balance.

John M. Hull
The Queen's Foundation for Ecumenical Theological Education
December 2012

INA TER AVEST

ON THE EDGE:
A BIOGRAPHICAL APPROACH TO PEDAGOGICAL
THEORY DEVELOPMENT

*The 'making of' Pedagogical Theories on Religious Education and
Citizenship Education*

INTRODUCTION

Life on earth is a given, living together is a human construction

In this contribution, at the start of a volume of biographical narratives of leading
scholars in the field of the pedagogy of religion and citizenship – or as Siebren
Miedema prefers to call it: the pedagogy of religious citizenship – I will focus on
the concept of narrativity and the role of stories in the biography and the
development of a personal and professional identity. In her dissertation Swennen
quotes Holland et al. (1998) who describe identity in the following way:

> Identity is what people tell others who they are, but even more important,
> they tell themselves who they are and then try to act as though they are
> who they say they are. These self-understandings, especially those with
> strong emotional resonance for the teller, are what we refer to as identities.
> (Holland et al., 1998, p. 3, in: Swennen, 2012, p. 38)

It is this description of identity, with its central focus on 'telling' that I would like
the reader to keep in mind when reading the following paragraphs.

First I elaborate on the concept of 'stories' or 'narratives' and the development
in their meaning and role. Then in the second paragraph I come back to the concept
of 'identity' and point to the pivotal importance of an audience in telling who you
are. The third paragraph is dedicated to the fragmentation, or the multi-voicedness
of the construction of identity these days – in contrast to a given identity of earlier
days. The development of identity in psychology is the focus of the fourth
paragraph. Nowadays in developmental psychology identity development is seen
as a prospective development, in contrast with earlier conceptions of retrospective
identity development. However, in the last paragraph I will tentatively conclude
that – after having read the contributions in this volume – at the end of the day the
development of a personal and professional identity and the construction of an
authentic theoretical perspective looking back seems to be more a 'given' than I'd
ever like to admit, and is far better understood in terms of retrospective
development than in terms of prospective development. The reader is invited to

*I. ter Avest (ed.), On the Edge: (Auto)biography and Pedagogical Theories on Religious
Education, 1–10.*

come to an own conclusion after having shared the narratives of the scholars who contribute to this volume.

A STORY TO TELL

The concept of narrativity finds its origin in contentious jurisdiction (De Haas, 1999, p. 2; Ganzevoort & Visser, in: Steegman, 1993, p. 9). The concept of narrativity in the first place relates to telling an audience the facts of an exceptional event in a well-described context involving specific persons. Informing listeners in earlier days was a verbal act, heavily relying on rhetorics, the art of convincing people by eloquent and convincing speech acts (Toulmin, in: Kunneman, 2005, p. 39 ff.). The story always was about 'particular people in specific situations dealing with concrete cases where varied things were at stake' (ibid., p. 40). The story in that situation has the function of finding out the truth of what happened in that specific concrete situation. The focus is on practical and context-related knowledge. The starting point in this line of thought is the correspondence between the facts and the story; something happens resulting in something else and these two happenings are sequentially brought together in the time-span of the story. In the story the event is copied and the facts of an objective world re-presented, including the 'condition humaine'. The structure of the story in itself is already an interpretation of what happened and makes the events meaningful, which makes the role of the storyteller pivotal (Benjamin, in: Ankersmit et al., 1990, p. 12). Characteristic for this kind of representation of the facts is its teleological frame of reference. Facts, their value and their meaning are undivided (McIntyre, in: Haas, 1999, 142 ff.). The description of the facts and their meaning come together in the narrative; they can be distinguished but are undividable. For the addressees in earlier days it is unquestioned that factual incidents and situations will eventually lead to the completion of creation. What happens to a person in that specific concrete situation for them is part of a Great Narrative in an ongoing process culminating in an ultimate situation of peacefully living together. The Great Narrative is central in the story and expresses everlasting virtues and values – unconditional imbuing a person's life.

Emplotting Critical Incidents

In earlier days the centrality of a Great Narrative as well as the connection between facts and story was accepted as a general basic assumption – for the community as for any individual in. The idea of an ongoing process following a person's historical life span though, is challenged by the psychologist Bruner. "I want to assert that an autobiography is not and cannot be a way of simply signifying or referring to a 'life as lived'" (Bruner, 1995, p. 161). Bruner draws attention to the fact that a person starts to tell a story the moment that this ongoing process is disturbed. The moment that the world in its familiar emergence is shaken by drastic situations with far-reaching consequences, a person gets in need of an interpretation of the at first sight unintelligible events, according to Bruner; in need of a sense of causality and continuity in one's life. In that case a historical or scientific report does not account in a satisfying way to what happened, or to put it more clear: to the situation or the events as they are perceived and received by the person(s) involved. Only a narrative account does justice to the subjective reception of the facts. Only an encompassing narration can provide a new interpretation and a new emplotment for the actual 'strange' situation; not only the actual situation is included in the narrative, also situations form the past might need another response and might necessitate to be emplotted in a new story due to the disturbance caused by the drastic situation. The plot of the narrative gives meaning to the events emplotted; the plot includes what is important yet threatened with exclusion because of its opaqueness and incomprehensibility (Kunneman, 2005, p. 226).

Just imagine, a person walking the same street, meeting the same neighbours at exactly the same time every day, has no story to tell. But the very day one of those neighbours approaches this person, and stops him saying "You know what? The Queen is coming to our place since this neighbourhood is exemplified for the whole country as 'the place to be' due to tight networks of social cohesion" – that very day this person will come home and will say to the other family members: "I can tell you something." 'Critical incidents' like this force people to integrate the disturbing event or situation in their life view and life orientation.

A person's life orientation is part of and situated in contextually related stories, 'folk tales', including 'practical wisdom' as this emerged from many real life experiences urging people to make sense of their life. An overall umbrella, the plot of a story, brings back the continuity in a person's life and the discontinuity caused by the 'critical incident'. 'Emplotting' of a 'critical incident' is part and parcel of a person's meaning-making process. Emplotting is the process that bridges the tension raised by the contrasting experience of discontinuity in a course of life characterized by historical continuity.

Look who's telling! The audience, to whom a story is told, is a very influential factor in focussing and shaping the narrative. As said above: the description of the facts and the structure that is given to the story in itself is an interpretation. This interpretation is not univocal. The storyteller in the narrative discloses her or his own point of view, the way the person perceives 'the other' in the current of events. Childhood memories and tensions are part of the new story. Profession related stories, like the ones in this volume, express the uniqueness of an individual and explain what guides the person in the way dilemma's are solved and explicates the meaning given to the solution that is reached (cf. Meijers & Lengelle, 2012, p. 2). However, there is always an other story to tell – there are many stories to tell triggered by the same event. In the example given above, it might be the arrival of the Queen that will be accentuated for a member of the family, but it could as well be the aspect of social cohesion for the neighbours as listeners or it might be that for the addressees 'tomorrow' is accentuated – contrasting the event to today's life 'as usual'. Professional story telling is a practice 'on the edge' of articulating and negotiating different possible positions. The story told is received in a whole world of symbols, odour, colour, gestures, and actions that are full of meaning. Sharing a story with different addressees strengthens certain aspects in the story, and might bring about different ways of structuring the story.

Look who's listening! Listening to a story is a process of de- and re-construction. The produced text has to be adapted into a received text (Hahn, 1993, in: Steegman & Visser, p. 110). Listening to a story, active restructuring already developed mental images, is hard working! In the first place the listener cuts the story into pieces that are easily digestible. This process of fragmenting is a selection process in which certain fragments are set apart as recognisable, challenging or meaningless for the moment. The perception and reception of the story is highly dependent on the person's cultural (including religious) experiences in early life and during the life span development. 'Significant others' shape imprints in our childhood memories and provided us with artifacts that carry meaning.

The produced text is transformed into the received text – a different received text in the mind of each listener. Sharing received texts challenges each person's understanding of the text. The fit between the produced text and the received text is called the 'recognizable analogy' (Hahn, 1993, p. 111). The better the 'recognizable analogy' of the chosen fragments, the better the reader can integrate these parts of the text into an own reconstruction of the text as part of the own narrative. The listener's frame of reference and earlier experiences are leading in the process of de- and re-construction of the story. However, in this process the storyteller influences the listener by structuring the story .

Her/His-story and the Story

Not only the audience is decisive in the re-construction of the event into a story, also the teller him/her self is of pivotal importance; s/he makes it her or his story respectively, responding to a question, an encounter with a colleague or to an other interruptive situation. A student in History might articulate in her story the historical context of the neighbourhood as an area in town where from way back social cohesion in the sense of 'duty to one's neighbours' has been part and parcel of life. For a fan of the Royal Family the visit of the Queen will be the central part of the story, probably even elaborating on details of her dress and the hat the Queen will wear. And another person might articulate the importance of the role of a King in the history of a nation. This person might make use of other narrations about Kings' visits as an example of the symbolic meaning of such a visit. In this case, the other narrations referred to are not mere illustrations of a royal visit, but are model of and a model for the way a King pays attention to the wellbeing of the subjects of the kingdom and represents 'caring' as an aspect of the leading elite represented by the King. The examples of Kings visiting their subjects in that case are de-contextualized in order to be re-contextualized in the actual situation of the own neighbourhood. The storyteller in the re-construction makes a backward movement (to a certain extent imitating the model) in order to move forward (re-telling the facts in the actual situation). The way de- and re-construction takes place depends on the perception and reception of 'the facts' by the storyteller. Narrative structures incorporate the storyteller in the wider cultural context of which teller and listener, sender and receiver of the story, are part of.

Telling a story is more than repeating facts, as we have seen above. The story also may incite to actions. If we celebrate a birthday and somebody says 'Drinks are finished', this remark points to the fact that somebody should bring some more drinks. Whether or not somebody really gets more drinks for the guests depends on the position and the authority of the person who pointed to the empty glasses. The fact that words have the power to evoke emotions and to incite actions is true not only for spoken words but also for written texts. A written text, like the texts in this volume, has the power to call for associations and evoke readers' images and memories. This relationship between text and reader is a mutual relationship. I as a reader of a text have my own associations and interpretations, the text in itself steers the direction of the links in my memories. Reading a love letter evokes different emotions and memories than an advertisement, which differs from the associations reading a tax assessment. Texts are not only subjected to the memories of the reader; texts also evoke associations that reach further than the concrete situations described. Texts have the power to disclose worlds, new and future worlds, and as such introduce the reader to yet unknown ways of living and incite the reader to new actions (cf. Ganzevoort & Visser, in: Steegman & Visser, 1993, p. 21).

LIFE SPAN DEVELOPMENT

A narrative is characterized by characters that live through certain events within a certain time span. A biographical narrative is characterized by a leading character, undergoing certain experiences during their life span. In these experiences different voices are heard; different persons or certain events function as 'critical persons', or 'critical events' in the sense that in retrospect they are perceived as very influential for the line in her or his story of the life span. An autobiographical story makes use of historical aspects situated in a cultural context and displays on the one hand a personal interpretation of situations and events in the course of life, on the other hand gives insight in the way a person situates her or himself amidst others. In an autobiographical narration the storyteller is subject as well as object; the storyteller that tells about her or himself at the same time reveals her or his identity. There is a mutual relation between history, the interpretation of history and the personal life story (her-/his-story) resulting in a narrative identity (cf. Ricoeur, 1985, p. 442).

Life span development and identity construction starts the moment a baby is born; or maybe even before the moment the new born baby cries its first cry. Since from the very first day the mother is pregnant, the child is adopted into a world that is already there. A mother and a father and their ambitions in their professional life, as well as grandparents and their achievements in life, are a given; a whole family with its social-economic status, the ethnic and religious family background, the historical context – it's all there and this all together constitutes the ecological

5

context of the child's development. In the ecological pedagogy of Urie Bronfenbrenner, life span development includes the different contexts the child enters as s/he grows older; contexts that have a certain influence on the child's development, contexts that in their turn are affected by the child's manipulative power. Following the line of thought of Bronfenbrenner, the change from one context to another (from the family context to the context of day-care or nursery school) is stressful and stress-provoking. However, this stress according to Bronfenbrenner is needed as a stimulus for children to grow and flourish.

Narrative Identity

The Dutch psychologist Breeuwsma, elaborating on the line of thought of the Russian psychologist Vygotsky, points to the fact that development takes place due to biological, psychological or sociological changes in the context of the child – the inner context (e.g. physical growth) or the outer context (changes in the micro-, meso- or macro system of the child). Breeuwsma describes four main factors extensively (Breeuwsma, 1993). In the first place Breeuwsma mentions physical growth as an influential factor in life span development. The growth of for example the brain, and the growth of muscles giving the child physical strength and power are influential factors in life span development and identity development. What a child can do, constitutes the identity at a certain age. "I can climb a tree" is an important contribution to a positive self image. Next to that, Breeuwsma mentions in the second place the historical and cultural context in which a child is born and which makes the child belong to an age cohort or a generation. This age cohort determines to a large extent the life span development. In the Dutch context we speak of 'the baby boom generation' whose life span development is to a high extend influenced by the post-war reconstruction of the Netherlands. We also speak of 'the generation X', 'the generation Nix', 'the lost generation', and 'the Einstein generation'. Each of these generations represents a certain ideology and life style, and the other way around the life style of such a generation establishes an imprint on people that are included in such a cohort. In the third place Breeuwsma pays attention to age-unrelated and history-independent factors that determine the life span development, for example the death of a baby brother or the change from one country to an other (migrant stories). And last but not least Breeuwsma mentions the different contexts in which the child lives and functions in different roles: at home the daughter or son of the parents, at school a pupil amidst peers, at the sports club a team-player, and at the church choir the solo singer. In each of these contexts the child is influenced and is influential him/her self. Each of these factors has a voice in the narrative of the child, of a person, and is more or less influential in the narrative identity construction.

Narrative identity: Given. The developing identity of the child is interrelated with the life stories of these persons, who become 'significant persons' or 'critical persons' in retrospect when the person narrates the life span development to others. Persons and situations become 'critical' in the process of emplotment, in retrospect. Life on earth is a given; living together is a human construction, a process of sensing, sifting, focussing and understanding (cf. Meijers and Lengelle 2012). A variety of 'critical situations' and 'critical persons' ('sensing') are given decisive roles in retrospect ('sifting' and 'focussing') in the construction of a person's narrative identity ('understanding') and of a nation's narrative identity. Objective facts in the history of single persons and of communities are brought together in the subjective interpretation and structuring of their story/stories; they constitute a narrative identity. 'Critical situations' and 'critical persons' are a 'given' in a person's life; in retrospect they are given a decisive role by the person her or him self.

NARRATIVE FABRIC

The school, according to Bronfenbrenner (1979), is a place-in-between family and society, and as such a place to bridge different lines of thought – narrative lines and cognitive, scientific and historical lines. School offers the young learners existing knowledge: historical knowledge on the objective course of events in the history of a country, of leading persons (religious leaders like Jesus and Mohammed) and present day 'prophets' (like Nelson Mandela and Martin Luther King) and of 'critical events' like the Second World War and 'nine-eleven'. At school, the child is enabled to relate personal family stories (about grandpa starting of his enterprise; of grandma settling down as the wife of a migrant worker in a new country). The cognitive knowledge about 'guest workers' together with accounts of these events in personal stories of parents and grandparents form the fabric of the child's own developing narrative identity. The stories of significant persons like parents and teachers ('folk psychology') provide the child in the process of 'sensing', 'sifting', 'focussing' and 'understanding' with poss ibresponses to existential questions – responses rooted in religious and secular life orientation traditions.

School and Education

To become familiar with the fabric of cognitive and narrative knowledge as this is a given in the cultural context of the child, teachers in schools are of decisive importance. They are responsible for the creation of a safe environment to teach the child to respond to opaque and incomprehensible situations (Roux et al., 2012). Historical, technical and juridical knowledge together mark the space in which the child explores the possibilities to respond to new situations; the teacher makes use of scaffolding techniques to guide the child in finding an own unique narrative identity where cognitive knowledge and family stories come together and evoke an own repertoire of actions. A safe environment in the classroom allows for direct relationships between cognitive and narrative knowledge. A safe environment also allows for 'sitting on the edge' in the exploration of presented texts and their relation to the development of an own 'text', a unique responses to existential questions and an authentic situatedness in the fabric of the surrounding culture.

Scaffolding. Every child should feel free to explore to develop its own responses to incomprehensible situations. The teacher should teach the child to narrate, that is: to learn to invent a story, to dream of a tale in which what is not understandable will still obtain a meaningful place. The teacher should encourage the child to explore and develop its own design for a meaningful life, for 'the good life' based on the given scientific knowledge, and inspired by family stories (including narratives from religious and secular traditions), and the own experiences – by trial and error in a safe classroom environment. In our post-modern society the development of a narrative identity is no longer situated in a given Great Narrative, as an ongoing process culminating in an ultimate situation of peacefully living together as it was in earlier days. Today in the construction of a narrative identity the spirit to explore new possibilities is at the centre point, challenged by the associations and memories evoked by the stories of others. The tension characteristic for this process of exploration, or what is called a 'conflict' following the line of Vygotsky, is indispensable, or better: pre-conditional in the process of narrative identity development. Diversity forces us not to lean back in comfortable ways of understanding the world, but to sit 'on the edge' and be alert on divergent understandings of the same text as a trigger to reconstruct our familiar readings.

Plurality. The tension in the process of identity development is related to the plurality and diversity in responses to existential questions, which form the fabric of our post modern society. A plurality in which the answers given do not only differ from each other, but sometimes even are on an tense footing, or even conflicting. Plurality is not only enriching, as the supporters of pluralism like us to believe, but is also challenging or in some cases experienced as frightening. For the teacher in the classroom it is important to familiarize learners with different components of the cultural and religious fabric, at the same time not upset them because of the explicit or more implicit differences (Streib, 2006). It is a challenge in education today to induce 'instructive friction' (Kunneman, 2005, p. 131), which is to present scientific and narrative stories that are food for thought. Such stories are not characterized by a given meaning, a given message that in a unidirectional way can be presented to the listener to be included in the own memory without giving a second thought. The stories that have the potential to transform the addressee are 'an open space', not filled up with one clear message to colonize the listener, but an open space as an invitation to explore what is until then a non-place, and transform it in a process of co-creation in conversations with others into a meaningful place (cf. Augé, 1995; Witvliet, 2003).

PRODUCTION, RECEPTION AND PRODUCTION

In this volume, scholars in the field of Religious Education and citizenship education tell others who they are, but even more important, and by doing so, they tell themselves who they are and how they tried during their life span to act accordingly; they disclosed their professional identities. The text of this chapter provides the reader with lenses for the perception and reception of eighteen biographical narratives. 'Critical incidents' and 'critical persons' prospectively opened a variety of pathways for their professional development. In retrospect these seventeen scholars relate – sometimes consciously and sometimes less so – certain events and situations to the development of their pedagogical theory on Religious Education and Citizenship education, or – as Siebren Miedema prefers to call it – religious citizenship education.

Narratives have the power to disclose worlds, new and future worlds, and as such introduce the reader to yet unknown ways of living and incite the reader to new actions. It is up to the reader – making use of the narratives in this volume as part of the fabric of the pedagogical culture we live in – to de-construct the produced texts and re-construct the contributions into receptive texts challenging the production of an own narrative identity, an own personal flavour. A milestone to celebrate while at the same time not knowing where to go next. There are many ways (plural!) to go. A milestone to be shared with others as part of the 'making of' of pedagogical theories as an ongoing process of production – reception – (re-) production.

REFERENCES

Ankersmit, F., Doeser, M., & Kibédy Varga, A. (eds.). (1990). *Op verhaal komen. Over narrativiteit in de mens- en cultuurwetenschappen* [Recovering by story telling. On narrativity in humanities]. Kampen: Kok Agora.

Augé, M. (1995). *Non-places. Introduction to an antropology of supermodernity.* London/New York: Verso.

Bal, M. (2006). *A Mieke Bal reader.* Chicago/London: The University of Chicago Press.

Breeuwsma, G. (1995). Alles over ontwikkeling. Over de grondslagen van de ontwikkelingspsychologie [All about development. On the foundations of developmental psychology]. Amsterdam: Boom.

Bronfenbrenner, U. (1997). *The ecology of human development; experiments by nature and design.* Cambridge MA: Harvard University Press.

Bruner, J. (1996). *The culture of education.* Cambridge/Massachusetts/London Engeland.

Haas, W. de (1999). *Verhaal als opvoeding* [Narrative as education]. Kampen: Uitgeverij Kok.

Kunneman, H. (2005). *Voorbij het dike-ik. Bouwstenen voor een kritisch humanisme* [Beyond egocentrism. Building bricks for a critical humanism]. Amsterdam: Uitgeverij SWP.

Meijers, F., & Lengelle, R. (2012). Narratives at work: The development of carreer identity. *British Journal of Guidance & Counselling.* DOI: 10.1080/03069885.2012.665159.

Ricoeur, P. (1991). Narrative identity. In D. Wood (ed.), *On Paul Ricoeur; Narrative and interpretation* (pp. 188-200). London/New York.

Steegman, P. D. D., & Visser, J. (1993). *Zin in verhalen. Over de betekenis van verhalen bij de overdracht van geloof, waarden en normen* [Meaning in stories. On the meaning of stories in the transmission of faith, values and regulations]. Zoetermeer: Uitgeverij Boekencentrum.

Streib, H. (2006). Strangeness in inter-religious classroom conversations. In D. Bates, G. Durka, & F. Schweitzer (eds.), *Education, Religion and Society. Essays in honour of John Hull.* Routledge. Taylor and Francis Group.

Swennen, J. M. H. (2012). *Van oppermeester tot docenten hoger onderwijs. De ontwikkeling van het beroep en de identiteit van lerarenopleiders.* [From first class teacher to teacher in higher education. The development of the profession and the identity of teacher-educator]. PhD thesis VU University Amsterdam. Hilversum: Uitgeverij Verloren.

Vygotsky, L. (1926/1996). The historical meaning of the psychological crisis. A methodological investigation. In R. Riebert (ed.), *The collected works of L.S. Vygotksy. Vol. 3. Problems of theory and history of psychology.* New York/London: Plenum Press.

INA TER AVEST

Witvliet, T. (2003). *Het geheim van het lege midden. Over de identiteit van het westers christendom* [The secret of an empty space. On the identity of western christianity]. Zoetermeer: Uitgeverij Meinema.

AFFILIATIONS

Ina ter Avest
Vrije Universiteit/Inholland University of Applied Sciences
Amsterdam, The Netherlands

COK BAKKER

THE REAL TALKS

On the Ambition to Deconstruct and Reconstruct Teachers' Identity Claims

INTRODUCTION

(Professional) life is like hiking. Arrived at one point, there is a
milestone to celebrate and at the same time it is not quite clear where
to go next. There are many ways (plural!) to go.

Being interested in the biography of teachers and the way their biographies
influence professional I must admit, looking back at a period of 20 years of
academic work, I can not deny that a specific focus, interest and emphasis are easy
to distinguish, closely related to a subjectivity that is rooted in my own biography.

At Utrecht University from 1990 on, in collaboration with many colleagues
(inside and outside the University), I have been involved in research in Religious
Education (Dutch: Levensbeschouwelijke Vorming). I will start this contribution
with an overview of the research referring to various phases in my academic life
(par. 2). Then I present my personal journey (par. 3) distinguishing between a
recent and an earlier biography, finally sketching some common ground between
my personal story and the research that is done (par. 4).

To work in an academic environment, having an intellectually challenging job is
a real privilege. Besides this I realize that doing academic work – and to keep on
having the motivation for this – is only possible in an inspiring and cooperative
team. Apparently and interestingly, the demarcation lines of this 'team' could not
be clearly drawn. Very often academic work is done in 'fuzzy' cooperation and
relationships, and so is mine. Of course, one could refer to the organizational
structures my projects are embedded in, like a University and a Faculty (Utrecht
University, the Humanities), a Department (Religious Studies and Theology), a
Research Institute (Integon), a national research school (NOSTER) and a
consultancy group. But where I find the inspiration to initiate research projects and
to develop new ideas only sometimes matches with these structures. Very often
ideas, inspiration and initiatives come by coincidence, and in fuzzy contacts, in
national and international relationships, and sometimes even in friendships,
research projects are initiated and developed. Preparing the overview for this
article I must admit that Wenger's theory on communities of practice is true.
Shared ambitions and interests, the personally felt need to discuss them, the good
academic symposia combined with the good talks in the bar, storytelling about

*I. ter Avest (ed.), On the Edge: (Auto)biography and Pedagogical Theories on Religious
Education, 11–21.*

research all the time and ever changing collaborative patterns, have brought me this far (Wenger, 1998).

Before taking up the route map as sketched out before, let me start with an anecdote to illustrate the community of practice as I have experienced this with Siebren Miedema, the key figure of this book.

An Anecdote

Between 1999 and 2006 Siebren Miedema and myself were, as a couple, responsible for a course module with the title 'the identity of the school'. This module was constituent part of a nationally organized 2-year course on school leadership. Every year we had an intensive two week-period that we were sharing sessions with school leaders all over the Netherlands. We had to get up early, step into our cars and try to be there on time. The one day it was in Leeuwarden in the North of the country; the other day it was in Rotterdam; different places all the time. Almost every day we start phoning from our cars to discuss the final touches of the daily programs that we had developed tailor-made a few weeks before. Each version of a daily program was based on the contributions of the school leaders of this very session as they had been written in advance. In their papers they presented an analysis of their own school's ethos and identity. Every session was organized for 15 to 30 school leaders and was richly provided with observations and evaluations of their own schools and leadership practices. Working together with Siebren, as a colleague and friend, was big fun, which was articulated by the daily, early phone calls. Notice that we were affiliated to different universities and have different backgrounds and careers. Being different, but sharing ambitions and interests, finding ways to cooperate on an incidental occasion, was fun, academic fun, community of practice fun.

This anecdote could be seen as a metaphor to illustrate in what ways research ideas and projects come to life and are actually realized.[1]

UTRECHT RESEARCH ON RELIGIOUS EDUCATION

The Use of Educational Media in RE

Being trained as theologian and educationalist, and having worked for some years as a secondary school teacher, my first involvement in research was my own PhD project.

It was in the 80s that information technology was an absolute hype. Computers, computer games and communication techniques were developing incredibly fast. So, the question came up in what way schools could and should respond to these developments. For this reason it seemed to be necessary to equip schools with computers and so the Minister of Education did. In the mid 80s the leading idea was to train secondary school students primarily in the programming (!) of computers. Shortly after that the idea came up to see the computer also as an educational means. It became an issue how to use computers as educational media.

So, not as a goal in itself (computer-programming), but as a means to realize the objectives of the regular school subjects. In these dynamics also the more specified question was raised how educational media were used in the subject RE.

The PhD project I did, was developed to fill this gap. It contained a state-of-the-art study of the subject RE in secondary schools in the Netherlands, a short history, some input from learning psychology, a review from educational media studies and an empirical research (both quantitative and qualitative) into media selection in RE (Bakker, 1994). For me this was an excellent opportunity to integrate my two background studies, Theology and Educational Studies, and to learn to move around in the two more-or-less different academic arenas and finally to find my own position and niche, somewhere in between.

Now, looking back, I could easily conclude it is the learning psychological 'red wire' through the dissertation, leaning heavily on socio-constructivist approaches, that has proven to be leading to the many projects that would follow in my career. I got deeply convinced, that the acquisition of knowledge is in its complexity totally integrated with the development of the personality of the learner. It was this constructivist view on learning that landed in my thinking: if there is a reality 'out there' at all (from the ontological perspective), the increasingly interesting thing for me is our *perception* of this reality (in the epistemological perspective), i.e. a continuous process of meaning making.

Interreligious Learning

After the phase of writing the PhD thesis I got involved for a period of four years in the Center of Interreligious Learning (CIL) at the Faculty of Theology of Utrecht University. Together with Piet Steegman and Trees Andree we were the management team of a group of researchers at CIL. Research was done to explore the ways schools and teachers deal with the variety of religious traditions, represented by children and learners in their classrooms. It was Andree's pedagogical stance that research should not only be descriptive but should also be turned into a prescriptive. Her action-oriented approach was made concrete, in the so called pedagogical strategy for 'interreligious learning'. She became the spokesman of the view that education in a multi-religious context should contribute to the following three processes simultaneously: (1) the development of the child's self understanding and self identity; (2) an openness towards others and (3) the readiness to learn with and from each other (Andree, 1996, p. 31). Some have said that with this message Andree was like a prophet in the field of education (in adoration as well as in critique), but that she probably was too early with this. Looking at the rather rigid pillarized structure of the Dutch educational system and the strong powers at that time to keep the system as it was, this qualification might be right (cf. Miedema, 2006).

The first problem with the notion 'interreligious' was raised in discussions with some critical persons we met during the organization of an international conference. It became clear that the conceptualization of 'interreligious' could no longer be maintained. The alternative to be preferred was the notion of 'diversity'.

'Interreligious' suggests as if two or more religious traditions are there, clearly to be distinguished, and that the 'inter'-aspect would mean that something is done in between. We came to the interesting conclusion that 'interreligiosity' is a too academic approach, which does not meet the everyday reality 'Diversity' on the contrary appeals to a variety of inter-dependent variables that play their roles and have their impact in a dynamic interplay. And so, sometimes *religious* diversity is an issue, but more often it is not. And if it is an issue then this is in a complicated way almost always interrelated with an ethnic, cultural, skin color, reading skill or gender diversity (Bakker, 1999).

The second problem with the notion of 'interreligious' was my profound surprise that many religiously affiliated schools in the Netherlands, counting for almost 65% of all schools, had a prejudiced resistance against the notion of 'interreligious learning'. To talk about interreligious learning very often was interpreted as a threat to the *Christian* school ethos. At the same time we know from empirical research that the contents of Christian school identity cover a very broad range of varying theological and pedagogical claims (Bakker & Rigg, 2004; Bakker, 2006; Bakker & Ter Avest, 2010). So, *the* Christian identity does not exist in an undisputed sense, being multilayered. This could lead to the challenge to explore the variety of individual understandings and different interpretations of the Christian school ethos (in order to see to what extent it might meet with interreligious learning strategies), but very often it was not. Why this reaction to say 'no', if you realize that both the 'Christian identity of the school' and 'interreligious learning' (as a proposal) are just mental constructs?, I was asking myself.

School Identity, Constructed by Teachers

After the CIL-period, and based on conceptual studies and empirical research, we analyzed that the societal and administrative debates on the pillarized system of education (on the macro level) and the religiously affiliated, corporate identity of the school (on the meso level) very often were disturbed by a pre-supposed deductive reasoning. The assumption seems to be that a Christian school 'has' a Christian identity, which is experienced to be like a concept of Christian education that should be applied to the educational reality. The actual problem with this deductive representation is (1) that very often teachers are not aware of where and what that concept would be (where and how does this concept 'exist'?), and (2) that, suppose there is a central concept to point at, teachers make their own interpretations all the time, which makes the factual impact of the concept diffuse (Bakker & Rigg, 2004). Taking this observation seriously it seems urgent to start the debate on the identity of the school being aware of the fact that – whether or not debated and reflected – in their daily practicing teachers construct the identity of the school all the time. By their specific way of teaching they 'make' the school. Their professional behavior is to be characterized by its normative, subjective, individual dimension. By expressing and sharing the proceedings of teachers' reflective processes on a structural basis, a team could develop a line of thought from the individual to the collective level (Ter Avest & Bakker, 2010).

MOVING TOWARD THE BROADER PERSPECTIVE

From 1998 on research in this area was combined with a growing branch of consultancy work. Working together as a group of consultants, our shared interest was not only to do research in the field of education in order to better understand the mechanisms of identity formation, but also to facilitate schools, school boards, individual teachers and heads of school to create attractive and effective procedures to develop the school as an organization in such a way that the religious or value dimension of the educational practice was cared for. Academic work and consultancy work has proved to be a fruitful combination in many respects, with a challenging, reciprocal benefit.

The Link between Religion and Education

The attention that was paid to the role of the teacher and his or her religious biography in negotiating and creating the religious profile of the school is still one of the core issues in the Utrecht RE research group. It is important to emphasize that the research that is done is not only religious studies nor is it educational studies *per se*, but it is the mixture of the two. Taking up the best of the two worlds. It is not only *religious* studies, but it is the social sciences approach of religion with a specific interest how religion is manifested in the formal religious affiliation of the school as an organization and the individual professional behavior of the teacher. At the same time, the research that is done is not only *educational* studies, but it is the (mostly qualitative) empirical interest in the social phenomenon of school, education, teachers and teacher education with an explicit focus on and interest in the normative, subjective, religious dimension of these educational practices.

At this very moment the community of the Utrecht RE research group is basically composed out of at least 12 PhD projects, which offer a good illustration of today's broader program and perspective – ranging from teachers' perception of diversity to the characteristics of so called 'unaffiliated spirituals', the role of religion in citizenship education and a case study of RE in the Ukraine.

MY PERSONAL JOURNEY

How did personal experiences of the past influence my choices and the orientation of my research(-program) as described above, and the other way around. Of course there is a parallel to the time periods that research-projects were actually carried out (or still are). I will elaborate on this first (see 'recent biography'). But for sure the way I myself was brought up, the context of childhood, how I was educated in school and other 'interesting experiences' in earlier periods in life definitely are of influence on the unfolding of the research track record. I will elaborate on that later (see 'earlier biography').

Recent Biography

Looking back at this period of 20 years of RE research there has always been the need, but for sure also to pressure, to make plans for research. Let us assume that this has an impact in the sense that it directs the focus, the attention and also the concrete activities that are undertaken. However, these plans do not determine fully in what direction the research practice actually develops to. All along the way objectives and strategies are adjusted; and not seldomly unexpected but attractive opportunities pop up and it would be unwise to neglect them.

In our research into the biography of teachers we make use of Kelchtermans' methodology (Kelchtermans, 1991), distinguishing – in the reconstruction of someone's career in a retrospective – 'critical persons' and 'critical incidents' Let me list some of these critical incidents or critical persons in my own recent professional biography.

The ticket to the academic world. Having an MA-degree in Theology, and working as an RE-teacher, being a student in the final phase of an MA in Educational studies, the opportunity was there – by invitation – to step into a project as research assistant (aio) in order to write a PhD thesis (to start in 1990). Who was there to make that offer and what made the 'click' to say 'yes'? There was a University lecturer (Piet Steegman) with whom I used to have challenging talks, but also very open and personal talks. A largely experienced shared interest and the vacancy of an aio-position in the Social Sciences Section of the Faculty of Theology was a puzzling combination. He informed me about this position and we discussed the relevance and possibilities in the light of our shared interest. Looking back it seems to be all by coincidence. Now I must conclude that my application and appointment have had a big impact, not in the last place because it has led to the ticket to the academic world (PhD 1994).

The impact of supervisors. One of the promotores I have been working with on a frequent basis happened to introduce me into a constructivist approach in learning psychology (Kanselaar). I remember him referring to the articles without much emphasis. Not knowing how this was the literature that filled the gap I was waiting for, with a far more reaching impact than only 'learning'. Finally leading me to the study of 'pragmatism', getting involved in this perspective, also having consequences on my perception of religious and other truth claims.

Another example of the impact of the (other) supervisor I was working with (Andree): in the final phases of my own PhD-research she spoke the unforgettable words "to have trust in what I have done that far, and to accept that 'the better is always the enemy of what is already good". Though I am the first to say that it is a good ambition always to look for the better (and knowing myself: I know that I love this enemy), at that very moment it was by far the best a good supervisor could have said to me. Probably if this was not said I still would have been busy with improving the text ...

An academic career? Some colleagues at that time have been crucial in creating space to continue my academic research in a combined job at two different institutes at Utrecht University (The Faculty of Theology and the IVLOS Institute for Teacher Education). In the combination of the two opportunities were created to start academic teaching and post doc research. One could say that again it is a coincidence to be surprised with a 'match' like this. On the other hand, for 5 years already I was also a practicing secondary school teacher, which I decided to do, knowing that if I would ever be in the opportunity to get a permanent academic position that experience from practice would be a great advantage. So, deliberately planning and coincidences go together.

Fuzzy Boundaries

To meet committed researchers with comparable interests, approaches and working-styles is as easy inside as it is *outside* one's own university as is shown above in the working relation with Siebren Miedema (and many more concrete examples could be mentioned). A community of a research practice blurs the formal distinction between colleague and non-colleague, there are 'fuzzy boundaries'. Some personal contacts have turned out to be very valuable. And the other way around, some professional contacts have deepened into friendships. Overviewing the many research projects, some contacts have been very stimulating on a temporary basis; some contacts seem to be for a lifetime. It is very valuable to collaborate with academics with whom you can stand the heat. It is funny to see that over time – whenever or not there is a formal collaborative link – with some professional people I am collaborating all the time: lecturing, doing research and in consultancy jobs we are in different roles attached to each other. In my case this is with Ina ter Avest. We have been working for many years together, which has led to a continuous exchange on theories, possible approaches, but also the mutual appreciation of the personal style of doing the work and how activities engage with each other; in the broad range from conceptual (dis-)agreement, and the good talks on that, to the intensive travelling together (from time to time). It was (and is) only for a few hours a week that we are colleagues, officially speaking. For the rest we have other, different jobs, which in fact does not block us to cooperate wherever necessary or valuable.

The recent biography makes clear (at least to me) that there is not a clear cut path to go, but that it is like hiking. Arrived at one point, there is a milestone to celebrate and at the same time it is not quite clear where to go next. This is open and I think that it is principally right to experience this phase as such, realizing that for sure there are many ways (plural!) to go. I retrospect one could say that there has been a program and intention; but all along the way both new insights are developed and books and articles are published and a research team is built.

Earlier Biography

I was born and raised in an orthodox Protestant family. Both my father and mother were pious and devoted believers in an Almighty God who was seen as being directly and personally involved in their lives. And so they expect their children to believe in the same way and to participate in the self-evident patterns of worship and church life, as this was essential to them. A reflection on my own life span development from that early period to today's believing is too much to discuss in this chapter (and might also not be that interesting for the average reader). So let me point at only three interesting aspects in this earlier biography that illustrate the link to today's activities, interests and developments.

First, as a 14-year-old I boldly decided to stand up against all these patterns of lingering and talking, old fashioned church self-evidences, etc. Looking back it is surprising to see how much impact it had, including the necessary conflicts with my parents, to join an evangelical youth movement. At that time, in my own experience, it was a real decision to do it differently. And indeed, the daily life and how daily life was related to beliefs, was really different to what I experienced at home: a lot of fun and adventure, summer-camps, going-out, drinking and laughter in a group with 15 to 20-year olds, etc. (different and therewith very challenging). At the same time there was the singing of Christian hymns, prayer meetings, and somewhat a comparable theology as it was at home. I experienced this phase as totally different, opposite and new. I learned a lot: discussing, presenting, organizing, taking responsibilities, handling all kind of 'pastoral problems', etc.

After some years in this movement I slowly start to realize the growing discrepancy between the harmonic youth culture (I was part of) and the prevailing theology (I found myself in trouble with). I loved the culture which was much more attractive to me than the traditional church: the community life, the atmosphere of connectedness and friendship, the (inclination to the) good and 'real' talks, but the dominant and cherished theology became more and more problematic.

Secondly, as a first year student of Theology I discovered that almost all fellow students were straightly heading towards the pulpit; they were very much church-oriented. However, the pulpit in the traditional church was clearly a bridge too far. I decided not to quit, but to continue the studies on a part-time basis, combining this with a job in 'the real world' (being a planning officer in the health care business). After some time I became a full-time student again finalizing an MA in Theology, finding new ambitions, more convenient with me, in becoming a secondary school teacher by doing a Certificate of Education. To broaden the scope I started Educational Studies, expecting once to have a challenging profession in the combination of the two very different disciplines and qualifications.

The re-framing of my own theology was quite a long way to go. Being a convinced evangelical (after some years even as the principal leader of the local youth movement), but slowly discovering that this was the same disappointing theology as it was at home, be it in disguise. After a long process of reframing I start to discover that 'some fragments' of that good old tradition, or just single stories, could touch me more than the entire well-designed and optimally tuned theological system of the former days had ever done. Of course this was a growing away from black & white thinking schemes, but it was also a satisfying phase of re-construction after a necessary phase of de-construction.

COMMON GROUND

Endlessly complex of course would be the list of links between my personal biography as researcher and the actual research and research projects I have been involved in and contributed to. Let me conclude this contribution with listing up some of the links – as I could see them – between the short description of this earlier biographical details on the one hand and the research projects and themes I am involved in on the other hand.

I am impressed when people are existentially focused on what they do. It is not what they say, but it is what they do, intrinsically motivated (as I experience them, of course). I have some resistance, I feel disappointed when people act by playing a game. In line with this I like to 'seduce' teachers to reflect on their 'real motives' for their professional behaviour. Tell me (either in research interviews or in seminars) what you 'really' think, instead of just explaining what you do in phrases and terminology that is socially desirable. I feel irritated or sometimes even disappointed when people speak, live, and say to believe, without any reflection on their actual position and claims. Life and also societal life is not self evident, and while talking, people create categories, societal boxes, stratifications, etc. all the time, but also unavoidably. In other words, they are constructing their realities in their narratives. While talking you cannot avoid to construct, but this is only acceptable if one is critical on his phrasing and also prepared to de-construct. I could understand very much that a religious affiliation (of whatever type) could be very important for some people; and that religious claims could be experienced as fundamental and existential claims. But at the same time, easily every believer could (and should) establish empirically that the same religious claims could have other meanings to other persons. So, religious claims, or: religion, is nothing and everything at the same time. In line with this I have the ambition to (help to) deconstruct religious claims and to see how these claims are interrelated with other claims, needs and desires.

Being religious means to me to search for deeper meanings (rationally and emotionally) which makes the good talks and an open mind necessary. Good talks, in which we both de-construct and re-frame and re-construct; the good talks, in which we create the more complicated understanding of life itself by the more complex narratives. This is what we need in daily life and in professional life: the good talks, being captured and analyzed by research methods, and the good talks in consultancy procedures helping to (re-)construct a school's ethos and identity.

COK BAKKER

THE FUTURE OF RELIGIOUS EDUCATION

Finally, for me it is not religion for the sake of religion, or religious studies for the sake of the Academia, but it is religion for the better understanding of life. In the search and talks about the essence of the 'good life', a (religious) tradition could function as a source and as a critical friend. Me is just me, very much restricted, but what really counts is that what is bigger than me, what transcends my daily life, what (helps to) make(s) meaning of life and give(s) joy. The richness of whatever tradition could help with this, widening the perspectives and horizons.

Religious and theological claims are socially and historically constructed. The status of academic, clerical or layman claims may differ, but all of them remain to be constructs. As a theologian, realizing that academic theology is also 'just' a construct, I am mostly interested in the religious claims teachers make. For sure, they are no professional theologians or clergyman, but they do make their claims and their claims have their impact and consequences in their educational realities. For that reason I would like them to be preferred, not at least because they have this huge impact in teaching and education. It is a passion to have them observed, analyzed and criticized. In other words: to have them de-constructed and re-constructed.

Let us start talking, trying to realize the real talks, on how we want to educate our children, students and learners.

NOTES

[1]   See Bakker, Miedema, and Van der Kooij (2007).

REFERENCES

Andree, T. G. I. M., & Bakker, C. (eds.). (1996). *Leren met en van elkaar; Op zoek naar mogelijkheden voor interreligieus leren in opvoeding en onderwijs.* Zoetermeer: Boekencentrum.
Avest, I. ter & Bakker, C. (2009a, May). Structural identity consultation: Story telling as a culture of faith transformation. *Religious Education, 104*(3).
Avest, I. ter & Bakker, C. (2009b). *Werk-in-uitvoering; Samen nadenken over de identiteit van de school.* Amersfoort: NZV Uitgevers.
Bakker, C. (1994). *Media in het godsdienstonderwijs; Een onderzoek naar de betekenis van de informatietechnologie voor het godsdienstonderwijs op scholen voor voortgezet onderwijs.* Zoetermeer: Boekencentrum.
Bakker, C. (1999). Diversity as ethos in Intergroup Relations. *Journal for the Study of Religion, 11*(1).
Bakker, C. (2002). Hoe geef je vorm aan de identiteit van de school? In S. Miedema & H. M. Vroom (eds.), *Alle onderwijs bijzonder: Levensbeschouwelijke waarden in het onderwijs.* Zoetermeer: Meinema.
Bakker, C. (2006). Een christelijke identiteit vanuit het alledaagse; Over het theologiseren van de leerkracht op de christelijke school. In S. Miedema & G. Bertram-Troost (eds.), *Levensbeschouwelijk leren samenleven. Opvoeding, Identiteit & Ontmoeting.* Zoetermeer: Meinema.
Bakker, C. & Avest, I. ter (2010). Self-understandings of RE-teachers in structural identity consultation; Contributing to school identity in a multi-faith context. In K. Engbertson, M. de Souza, G. Durka, & L. Gearon (eds.), *International handbook of inter-religious education.* Dordrecht/Heidelberg/London/New York: Springer.

Bakker, C., Miedema, S., & Kooij, J. C. van der (2007). Dimensions of school identity formation. Research about and with principals of Dutch elementary schools. In C. Bakker & H-G. Heimbrock (eds.), *Researching RE teachers. RE teachers as researchers.* Münster/New York/München/Berlin: Waxmann.

Bakker, C., & Rigg, E. M. (2004). *De persoon van de leerkracht; Tussen christelijke schoolidentiteit en leerlingendiversiteit.* Zoetermeer: Meinema.

Kelchtermans, G. (1991). De professionele ontwikkeling van leerkrachten vanuit het biografisch perspectief. *Nederlands Tijdschrift voor Opvoeding, Vorming en Onderwijs, 7*(3).

Miedema, S. (2006). Levensbeschouwelijk leren samenleven: een godsdienspedagogische balans. In S. Miedema & G. Bertram-Troost (eds.), *Levensbeschouwelijk leren samenleven; Opvoeding, identiteit & ontmoeting.* Zoetermeer: Meinema.

Wenger, E. (1998). *Communities of practice: Learning, meaning and identity.* Cambridge: Cambridge University Press.

AFFILIATIONS

Cok Bakker
Department of Religious Studies & Theology
Faculty of Humanities
Utrecht University
Faculty of Education of the Hogeschool Utrecht

GÜNTHER DIETZ

THE CHALLENGE OF DOUBLE REFLEXIVITY: ETHNOGRAPHIC METHODOLOGY IN INTERCULTURAL EDUCATION

INTRODUCTION

I once experienced being an 'other'.
This has become a connecting thread
in my life as in my work:
the tensions rooted in otherness.

I grew up as a German in southern Chile, where my parents worked as teacher. Through immigration many Germans worked in southern Chile, where most people were of Mapuche indigenous background. In that context I belonged to a privileged minority of Germans in a very asymmetrical situation. I felt an 'other', but was privileged as the 'other'. Returning to Germany at the age of twelve/thirteen, I again felt as a member of a minority, because I was schooled in Spanish and in a certain way I identified with Chilean and Latin American culture. Due to this background, I had to repeat a whole year in school: I did not understand the teachers, because my academic language until then, apart from the German classes, had been Spanish. I was treated as an outsider; I again felt an 'other', a stranger. However, from an 'other' belonging to a privileged minority in the Chilean context I suddenly was an 'other' belonging to a non-privileged minority in the context of northern Germany. When I finished high school I got a fellowship for a year and went to Spain. Living in the Granada area I became very interested in the so-called Gitanos, the Roma. I lived with the Roma in their community, in their houses. Living in a community of a minority with a strong stigmatized identity imposed on them by the Spanish majority I once again experienced being an 'other' in again a different minority-majority balance. Although Spaniards and particularly Andalusians celebrate Roma culture, they at the same time they discriminate Roma people. This reminded me of the situation of the Mapuche in Chile: celebrated because of their culture, discriminated as people. This has become a connecting thread in my life as in my personal work: the tensions rooted in otherness.

Migration in my life is not only cross-national from one country to another, but also cross-disciplinary between and within different disciplines involved in intercultural education. In this nomadic journey I discovered a surprising scarcity of empirical studies about intercultural and interreligious processes and relations, as they actually occur in the school and extra-school educational spheres. This

I. ter Avest (ed.), On the Edge: (Auto)biography and Pedagogical Theories on Religious
Education, 23–35.

striking gap that exists between the normative-prescriptive and the descriptive-empirical area is a feature of educational systems. Even in those countries in which different strategies destined to 'interculturalize' educational praxis have been debated and experimented with for decades, the imbalance between the discourse about 'what is intercultural' in education and the evaluation of intercultural practices persists. I my view, ethnography can contribute to overcoming this gap by empirically analyzing the interwoven and often dialectic relationship between the discourses of the pedagogical-intellectual sphere and daily educational praxis.

In this contribution, I will describe in relation to my nomadic biography an approach I am developing in the field of intercultural and interreligious education. In order to do this, I will start to present and discuss the elements required for a conceptual-methodological model that can integrate 'syntactic', 'semantic', and 'pragmatic' dimensions that will articulate the dialogical/conversational relationship between (ethnic) discourses of same-ness and other-ness and (cultural and intercultural) practices if diversity.

COMPARING MULTICULTURALISMS

Multicultural discourse in the educational context of Western societies has become the principal ideological basis of intercultural education, conceived as a differential approach towards the education of allochthonous, immigrated minorities. As the long-standing tradition of indigenism illustrates, however, in the Latin American context and under nationalist, not multiculturalist ideological premises, very similar policies of differential education have been targeting autochthonous, indigenous minorities, not allochthonous ones. This paradoxical similarity between mutually opposing approaches reveals the necessity of analyzing intercultural, multicultural, bilingual and/or indigenist educational responses from a larger perspective than the disciplinary pedagogical one. The closely-knit network of normative, conceptual and empirical inter-relations which are perceivable between 'interculturality' and 'education' is therefore not reducible to the educational sciences, but requires a contrastive and interdisciplinary analysis. It is this interdisciplinary approach I favour the study of 'intercultural education'. Intercultural education as an anthropological and pedagogical analysis of inter-group and intercultural structures and processes which constitute, differentiate and integrate contemporary society.

In the continental European arena of the debate, on the contrary, the need for interculturality in education is not claimed on the ground of the minorities' identity necessities; the struggle for intercultural education is justified by the apparent inability of majority society of meeting the new challenges created by the increasing heterogeneity of the pupils, by the growing socio-cultural complexity of majority-minority relations and, in general, by diversity as a key feature of the future European. Whereas in Latin America a minority empowerment education is being developed, continental Europe is shifting towards an education which mainstreams the promotion of intercultural competences inside both the marginalized minorities and the marginalizing majorities. This differential treatment – be it assimilationist, integrationist or segregationist – provided by official educational systems to certain minority groups is an integrated part of the respective nation-state's own 'identity politics' and as thus has to be analyzed and compared. The current pedagogy of multiculturalism, both in its orthodox mainstream and heterodox critical versions, has to be analyzed not as mere 'response' to the internal diversification of the classroom, but as contemporary expressions of the West's identity project.

The nomadic journey of the analysis of intercultural education in my view should not start from the classroom nor from academia, but from 'the street'.

I claim that only a contrastive and mutually inter-related definition of culture and ethnicity allows for conceptually and empirically distinguishing between intra-cultural, inter-cultural and trans-cultural phenomena. Habitualized cultural praxis and ethnicized collective identity discourses have to be both synchronically delimitated from each other and diachronically de-constructed as culturally hybrid products of ongoing and closely-knit processes of intercultural ethno genesis and routinization.

THE NEED FOR REFLEXIVITY

Reflexivity is one of the main contributions of ethnography to the field of intercultural and interreligious education. I understand reflexivity to be "the regularized use of knowledge about the circumstances of social life as a constituent element of its organization and transformation" (Giddens, 1991, p. 20). The explicit positioning vis-à-vis the subject to be studied that I propose starts out with the identification of two different reflexive processes. The social actor, on the one hand, who constantly reflects on his daily tasks, and the meta-daily activity of the social researcher, on the other hand, interact in a 'double hermeneutics', in a "double process of translation or interpretation which is involved" (Giddens, 1984, p. 284).

The growing penetration of scientific knowledge in contemporary life worlds disseminates social scientific and anthropological knowledge. In the case of multiculturalism and its educational policies, this self-reflexivity of the social and educational actor must be taken seriously and faced by a committed, engaged anthropology. Nevertheless, as this commitment with the actor studied does not imply full identification with his/her objectives, the task of a 'double hermeneutics' broadens the study of the actor to include the uses that this actor makes of the constructed anthropological knowledge. Through a reciprocal negotiation of academic and political interests, it is possible to generate a mixture of theory and practice that translates into a 'triadic methodology' (Álvarez Veinguer & Rosón, 2009), which consists of phases of empirical research, of academic theorization, and of transfer to the researched political and/or educational praxis. This transfer is not reduced to an act of 'consciousness raising', but constitutes an exchange between the two kinds of knowledge mentioned: between the knowledge generated in the 'first order' by the 'experts' of their own life world, on the one hand, and the anthropological knowledge generated in the 'second order' by the academic 'expert', on the other. The possible contradiction that arises from the exchange of both perspectives has to be integrated by the ethnographer in the research process itself, which will oscillate dialectically between identification and disengagement, between phases of full commitment and phases of analytic reflection.

Double Reflexivity in the Ethnographic Process

The inter-subjective, dialogical relationship that thus arises between the researching subject and the actor-subject that is being researched generates a continuous and reciprocal process of criticism and self-criticism between both parties. Let me give an example in which the theoretical concept of double reflexivity is practiced. In a research project on social welfare, we worked together with Spanish NGO's and communities of Muslims (Dietz, 2004). After interviews and participant observations and after transcribing and interpreting the texts ourselves, we did workshops firstly with the Muslims of the participating communities, and separately with the Spanish NGO's. In so-called intercultural workshops we brought the two groups together and discussed questions of conflicts, of confluence and about the influence of the Roman Catholic Church. Again we transcribed and analyzed these conversations and gave the results back for further interpretation by the participants of the two groups. Research in this way is a continuous coming and going of observing, dialoguing and interpreting from different perspectives – the perspective of academia intermingling with the perspective of the collaborators in the research. In such a way, we come across divergent interpretations, which are normal of course due to the different interests, but we also discover confluences. Often in this research project the confluences were more often than the divergences, and this happened even between very laicist NGO's at the political left side of the spectrum, and the participants of the Islamic communities, on the other hand. To make it more concrete, to start with the Spanish NGO's, although having feelings of solidarity with the Islamic immigrants, strongly opposed the introduction of Islamic Religious Education (RE) in primary schools. In their view, this would empower the confessional field – which in the Spanish context is the empowerment of the Catholic Church. On the other hand, the participants of the Islamic communities emphasized that the laicist argument was somehow false in Spain, a kind of laicist lip-service, whereas in reality the Catholic church maintained a monopoly on RE. The Muslims' statement was: either no confessional RE in schools but some kind of interfaith education or an equal treatment of Catholic RE and Islamic RE – which includes equal financing of the salaries of RE teachers from both faith traditions. In these conversations the Spanish NGO's finally realized that they where (indirectly and without knowing) discriminating against Islamic RE. At the end of the conversations, both parties strongly promoted the inclusion of training courses of imams in Spanish and inside Spanish universities for becoming Islamic education teachers. Double reflexivity is practiced here in the mutual process of confrontation of the results of reflection and interpretation of the participants and – above these conversations – about these results with researcher(s) and members of NGO's and Islamic communities together.

Another example of double reflexivity in ethnographic research stems from the struggle for safe spaces for Muslim women (Dietz & El Shohoumi, 2005). Many women representatives of Islamic communities in southern Spain claim to have their own spaces to do activities together, apart from the Spanish NGOs with whom they collaborate. In the beginning many of the NGO-representatives and local town-hall representatives, people from the social service department of the municipalities in Andalusia rejected these spaces because this in their view would result in isolation and ghettoization of Muslim women. The women themselves explained in the conversations that for them it was very important to have their own meeting ground, to have their own assemblies as Muslims and as women, without the participation of men and without the participation of Spanish people – of non-Muslims. According to them, it is very important for them to question ourselves on questions like 'being second generation', about mother-tongue questions and practicing Islam (e.g. the celebration of Ramadan) in a Catholic majority society. Finally, both parties agreed upon the importance of 'safe spaces', and nowadays Muslim women can meet and even the more conservative Muslim women who come from a rural background have the 'permission' of their husbands and family to go to a gathering with other Muslim women. What happens in these conversations is that the reflection on the results and interpretation of each party ends up in questioning very Western notions of what is good for minority women and what is seen as progressive and what is seen as against women's rights. Double reflexivity is a mutual process of learning through questioning. I need to question my otherness and liberate myself and the other from prejudices. In these conversations, we as researchers show the participants how there is a certain prejudice in the way they see 'the other' and confront them with other kinds of prejudices against themselves as a minority. That is one of the reasons that we always end with mixed groups for these conversations, because it is much more fruitful in diverse groups, as there are in a natural way diverse ways of perceiving each other. What people learn from these conversations is that they produce and transmit prejudices, not only about others, but also the prejudices against themselves – a process that disempowers them. Mentally these conversations can also have a de-colonizing, liberating effect for those who participate. They invent new identities and perform them by combining different sources of identity, which gives back to 'the victims of minority' their agency.

Between structures and actors, between discourse and praxis

As is shown in the examples above, conceiving social structures of majority and minority independently from social actors, or vice versa, is not fruitful: the actors are born into and socialized amidst pre-existing structures that will prefigure their specific cultural practices, but that, in turn, will be actively reproduced, modified, and adapted by these same actors according to changing interests, identities, and contexts. In order to overcome the simplistic dichotomies of objectivism *versus* subjectivism and materialism *versus* idealism (Bourdieu, 1990), this dialectic and 'praxeological' notion of the inter-relationship between structure and actor is explained by Bourdieu through the concept of *habitus*, described as a set of 'structured structures' that can actualize and articulate themselves as 'structuring structures' (Bourdieu, 1990). For me this approach in the analysis, which focuses on the actor him/herself, is complemented by Giddens' analysis, which starts from the opposite end, from structures and their dual character (Giddens, 1984).

The habitualized practices that are reproduced from one generation to the next, such as the culture of a specific group, constitute 'structured structures' that, in situations of contact and interaction with other human groups, unleash phenomena of ethnicity – processes of reorganization, re-signification, and re-normativization of what is considered to be 'one's own' and what is supposed to be 'someone else's'. These processes of ethnicity imply that the habitus is instrumentalized as a 'structuring structure' in order to generate a new intra-group homogeneity, starting from which cultural content is re-internalized, becoming sedimented once again as a 'structured structure'. This resulting notion of habitus is constructivist, but at the same time it explains the mechanism of primordialization that turns routine practices into supposedly ethnified, ontic entities. The permanent contrastive combination of an *etic* perspective with an *emic* one is the only resource capable of distinguishing between the construct – observable as praxis – and its primordialization – only interpretable in dialogue.

For the construction of ethnicitized entities, I take my starting point in a tripartite typology of 'capitals': economic capital (material property that can be converted directly into money), social capital (resources such as prestige, honour, networks, and social relations, whose 'symbolic' value can, under certain conditions, be converted into economic capital), and cultural capital (educational resources that, in certain circumstances, can also be converted into economic capital). The unequal distribution of the three kinds of capital among the members of a certain society or sub-society generates systematically different social positions, each one of which corresponds to a specific composition of the volume of the three kinds of capital available; a composition constructed by the person him/herself by way of the competency to make fruitful and adequate use of the capitals at his/her disposal. For this competency we use the concept of identity capital (Matthys, 2011). The disposal of and hierarchy in these social positions makes up the social space, identical to the space of distribution of capitals in a society. As a function of this distribution of capitals, the individuals who occupy an identical position in the social space generate a distinctive specific and recognizable habitus, which, on the one hand, as a 'structured structure' reflects their access to some of the society's resources and, on the other hand, as a 'structuring structure', conditions the possibilities of reproducing and/or transforming their position. It is the cultural capital, above all, that – incorporated in the individual – nourishes his/her distinctive habitus.

The study of educational processes in multicultural contexts will have to empirically elucidate this relationship between habitualized cultural practices and the strategic uses that a particular group makes of a certain cultural capital in a given social space – that is the development of identity capital. At present cultural capitals coexist that are not only unequally distributed, but lacking a social space that is shared and competed for among everyone. These cultural capitals, springboards for an ethnic and/or a religious identity are articulated around a logic of their own, which often manages to preserve their counter-hegemonic character.

In order to analyze and visibilize these complex interrelations between habitualized cultural and/or religious practices, hegemonic as well as counter-hegemonic identity discourses and the role of pedagogical institutions in the structuring of intercultural and inter-religious educational responses, an interdisciplinary and comparative approach is necessary. For this purpose, ethnography, in its characteristic oscillating between *emic* – inward looking, actor-centred – and *etic* – externally comparative and structure-oriented – visions of educational, social and cultural realities, is conceived as a reflexive endeavour which retrieves from within the social actors' own discourses while contrasting it externally with their respective habitualized cultural praxis. An ethnography of education in intercultural constellations will necessarily have to widen the analytic scope of these discursive and praxis dimensions towards a third axis of analysis: the particular institutional structurations (Giddens, 1984) which result from the role played by the 'pedagogies of otherness'.

In order to elaborate on the concept of 'pedagogies of otherness', I compare and analyse different interpretations of such a pedagogy and take my starting point in the collective imaginaries of 'otherness', as they are politically institutionalized and instrumentalized by the state. The comparative study of educational policies illustrates first of all the constructed, relative, and contextual character of the underlying nationalizing identity discourses. From the infinite number of possible criteria of institutional 'discrimination' for categorizing and 'problematizing' the pupils – such as, for example, age, gender, geographic origin, current residence, mother tongue, religion practiced, 'culture', 'ethnic' identification, citizenship and/or nationality, behaviour patterns, school performance, parents' socio-economic level, etc. – institutions define particular 'educational knowledge codes' (Bernstein, 1975, p. 90) and generate a specific combination of criteria for detecting or denying the existence of 'diversity in the classroom'.

TOWARDS A METHODOLOGICAL MODEL

The combination of these criteria of problematization and their application to educational systems and highly heterogeneous national contexts has sparked off an exorbitant proliferation of approaches, models, and pedagogical programs to deal with 'diversity in the classroom'. The resulting typology of these possible combinations of the public and private spheres cannot be subsumed under the conventional concepts of 'assimilation' *versus* 'segregation' (Verlot, 2001). The combination of postulates makes up the 'basic intuition' of a certain institutional actor generates a certain 'syntax', a habitual framework of 'structuring structures' that pre-shapes the behaviour and widens or narrows the 'room to maneuver' of the institutions and actors. Despite the evident need to detail and validate empirically

Verlot's conceptual contributions, the value of these first comparative studies resides in their heuristic potential. In order to carry out an ethnography of interculturality that transcends the level of mere discourse, it is necessary to inquire into the collective structurations that, as 'syntax of pedagogy of otherness', underlie the institutional when faced with the heterogeneous challenges of cultural diversity.

The analysis of the discursive strategies used by the different pedagogical-institutional actors requires a combination of three levels: in the first place, the level of approaches and models of 'intercultural education', as developed and promoted by the academic, political, and school discourses, which contribute to the semantization of 'the other' and which end up conforming the underlying syntax of pedagogical 'otherness'; secondly, the level of teaching and curricular designs specifically created to respond to the 'school problem' of cultural diversity, which endow these models with semantic concreteness; and, finally, the level of individual discourses generated by the social and institutional actors that converge in school practice.

In every day classroom practice of semantization, the pretended concretization of interculturalization is only carried out in those areas in which, according to pedagogical judgment (or prejudice), the phenomena related with cultural diversity materialize most easily: the subject areas of social and cultural studies, religious education, language and literature, foreign language, and lately also mathematics. This curricular interculturalization practiced to date reifies and reduces cultural diversity by introducing 'items' coming from other 'cultures' into the official canon of 'our heritage'. The result is a slightly folklorized curriculum that exoticizes 'otherness' without questioning the hegemonic canonization processes to which it resorts. Evidently, the reductionist and reifying treatment of cultural diversity in the curriculum molds, at the same time, the didactic material used by the teaching staff. No matter how refined, complex, and reflexive the intercultural didactic material is, if it is only employed anecdotally within a hegemonically monocultural school praxis, the impact that is desired and promoted from the grandiloquent models of intercultural education will be equally anecdotal.

Transformed from a social movement to a pedagogical strategy, multiculturalism seems to project on one single actor, the teaching staff, all of its old hopes. The tendency to overload the teaching staff with functions and competences that are complementary to their canonized monocultural training once again generates 'cognitivist' solutions: reified information about 'the' culture of the pupils with whom they will be working daily is transferred through an endless list of courses. This generates openly defensive attitudes with respect to cultural 'otherness' that, instead of questioning the teacher's monolithic hegemonic identity as representative of the 'national culture', reinforces it even more. The result is a reciprocal, mutually invigorating ethnocentrism.

I hold that, in school practice, the officialised reduction of cultural diversity to 'items' that indicate 'otherness' as well as the reifying thematization of intercultural phenomena end up ethnifying the discourses of the different actors who interact within school and outside of it. Due to the mentioned power asymmetry, in practice these ethnified discourses may easily evolve towards an 'institutional racism' (Verlot, 2002) directed against stigmatized and 'minoritized' others. An ethnography of intercultural education, therefore, will have to broaden the narrow margin of the traditional 'school ethnography' in order to include the impact that both the underlying structuring syntax of a pedagogy of otherness and the institutional discourses that semanticize intercultural praxis of a pedagogy of otherness *ab initio* have on 'school culture'.

In my view, a 'pragmatic' dimension (Verlot, 2001) analyzes school praxis as a place of interaction and confrontation among diverse rutinized and habitualized 'life worlds' and 'lifestyles'. School conflicts and misunderstandings are analyzed as results of the growing gap that separates the pluralisation and multilingualization of the pupils' 'life worlds', on the one hand, and the persistence of a monocultural and 'monolingual habitus' on the part of the teaching staff and the school institution as a whole, on the other hand (Gogolin, 1997). This 'monolingual habitus' transcends the merely linguistic sphere in order to become the sign and refuge of the teaching staff's identity under conditions of increasing professional complexity (Gogolin, 2002).

In a longitudinal ethnographic study of a primary school in an urban-migratory context, Gogolin (1997) shows how this monolingual and monocultural habitus practiced by the teaching staff and institutionally backed by the educational system coexists with the obvious multiculturalization of the school, family, and residential environments. Above all in immigration and/or transmigration contexts of urban agglomerations, daily life worlds are increasingly bilingual or even multilingual, a process which affects both native and migrant populations. This 'life world bilingualism/multilingualism' is often becoming a 'cultural resource' and a future source of cultural capital, a trend which is growing from the 'bottom up', but which is not being recognized until now by monoculturally and monolingually socialized educational actors. Institutional monoculturalism and life world multiculturalism thus coexist. This contradictory coexistence is accepted by the affected pupils, their families and neighbourhoods. This acceptance would be, then, a 'common sense' matter that is internalized as a kind of compromise or *arrangement* by the minority groups. The proclaimed 'tolerance' and 'empathy' with respect to the 'different' child is surpassed and dissolved throughout an interaction that is characterized by a constant oscillation between different verbal and non-verbal codes that can come from one cultural context or the other, but that are hybridized in the joint dramatization and interaction. Consequently, a decidedly pragmatic focus surpasses the essentialism inherent in the conventional pedagogical uses of the concept of culture.

Seeking to deliberately and consciously include syncretic and/or supra-cultural modalities that come from contemporary youth cultures, in the modes of interaction acknowledged in the school sphere, however, would evidently mean to 'revolutionize' not only the current conceptions of intercultural education, but the school institution itself. The true problem posed by the binomial of 'interculturality and education' becomes evident. The problem is not 'the immigrants' or 'the youngster'; the main obstacle that any strategy directed towards interculturalizing education will have to face is the school institution and how deeply rooted it is a national pedagogy of otherness.

For the development of my own approach of a pedagogy of otherness, the social-psychologist Georg Kleining has been and still is very influential. He fled from the nazi regime and worked in the U.S. in line with Adorno and Horkheimer and then came back to Germany. He questioned dichotomies such as qualitative vs. quantitative research, of sociological vs. psychological research (Kleining, 1988). Considering my Chilean background, I learnt from him how to do critical and self-reflexive research in the community of Chilean refugees in Hamburg, who fled the Pinochet regime. This was again a huge experience of otherness with people who somehow shared my experience of otherness, but who were political refugees who came directly from the camps of Pinochet into the German welfare state – me being from a German background, related to a German minority in Chile who had supported the Pinochet regime. This brought me to the insight that our views and opinions need to be relational, and not essentialized. It is not worth to essentialize identities and academic standpoints since it impoverishes our views. My British colleagues Jagdish Gundara and Bob Jackson have then been very influential for my own professional development in the field of intercultural and interreligious education. Gundara (2001), working comparative interculturalism at the Institute of Education in London, taught me that it is not possible to perceive the richness of interculturality if you only work inside one national, political, ethnic context because you yourself are part of that context. He would say that you have to cross borders of nations, but also of academic disciplines in order to be able to perceive how much your own view is shaped by your national etc. background.

And, last but not least, I learned a lot from Bob Jackson's interpretive approach (1997), through which he combines ethnography, hermeneutics and our view on religious diversity – not as a problem but as a resource, a pedagogical resource, not from the point of view of any given church, but from the point of view of the interviewed – be it an older person or a student, a women or a man. But most of all I developed my dialogical competencies so badly needed in ethnographic studies, from the people I worked with, the people from the Spanish NGO's, the Muslim women, the Chilean refugees in Hamburg, the indigenous Mexican peasant families and their children I am currently working with.

According to these experiences, it is in the ethnographic potential that I see the main contribution that anthropology can and should offer to the contemporary debate on multiculturalism and interculturality. Nevertheless, in order to take advantage of this potential, it is indispensable, in the first place, to rethink and reiterate the close relationship that must exist between theoretical conceptualization and empirical realization. Going beyond the alternative between academism and 'empowering'- tranformationism, my approach in ethnography is a systematic oscillation between an *emic* – internal, actor-oriented – and an *etic* – external, interaction-oriented – vision of social reality as a reflexive task that recovers, from within, the discourse of the social actor being studied, while simultaneously contrasting this discourse, from outside, with the actor's respective habitualized praxis. This oscillation and contrast between an *emic*, semantic and discursive axis

and an *etic*, praxis and interaction driven axis has to be finally integrated into an ethnographic study of the institutional structurations in which intercultural education develops, schematized in a three-dimensional ethnographic model, which combines (Dietz, 2009):
- a 'semantic' dimension, centred on the actor, whose identity discourse is studied – basically through ethnographic interviews – from an *emic* perspective and is analyzed in relation to his/her strategies of ethnicity.
- a 'pragmatic' dimension, focussed on the cultural praxis as particular modes of interaction, which are studied – above all through participant observations- from an *etic* perspective and are analyzed in relation to their functions both as intracultural habitus and as intercultural competences.
- and a 'syntactic' dimension, centred on the institutions inside of which these identity discourses and interaction practices are developed; these institutional settings are analyzed when brought into a dialogue of an *emic* versus *etic* type of ethnographic data and that have to be interpreted not as mere data incongruities, but as those 'coherent inconsistencies' which reveal the underlying particular logic of the actor(s) and researcher(s) concerned.

CONCLUSION

Let me conclude with another example, in which the oscillation between *emic* and *etic* perspectives, and the translation from one field to another is illustrated, giving thus access to new knowledge for all participants involved. In northern Veracruz, at the Mexican gulf coast, we designed a short course with so called community authorities, peace judges who are in charge of social and peaceful relations inside communities on customary law, in relation to the nation state law and citizenship rights. Representatives from different communities, and even from different indigenous languages shared the problems they have with combining local customary law with national law. The training that we had given the participants of the conversation before, and through video material we had given to them of other case studies, they recognized that the current reforms in Mexico on human rights and their implementation on the local and civil level gives them an ally in the struggle for recognition of local traditions and laws. They felt re-empowered by knowing about these national laws and translating them: what they call women's rights, we call dignity; what they call local autonomy, we speak of village assemblies once a month; they just did not call it that way. And the other way around: We at the local level speak of punishment of crime by restoration of loss in the economic domain, which at the national level is called 'compensatory measures'. The course gave the local authorities access to a new language not only in Spanish, but also an updated judicial language. At the end they decided that for the 2012 federal elections they would invite all the candidates of the different parties for an assembly with them, an assembly to expose the political leaders their minimal recognition of their rights on the local level in order to be able to vote. If local authorities would not arrive on a consensus with regard to these candidates, they would not allow the election-institute to carry out the elections in their region;

they would not distribute any ballots because they feel they are not treated as citizens. As a local peace judge explained,

> we experience this as a discrimination of our customary laws by the whole system. If political parties want to take serious human rights, then the local authorities demand from them to sit down and discuss with them their topics; if political leaders have no time or are not interested, then the local authorities are no longer interested in participating in their political 'games'.

The course on social and peaceful relations, that started with discussions on crime and punishment at the local level, at the end of the day empowered local authorities not only at the local level, but even on human rights and citizenship at the national level; a result that we would not even have dreamt of when designing this course.

As shown in the above example, the distinctively anthropological contribution to the study of intercultural education lies in its particular, theoretical-empirical binomial. The dialogue provides a theorization about interculturality and an ethnography of the intercultural and intercultural phenomena generates an integral vision, both emic and etic, of the object-subject of study. Biographic, identity-related dimensions of the participant actors are as important in this kind of research as structural features and constraints. The 'nomadism' of the ethnographer engages in a dialogue with her or his non-nomadic research counterparts, collaborators and co-interpreters. The semantic and pragmatic analyses complement each other and complete an ethnographic vision of the institutions that, like an omnipresent but underlying syntax, structure the identity discourses of each of the actors studied as well as their respective cultural practices. Academics and activists, teachers and learners reflecting together on these structural constrains as well as on the implied opportunities for pedagogical and social change – this is the main task and challenge for double reflexivity in educational research.

REFERENCES

Álvarez Veinguer, A., & Rosón. J. (2009). Pupils, teachers and researchers: Thinking from the double hermeneutics. An ethnographic approach to a triadic methodology. In I. ter Avest et al. (eds.), *Dialogue and conflict on religion: Studies of classroom interaction in European countries.* Münster/New York: Waxmann.

Bernstein, B. (1975). *Class, codes and control. Vol. 3: Towards a theory of educational transmissions.* London: Routledge & Kegan Paul.

Bourdieu, P. (1990). *The logic of practice.* Stanford, CA: Stanford University Press.

Dietz, G. (2004). Frontier hybridization or culture clash? Trans-national migrant communities and sub-national identity politics in Andalusia, Spain. *Journal of Ethnic and Migration Studies, 30*(6), 1087-1112.

Dietz, G. (2009). *Multiculturalism, interculturality and diversity in education: An anthropological approach.* Münster/New York: Waxmann.

Dietz, G., & El-Shohoumi, N. (2005). *Muslim women in southern Spain: Stepdaughters of Al-Andalus.* San Diego, CA/Boulder, CO: University of California at San Diego, Center for Comparative Immigration Studies/Lynne Rienner Publishers.

Giddens, A. (1984). *The constitution of society: Putline of the theory of structuration.* Cambridge: Polity.

Giddens, A. (1991). *Modernity and self-identity: Self and society in the late modern age*. Cambridge: Polity.

Gogolin, I. (1997). *Grossstadt-Grundschule: Eine Fallstudie über sprachliche und kulturelle Pluralität als Bedingung der Grundschularbeit*. Münster/New York, NY: Waxmann.

Gogolin, I. (2002). Linguistic and cultural diversity in Europe: A challenge for educational research and practice. *European Educational Research Journal, 1*(1), 123-138.

Gundara, J. (2001). *Interculturalism, education and inclusion*. London: Paul Chapman Educational Publishing.

Jackson, R. (1997). *Religious education: An interpretive approach*. London: Hodder & Stoughton.

Kleining, G. (1988). Wie ist kritische Sozialforschung möglich? In A. Deichsel & B. Thuns (eds.), *Formen und Möglichkeiten des Sozialen: Eine Gedenkschrift für Janpeter Kob* (pp. 235-251). Hamburg: Weltarchiv.

Matthys, M. (2010). *Doorzetters* [Get goers]. PhD study, Utrecht University.

Verlot, M. (2001). *Werken aan integratie: Het minderheden- en het onderwijsbeleid in de Franse en Vlaamse Gemeenschap van België (1988-1998)*. Leuwen: Acco.

Verlot, M. (2002). Understanding institutional racism. In Evens Foundation (ed.), *Europe's new racism? Causes, manifestations and solutions* (pp. 27-42). Oxford/New York, NY: Berghahn.

AFFILIATIONS

Gunther Dietz
Universidad Veracruzana
Instituto de Investigaciones en Educación

HANS-GÜNTER HEIMBROCK

MY PERSONAL CONTEXTS

Learning Religion in Context

INTRODUCTION

*Childhood memories about frequent moves from one place to another
and early life experiences, coined by the situation in post war Germany,
these are part of 'my context'.*

During the last decennia Religious Education (RE) theory in many European
countries became more and more aware of the essential importance of the
European context. Compared to older conceptions of faith education, contextual
orientated models of RE, despite considerable differences, share the strength, that
religion is grasped seriously as a phenomenon of human self-understanding and
culture. The reference of processes of learning to experience is searched in
everyday life, pretending to show how RE under the conditions of secular multi-
religious societies can be an open contribution to the critical formation of the
human subject.

However, contextual orientation of RE asks for further clarification. This task
has been picked up at least in a twofold way. *On the one hand* scholars from all
over Europe more an got aware of their cultural and political context. Thus they
intensified their exchange and cooperation with colleagues in neighbour countries.
Among other associations, 'The European Network for Religious Education in
Europe through Contextual Approaches' (ENRECA) was set up in 1999 as a forum
for mutual co-operation and reflection on the changing role of religious education
in Europe.

> The group's commitment was to deal with the educational implications of the
> changing patterns of religious and secular plurality in European countries.
> Two perspectives have been important for the group's vision:
>
> – religious contextuality, with a focus on religious life in particular cultural
>   situations and local levels, and
> – religious competence as the ability of a student to negotiate on religious
>   meanings. (Miedema et al., 2004, p. 228)

On the other hand, the very concept of context was a constant objective of
theoretical clarification. Being of central importance for both, RE and theological
theories of formation, context and contextualisation have been understood quite
different, influenced by the various educational and theological theories in the

*I. ter Avest (ed.), On the Edge: (Auto)biography and Pedagogical Theories on Religious
Education, 37–46.*

background. Cutting things short, one could reconstruct typologically three different conceptions of context and contextualisation (Miedema et al., 2004, p. 228), which gained influence in RE:
- *the hermeneutical model: reading texts in contexts*
- *the liberation theology model: contextualisation as praxis*
- *the phenomenological model: context as life-world.*

Starting in the early 90s my own approach to RE drew heavily on life-world orientation

A LIFE-WORLD APPROACH TO CONTEXTUAL LEARNING

Life-world orientation goes along with a twofold understanding of religion. First, it is concerned with the educational introduction into religions as cultural traditions and collective symbol systems transmitted from older generations to younger people. Second, beyond this, it cares for the human searching for meaning, to make possible in both an educational productive grappling with reality and truth and with the experience of the other. This approach does not start with perceiving explicitly and distinct religious symbols, texts or artefacts, but rather with discoveries in the everyday culture of people: f.e. with perceiving the attempts of pupils to embody themselves, their anxieties and hopes, presenting and expressing their personalities aesthetically on the various stages of everyday-life. Nevertheless it is also perception that leads within the learning process to religion in the meaning of codified systems of collective symbols.

According to the classical description of Klaffki, the process of formation includes a twofold movement: to open up the world for the subject, and at the same time to open oneself to the things (Klaffki, 1964). It is not a contradiction, however a broadening of formation to say: Reference to life-world means a process of learning referring to local circumstances. Following this way, it is possible to get in touch with 'lived religion' (Failing & Heimbrock, 1998), in the individual's living context and its complex relations to everyday life. RE should therefore include the conditions of neighbourhoods and local life. If one is aware of the danger of overrating the own culture (including religion) and taking it absolute, this stands in no way in opposition to the intention of teaching openness and readiness for dialogue.

The aim of contextual RE includes a new approach to cultural and religious particularity. Taking context in a life-world-approach does not simply equate concrete situations just as a 'surrounding', which does not touch the essence particular religious phenomena, and thus could be simply replaced by other ones. Rather the approach reflects on the particular way the learning subject is encountering religion in everyday life as well as in learning situations. Important elements are:
- the ever-present given-nes of things, I am familiar with, versus the encounter of the unknown and the strange

- my experience and reflection of my surrounding on the basis of an embodied subject, thus the interaction of awareness, perception and reflection. This needs a conceptualisation of 'lived experience' (Failing & Heimbrock, 1998)
- the situational appearance of any object given in the senses as the basis of perception and meaning making.

All these elements can serve to prevent RE from the limitation to the use of contextless abstract sentences.

MY PERSONAL CONTEXTS

My contextual didactics as a concern of RE is located within decidedly personal, biographical contexts. Next to specific academic discourses, it highly benefited from people I met, and from situations I got in touch with. Thinking about particular instances, it is not books or papers that come to my mind. Rather, my imagination starts to fill with university classes in other countries, with local sceneries and urban squares, lovely cafés, familiar rows of houses. I see myself strolling down memorable streets. I revisit a countryside with its magnificent mountains and even more prominent vistas, views I once enjoyed. At the same time, memories of a different kind come to my mind: The search for luggage that went astray in Copenhagen. The picture of a friendly radiologist, who competently attended to my broken arm in a hospital 3000 km north of Frankfurt after I slipped and fell on ice.

Of course, there is much more to localizing my contextual learning processes than travels abroad: There are childhood memories about frequent moves from one place to another and early life experiences, coined by the situation in post war Germany. East Germany and West Germany – East Germany known by me only as a part of our country I had to pass through on my way to Berlin. Doubtlessly these are part of 'my context'. Another significant part is made up by stages of my career, by getting to know different universities and, at the same time, academic systems.

My approach to RE theory developed in Frankfurt, Germany. Geographically, for some people this means: right in the middle of Europe. Additionally, this development took place right at the turn of the centuries, more specifically right at the turn from the 20th to the 21st century. This approach to contextual didactics of religion deals with RE in the European context. For me personally, this main focus surfaced as a result of the large scale political and societal events, such as the launch of the Euro and the expansion of the European Union to Eastern Europe. My interest in a European take on RE, culture and theology did come about not only by various factual insights I collected throughout the past two decades. Rather, this theoretical work roots in and is shaped by personal experiences, internalized patterns as well as by new discoveries, made continuously along the way.

I grew up in a family with three sons and one daughter; I was the second boy. Since childhood I am familiar with mobility as constitutive element of lifestyle; a familiarity I became aware of in comparison with a family whose whole life was enacted in one little town in the country. At the same time, I always was just as deeply averse to provincialism as I was curious to get to know something new. This latter aspect probably is related to the closed private circle of our family. Nobody who has browsed my papers and books will be taken by surprise if I state here and now: I am extremely passionate about travelling abroad. Europe is not my sole, but increasingly a dominant destination, may it be Oslo, Groningen, Tromsø, Bern, Crete, Pisa, Granada or Prague. Beyond the European borders, frequent journeys in the past included places and regions like Boston, Chicago and Quebec.

I was born in Western Germany in 1948, right after World War II. I grew up in a period of history that is known now in Germany as the 'era of Adenauer' (the first post war chancellor of the Federal Republic of Germany) or the era of the German 'Wirtschaftswunder', the years of economic boom during the fifties and early sixties. Still a child, I learned about the war from photos my father had taken and from what we heard at school. I learned about this war, which Germany had dreadfully fought against next to all European neighbors, planting the seed of enmity. Nevertheless, concerning Europe the generation of parents and teachers rather unanimously handed down a mixture of presumption and ignorance. The essence of culture, the flourishing of mind and knowledge, was quite commonly depicted as something not to be found beyond the nation of the ones like Bach, Goethe and Schiller – our nation. At this time, many still fell for the illusion that masked the German occupation and subjugation of nearly the entire European continent as nothing but a minor accident, an accident that interrupted the flawless line of national success just shortly. It took years for me to free myself, to unravel and to unmask these prejudices.

During these early years, by means of maps and speeches more information was transported about our remote sister city in East Prussia than about the Dutch city of Nijmegen, quite close to our hometown. Sometimes famous names of foreign statesmen (de Gaulle or Schumann) were to be found in the headlines of newspapers. Pictures witnessed spectacular, groundbreaking encounters of the reconstruction of European relations. But all this seemed to happen in far distance, far from everyday life of a boy listening and playing music, and attending primary and secondary school. Growing up on the lower Rhine, however, I vividly remember regular visits to the Netherlands, just for a shopping tour or for lunch. Our first family holidays in Italy took place as early as 1957. In this period, the first 'Gastarbeiter' (non immigrant guest workers who substantially fueled the economic success) came to work in the Ruhr, the industrial heart of Western Germany, roaring during these days. The majority of these workers came from Italy and Turkey. As a matter of course, they brought little or no German language skills along. Still, it was all but usual to go 'to them' to eat pizza or döner kebab. Secondary school, a boys' school, opened my – until then – rather closed, world, non in the least place because I got to know and love four European languages: English, French, Latin and Greek (and, eventually: standard German, not frowned upon in the way regional dialects were). New languages that challenged me to leave the 'comfort zone' of the mainstream and explore new worlds. Next to that Bonhoeffer entered my life, when with a group of peers (a kind of 'counter culture') we started to critically read and discuss his 'religionslose interpretation von Religion', on a weekly basis; a contrasting experience to the closed private circle of my family. All this, in sum, did not yet fully allow for opening up worlds unknown before me as a boy. For years, Europe in my eyes still remained just a term to name the mere surroundings of Germany or the headline of another chapter the textbook for my geography class.

During my time as a student at the university, in this regard little change came about. It was not before I had finished my dissertation that I attended conferences and established contact with colleagues in my field. The qualitatively significant, groundbreaking step forward, however, took place in 1987 when I was appointed to a professorship in Groningen, Netherlands. My new professional home did not only bear the euphonic as well as dignified name 'Faculteit der Godgeleerdheid'. With pleasure I also experienced to be welcomed with arms wide open. Wilna Meijer and JanDirk Immelman were my companions in playing Beethoven and Bach, alternated with discussions about different approaches in RE. I was received by my colleagues in the faculty of Theology with sympathy and great expectations. At the same time, my colleagues did not deny to have had quite ambivalent encounters with Germans. This opened my eyes for another perspective on Germans (not only 'moffen', but also a respected powerful and influential country), and my own identification with Germany and the Germans. Having been employed for years as a civil servant in Germany, it came as both a surprise and a relief to me that I was appointed as an official by the queen of the Netherlands without ado. At a first glance, my time in Groningen did not yield much in terms of my engagement in RE per se. Yet, seen in retrospective, another light is shed on this stay abroad. It triggered abundantly many experiences and impulses, due to living for a longer period abroad and sharing common life of the 'Groningers', which I now find to be represented in my contextual approach to RE. I would like to point out four:

– Firstly: Both, participation in everyday life made me aware of the importance of the context of a rather closed circle of theological academic life in Germany, and intensive personal contacts with colleagues provided me – for the first time in my life – with a viewpoint decidedly from outside, seeing Germany through the lens of a small neighboring country. This learning process of mine was of particular intensity due to events of our contemporary history that came about simultaneously. The reunification of both German states was on the horizon and the country was about to 'grow' in size.

– Secondly: Despite the taunting judgment among Germans, ridiculing the Dutch language as a mere dialect of the German, Dutch is a genuinely independent language indeed. The nation and its people, of course, do own a quite distinct history as well as culture. By no means (and for the better as for the worse), not all energy is spent by concerning oneself with relationship and orientation toward the big neighbor in the east.

– Thirdly: Here, in the Netherlands, something was just matter of course: Theology is neither learned nor practiced within strict boundaries of one's own language or limited to national traditions of thought. While the own Dutch culture is upheld, the colleagues of the theological faculty freely move across European languages, they move way beyond their mother language, speaking English, French and German. At first, I often was puzzled by the bi- and multilingualism that unfolded on a daily basis. Yet, the benefit of being able to tap worlds formerly unknown and unfamiliar quickly began to surface before my eyes.

– Fourthly: This was when I began to grasp the eminent meaning of the term life-world – signifying a world that is common, familiar, both intimately and intuitively known. This understanding gained weight with every journey back to my family for the weekend: Their world, formerly intimately known to me, started to crack here and there, first hardly noticed, then in quite obvious domains. Travelling to and fro made me even more aware of the importance of context: I did not any longer watch the same advertisements on TV as my children did; the newspaper I used to read during the week differed vastly from the one my wife received her information on the events of the day from. When I came back to Groningen on Mondays, the same happened respectively, in the reverse manner. In short, I was constantly busy establishing the familiarity with friends and family anew time and again, backwards and forwards. I had a home for a time span only, lived a life in transition, not too romantic, and exhausting at times. Practice preceded the development of the theoretical concept of 'context'.

For 22 years now, I work at the University of Frankfurt on Main. Since my appointment here more than twenty years back, I also live in the 'Rhine-Main-area', this is, in various places in the region surrounding Frankfurt. Looking back, I am able to identify numerous impulses for a contextual approach to RE and practical theology that were fostered by this locality: by the greater Frankfurt area, by the Department of Protestant Theology in Frankfurt, just as well as by the urban culture in Frankfurt itself. While I was a student at a university in the western part of the Federal Republic in the years following 1969, Frankfurt on Main for me and for many politically active youth in Germany owned the fame of a Promised Land. The university in Frankfurt was close to messianic reputation. Promising names such as T. W. Adorno, M. Horkheimer, J. Habermas and A. Mitscherlich undergirded this aura of the place. Shortly after my appointment in Frankfurt 1990, however, I discovered flaws in this picture. Tensions and discrepancies emerge in the light of the drifting 'continents' that are made up by characteristics such as the open-mindedness of the metropolis, the sheer, concentrated power of money in the German heart of finance, and the often idyllic, partly rural and sometimes quite provincial mentality in the older parts of the city.

Driven by persuasion and commitment, I took up my own work on RE and practical theology. This meant taking up the focus of a theory of praxis in the line of Fr. Schleiermacher. This on the other hand meant in particular: doing theology in a decidedly urban culture, situated in an urban way of life. In a larger sequence of classes that collectively covers both homiletics and liturgy, which I conceptualized and tested together with colleague Matthias von Kriegstein, I had the opportunity to explore processes of learning in the field of contextual theology for the academic education of future pastors (Heimbrock & von Kriegstein, 2002). The trajectory of learning that we mapped out for this purpose nurtures my RE until today.

Starting early in the 90s, together with many coworkers in my research group I started to develop the life-world oriented approach, which proved to be a viable and sensitive instrument to perceive and experience the urban field, politically as well as in terms of the everyday life. In various teams, I organized classes, projects and field trips, which aimed at tracking 'traces of God in the metropolitan area'. My collection of photos, slides and audio documents concerning the 'Lived Religion' has grown significantly ever since. Now and then today, I surprisingly find myself collecting quite 'normal' arrangements or sights of the day to day life, taking over the role of a cultural anthropologist, who is collecting data of the local life. For this purpose, I use to carry a camera along, ready to be used whenever necessary or interesting: You never know what is to be encountered.

The tension between provinciality on the one hand and open-mindedness on the other reappears in quite concrete and practical instances. It emerged in conflicts within congregations, but also written in tombstone in a graveyard, likewise in discussions that centered on the extension of the Frankfurt airport. Not least, the attitude of students we work with on a daily basis is substantially coined by this ambivalence. Many commute from rural areas. Neither are they familiar nor comfortable with 'the city'. In our research group, we were on the lookout to identify theories that would boost our understanding of phenomena like these. Moreover, this cooperative search process came to be the context in which many major ideas of contextual didactics were presented for the first time. We discussed them intensely, sometimes controversially, most often in enormously fruitful ways.

Thanks to the contingencies of life-world, to me the recent years in Frankfurt University opened up a particularly promising chance for contextual didactics. In 2001, all faculties of arts and thus also the faculty of theology moved to a new building, the 'IG-Farben building', situated on the Frankfurt-Westend campus of Goethe university. Since then, the campus has developed, said to be picture-perfect among the campuses in Europe, a place where I enjoy working and living at. When we first arrived, however, we found nothing but an enormously huge construction site. It took a year to get rid of chaos, dust, hammering and sawing. Not before all this was overcome, a quite magnificent place for living and learning unfolded before our eyes. Yet, exactly these interruptions of everyday life, the jackhammer's noise during the exam or the stench of fertilizer on the lawn next to the window of our classroom led to a conscious and alert perception: perceiving surroundings of learning that are beneath and beyond our attention under normal circumstances. Due to the loss of the old structured environment, to the loss of the familiar places to get a cup of coffee, to make copies or to buy books, we had the one-time chance to meticulously explore the learning arrangements by means of exercises of perception and by reflecting that what was to be perceived.

Frankfurt on Main offered exciting contexts not only in this regard. The intensifying and intensified international cooperation in my field of research proved to be a primary inspiration. I got to get a closer look on approaches from various European countries and their ways of doing RE. Even the very first time, I read about 'Contextual RE' was not a German book, however a Norwegian one.[1] But, as mentioned before: More importantly, encounters with people, exchange on respective everyday routines, in other words the embodiment of other contexts of life fostered and triggered major impulses for my work in material regards. Hence, I did not have to start by looking up the term 'context' in textbooks before I felt motivated to formulate contextual didactics in the European horizon. Meetings, interpersonal experiences led quickly beyond just another expert talk. Worlds unknown came about when entangled in a personal chat, on the patio at home, for instance. Landmarks of contextual learning in Frankfurt emerged when jointly walking and discovering the city. Unfamiliar eyes immensely helped to see places and things anew that I only believed to intimately know. For instance, we discovered a depiction of Jesus on a scungy house wall. This exploration into my own life-world lead to several pieces of RE practice aiming at 'regional didactics'.[2]

Explorations at other universities and in other cities, where I stayed as a guest, were landmarks of another kind. Students and colleagues functioned as tour guides and facilitators of cultural anthropological insights into everyday life. Another way to push these thoughts even further was pretty simple: by temporarily just taking part in the daily routines of the university, by visiting a school, by attending a worship service somewhere in an urban district or by being invited to a celebration in a friend's family. Despite all growing familiarity and personal closeness, this, mediated by friends and neighbors, is not where the discovery of the new and of the other stops. Discoveries of this nature range from detecting a (from my perspective) less tidy appearance of the street to realizing the conditions bestowed upon the everyday life by local weather conditions. Unforgettable was the change from outdoor shoes to slippers that went without saying for the youth in the German school in Prague. I came to see and feel the winter sun gleaming over Frankfurt in quite a different way, after I had seen it disappear behind the horizon for the last time in months in Tromsø, far north of the polar circle, as early as in November.

The international accent of my work in RE broke through in 1986. It was this year, when I participated in the 'International Seminar on Religious Education and Values' (ISREV) for the first time, taking place at Dublin ISREV is a singular, international forum intended to provide a space to discuss issues of RE. My experiences amidst this forum irrevocably saved me from falling prey to an orientation that would focus on Europe exclusively. I met Norwegian colleagues Elisabeth Haakedaal, Heid Leganger-Krogstad and Geir Afdal who introduced me into their line of thought on contextuality and opened for me the field of contextual Religious Education More or less by chance I began to deepen my contacts within this extremely inspiring, global organization for RE predominantly on the European scale. Doubtlessly, starting from Frankfurt is of utmost help for a venture such as this: Many places in Europe can be reached via just one or two hours of flight. Getting 'to Europe' is not at all complicated. Anyways, all this nurtured the idea of founding a smaller, specifically European network, ENRECA.

During the conferences just as well as on the occasion of everyday contacts, via email or phone, some of the experience I had made for the first time in the Netherlands turned out to be even more true: Looking from outside, one can see and understand one's own situation far more clearly. Strengths and weaknesses can be identified more easily, concerning the profile as a whole as well as concerning little bits and pieces. The longer my friends in other European countries and I continue to deepen our contacts, the more clearly differences surface. These differences indicate the essential variety that is encompassed by this one name Europe – a variety ranging from the particular way of celebrating the Christmas dinner to the ritual opening a class in school or the legislation concerning opening hours for shops on Sundays.

For me, the exploration of other countries and of their respective developments concerning RE includes (for years now) encountering colleagues and students, both in universities and schools. The Erasmus-Sokrates program of the European Union provides a framework for academic exchange across Europe, both for students and professors. On this basis, we started in 1999 to establish partnerships for teaching exchange on a regular basis. Thanks to this institution and thanks to the hospitality of individuals abroad, I had the opportunity to frequently lecture as a guest in other European universities. Time to time, visit after visit, the cooperation in jointly planned seminars intensified. Besides, this has been and still is an excellent opportunity to get to know the routines of living and learning in different places. I gained abundantly many impressions, experiences and materials to take home with me. In particular, this proved to be of worth concerning the quite different arrangements of schooling. In the era of mobile computing, many texts have not been conventionally conceptualized at a desk, but while being on travels, with friends in a cottage close to the fjord, in the hotel room, in a waiting area of an airport, on a train.

The practice demonstrated on these very pages, the attempt to express contextuality in print, which certainly means: in decontextualized fashion, is somewhat awkward and limited. Thankfully, I look back upon my personal and professional contexts of my RE theory today. These contexts turned into much more than just professional stages and occupational surroundings, namely into contexts of life itself, even more, into very 'texts' of my life indeed, in a broadened sense of the term 'text'. At this point, I would like to invite my readers to set sail for an exploration of their own, taking a look at texts and contexts of their own biography concerning RE, both in thought and as embodied as possible.

For the near future, cultivation of contextuality is of pivotal importance for the discipline of Pedagogics of Religion. We should explore the possibilities of RE as a subject that facilitates the development of sensitivity of difference: difference in culture and religion. As such this will contribute to the sustainability of Europe. Relativasation of the own culture and of the own religious identity is necessary, in the sense of taking an other's perspective: 'walking the shoes of the other', without naïve attempt to copy them. For the future, as in the past, people are dependent on each other, for the economical development as well as for the cultural development. Knowing about the other's perspective on culture and religion is enriching in the first place and is preconditional for respecting the other. Knowing about the other and competent in communication with the other. In our research the focus should be on patterns in everyday life of people, and what this means for the discipline of Practical Theology and of Religious Education and the development of normative professionalism. Research in this field can only be done inter-disciplinary, as this was practiced in for example the project 'Perceiving the other'. Perceiving 'the other'; knowing about the other, precedes the reception of the other as a fellow human – this is what we should continue to work on in the near future, in our research as well as in our different practices, as well as in our encounters as scholars in this field – in real life as well as in publications.

NOTES

[1] See Afdal, Haakedal, and Leganger-Krogstad (1997). Important for me was also picking up the discussion in theology (cf. Bevans, 1992).

[2] Some pieces are presented in the chapter 7 of the book Heimbrock (2004), cf. also Heimbrock (2009).

REFERENCES

Afdal, G., Haakedal, E., & Leganger-Krogstad, H. (1997). *Tro, livstolkning og tradisjon: innfoering i kontekstuell religionsdidaktikk* [Faith, Life Interpretation and Tradition: Introduction into contextual RE]. Oslo.

Bevans, B. (1992). *Models of contextual theology.* New York.

Failing, W. E. & Heimbrock, H.-G. (1998). *Gelebte Religion wahrnehmen, Lebenswelt – Alltagskultur – Religionspraxis.* Stuttgart.

Heimbrock, H.-G. (2004). *Religionsunterricht im Kontext Europa. Einführung in die kontextuelle Religionsdidaktik.* Stuttgart.

Heimbrock, H.-G. (2007). Reconstructing lived experience. In H.-G. Heimbrock & Chr. Scholtz (eds.), *Religion: Immediate experience and the mediacy of research. Interdisciplinary studies in objectives, concepts and methodology of empirical research in religion* (pp. 133-156). Series Research on Contemporary Religion, Band 1. Göttingen.

Heimbrock, H.-G. (2009). Encounter as model for dialogue in RE. In S. Miedema (ed.), *Religious education as encounter* (pp. 83-97). Münster.

Heimbrock, H.-G., & Kriegstein, M. von (eds.). (2002). *Theologische Bildungsprozesse gestalten. Schritte zur Ausbildungsreform.* Frankfurt/M.

Klaffki, W. (1964). *Das pädagogische Problem des Elementaren und die Theorie der kategorialen Bildung.* Weinheim.

Miedema, S. et al. (2004). The European network for religious education through contextual approaches (ENRECA): Its policy and aims. *Informationes Theologiae Europae, 13,* 227-232.

AFFILIATIONS

Hans-Günter Heimbrock
Fachbereich Evangelische Theologie
Goethe-Universität
Frankfurt/Main, Germany

CHRIS HERMANS

RELIGION AS A SPECIAL WORLD OF MEANING SET APART

On Imagination, Experiences and Practices of the Other-Than-Rational

INTRODUCTION

*... a world of symbols, odour, colour, gestures, actions that
are full of meanings*

Being raised in a catholic family, I went to school with a view on the church. My parents were not particularly religious, rather average catholic in the early 1960s. As a child I was an altar boy whereby I assisted the priest at liturgy. During my time at primary school I was permitted to leave the classroom during school time in order to go to church for a wedding or a funeral. From all celebrations I attended, the funerals are those I remember most. A catholic liturgy is a world on itself: a world of symbols, odour, colour, gestures, actions that are full of meanings. The world of rituals is full of meanings, and those meanings constitute a world in itself. The everyday meaning is put between brackets: water is not for drinking but represents purity and purification; myrrh is not for the odour it emanates but represents the rising up of the prayer to God. The world of imagination is provided with a splendour of reality in liturgy (Geertz, 1966, 1973). For one moment it becomes Heaven on earth – just as real as everyday life. The experiences of that little boy in the churched shaped me to what I am. Add the loss of my mother at the age of ten to that, and you will understand that death and religious imagination will stick in my mind forever.

PRACTICE AND IMAGINATION

The world of imagination in symbols and rituals creates a world of meaning (Ricoeur, 1991). Symbols and rituals as embodied practices are a vehicle for our imagination. In these practices is the grief of people during a funeral lifted in a world of meaning that transforms this grief in new meaning. In this practice, it acquires an unexpected, yes even (seen through the eyes of the existing world) impossible meaning. Death suddenly has no longer the final world, nor brokenness, nor speechless grief, nor invisible suffering. The liturgical practice that pastor and church-goers shape together takes up the grief in a world meaning that – for a brief moment – constitutes a doorway to Heaven: an imagination of human wholeness or fullness (Taylor, 2007) where people long for. The world of meaning in these

I. ter Avest (ed.), On the Edge: (Auto)biography and Pedagogical Theories on Religious Education, 47–55.

practices need to be connected to the world of life of the participants outside the church (and liturgy). Religion is a practice, a way of life that orients human life towards fullness (see Ward, 2004).

Imagination

Mankind in search of meaning cannot evade imagination, because certain experiences of people cannot be mastered by reason. In the educational field in the Netherlands, there is a renewed attention for the so-called 'non-cognitive'. However, this idea remains rather vague in this debate. I believe that the concept of 'contingency' could to clarify what we mean by it. In religious philosophy in Germany, contingency is one of the core concepts (see specifically Wuchterl, 2011, 2012). Contingency refers to experiences that could occur to me as human being, but are not necessary. They are possible, not necessary – but for me as personal they have become topical. As a human being one can experience that a loved one (child, parent, partner, friend, family member, etc.) passes on. Just think how often this indeed happens at schools. This kind of situation cannot be controlled by reason. What happened, could have been different; it is not necessary or compulsory (i.e. it is ontological contingent). There is no way that I (or the other person) could not have acted in such way that it could have been prevented (i.e., it is absolute contingent). One is confronted with a situation which is ambiguous, open, has become a question. In these experiences, the taken-for-granted meaning of existence is interrupted; the world of meaning does no longer fits. A human being is literally not capable of living in this world anymore, as the saying goes: "I have no life anymore like this!" or "I don't know how to get on anymore".

Experiences of contingency are inherent to human existence. Before reason they constitute the other, strange, uncontrollable (see title of the book by Wuchterl, 2012). This does not mean that every human person acknowledges contingency: it is possible to 'manage' or 'control' is through reason (and its rational explanations). However, if one accept the unexpected and uncontrollable, in our imagination we have to search for meaning. Why imagination? Because, reason does not enforce a sufficient reason for what happened to us.

Religion is a play with imagination – a serious game. A game of symbols, stories, rituals. Just like you enter another world in a game, with different rules of play – a space that is delimited by the rules of the game – you enter in religion a world world of meaning where other rules apply with regard to what is and what is not important, what is and what is not true, what is just and what is not. In liturgy, this special world of meaning obtains a splandour of reality. During the game of imagination you are usurped in a design of world in which redemption of brokenness is promised. The desire for wholeness, fullness, human dignity becomes reality –albeit for a little while. What reason cannot grasp becomes reality through human imagination (poetry, symbols, rituals, sound, etc.). In a poem line by Huub Oosterhuis: "to be what cannot be, to do what is unthinkable – death and resurrection".

Practices of Imagination

> I am waiting with my bicycle for a traffic light to turn green. I am surrounded by students, youngsters, and mothers with children waiting for the same traffic light. Who provides new generations with the tools that are necessary in order to feed imagination and shape practices? Who provides them with the tools that are necessary in order to deal with questions of ultimate meaning in life; questions on life and death, of love and sorrow, on the contingency of existence?

This experience expresses my passion as pedagogue of religion in order to provide new generations with the tools of imagination, in order to provide meaning to experiences of contingency (existential questions). A tool box which enables them to enter a world of meaning and shape practices that provide meaning to experiences which reason is denied any possibility of control. I am passionate, to provide people with tools so that they are not without imagination in their longing for fullness. What cuts me like a knife is the situation that in these moments of contingency people do not have words, practices, traditions available in order to provide meaning to what happened to them. When people literally go up in smoke and fire in a crematorium, without any meaning can be given to this event this cuts me like a knife. If people are buried without practices of imagination, this violates all human dignity. Being embedded in practices of the past unites generations; but at the same time, people are invited to develop new practices of imagination that connects to generations to come. All use of practices is creative, never a mere copy of the past.

RELIGION AS A SPECIAL WORLD OF MEANING

Religion as experience is difficult to grasp. What distinguishes religious experience from all other experiences? What makes it unique and incomparable to other experiences? This approach is encountered regularly, but it is very problematic. In a psychological sense, religious experiences are an experience like any other experience, only the attribution of the meaning is different. Religious experiences are indeed special experiences that we set apart from other experiences (such as the experiences of contingency) (Taves, 2009). We attribute a religious meaning to certain experiences 'set apart': we associate them with the name of God based on stories from religious traditions we know, through our familiarity with symbols, stories and rituals. In short: we refer to a certain experience as being religious, since we have learned to associate this type of experience with the adjective 'religious'. Now let's return to the youngsters from my example at the traffic light: they do not have that language at their disposal and were not introduced into that special world of meaning which we call religion. The exciting question remains: 'How does one introduce people who have not become familiar with this type of systems of meaning into the world of religion? How will they obtain access to meanings that supersede our understanding, explanatory ratio?'

TOOLS

Let us return to the loss of a beloved one, the emotions of grief and pain that belong to that, and the ways in which people provide meaning to this experience and learn how to express it. Religious traditions provide forms of imagination to deal with the other-than-rational experiences. Via tools like in symbols, stories, and practices one enters a special world of meaning set apart. Legitimate participation of students in these practices enables them to enter this world of meaning: to learn to express their gratitude for the life of the deceased, to canalise grief, to express their feelings. We do not pull students in a community of faith – we don't regard that as acceptable in an educational setting. Still, we may challenge pupils in order to stand at the rim of that practice, to participate, and understand from the inside what the participants in this practices experience as meaning. Students have the right to decide to leave these tools behind (and the world of meaning incorporated in it) or appropriate them and become more deeply familiar with them.

The Practice of a Teacher

If you want to show understand the world of meaning incorporated in the tools of religious symbols, rituals, or texts from the Bible, you have to participate in the practice by which people deal meaningfully with these tools. Let me give an example: a teacher in reading Bible stories can show that this practice is something special when the teacher handles this Book in a special way, by lighting a candle, putting the Book in a special place in class, and asking students to be silent and listen, etc. By this situation the teacher embodies a practice of reading which is different from reading a story from a typical children's book (like 'Mary Poppins', or 'Pluk van de Petteflat' in the Netherlands). The whole practice in which this Book is read makes clear to students, that this is a Holy Text about the relationship between people and God. The whole learning situation reflects this reading practice: it embodies a special world of meaning set apart.

Freedom to Step away from a Practice

In the educational system it is important that the freedom of each pupil is respected to enter and leave this practice. You must enter into this practice in order to obtain access to the meaning, but not in a way that makes you fully surrender to it. With Wenger, I have called this legitimate peripheral participation. Through participating in a practice, the student becomes familiar with the world of meaning that unfolds 'in front of' this practice (Hermans, 2003). Without a hermeneutic interpretation of this practice, understanding is not possible (Pollefeyt & Lombaerts, 2004; Pollefeyt, 2008). The practices, rituals, or the life story of a person in another religion can only be understood if you become a participant in their world, and opened yourself for the other. Many students in our time are not socialized in a religious tradition – as that little altar boy did at the catholic primary school with a view on the church. Until the sixties, students were familiar with these practices, but did not necessarily understand their meaning in everyday life. In our times, we should (also) make pupils become acquainted with the world of meaning in certain practices, in order to be able to connect this meaning with everyday life (world of the reader).

Scaffolding

In education which invites students to participate in practices and creates the freedom to step back, is what I call 'learning from' religion. One needs to distinguish between 'learning in, about, and from' (Hermans, 2003). 'Learning in' refers to socialising students into a certain tradition. A student participates in a religious practice with the objective to adopt this practice. With 'learning about' refers to the goal that students become informed about various religious practices, e.g. a kind of phenomenological approach of Holy texts, practices, building, important persons, and rituals and symbols. A student observes from a distance at 'unfamiliar' practices without bridging this strangeness. In 'learning from' the identity development of pupils is the goal. A student is introduced to stories and practices of religious traditions but is free to appropriate its meaning or to leave it behind. This process is called 'scaffolding': the teacher constructs scaffolds which gives the pupil access to the meaning 'in front of the practice', and gradually removes these scaffolds in order to make the child independent. One the one hand, a teacher challenges students to become acquainted with a world of meaning from an inside perspective, and on the other hand gives them the freedom to incorporate this meaning in their personal identity or not.

PRACTICES ARE EMBODIED EXPERIENCES

The religious tool box, and practices are embodied experiences. An Easter candle, reading a Bible story, acting tolerant towards 'strangers' introduce participants in experiences of generations before us. The meaning of the resurrection is (hermeneutically) mediated by the 'tool' Easter candle. An Easter candle or action of forgiveness mediates the meaning that people attribute to these practices or tools. This meaning is shared with other participants in this practice. I must not 'forget' my own experiences in understanding this practice, but connect them with my own experiences. Interpretation ends when I have learned to connect the world of practices to my own life world (of the reader). Let me give an example: how do I know the meaning of forgiveness? I begin to understand what this means by participating in a certain practice of compassion or by understanding the actions of various persons in the story of The Good Samaritan. Finally, it is not all about participation in this practice, but about understanding the world meaning that is offered 'in front of' this practice or reading this story. The interpretation ends when I succeed in reading my own experiences from the experiences embodied in these practices. The story or the practice has become a tool of shared meanings.

Distributed Knowledge in Tools, Practices, Users, Context

The tool mediates between the meaning of experiences from the past and the meaning of experiences from the present. What has as yet remained underexposed is the enduring role that this tool plays as knowledge base of the community of users. We call this distributive knowledge, that is knowledge that is 'distributed' over tools, the situation, the use of this tool and other participants. How does a pilot 'knows' how to land an airplane? This knowledge is based on the expertise and skills of the pilot, the instruments in the cockpit of the airplane, the co-pilot, the situation of the landing strip, and the expertise available in the control tower of the airport where we will land. All these elements together (as well as their mutual relation) provide for the knowledge how to land; in other words: this is a very dynamic process, bound by its context.

This is something completely different from the context-dependent knowledge that we test in the educational system. We provide a child with a piece of paper and ask whether he or she wants to write down individually what he or she remembers. And if this knowledge is reproduced 'properly', the child has learned what we intended to teach. I think that this belief also ruled my ideas on learning when I started in the eighties and nineties. It also constituted the foundation of my doctoral thesis: learning as cognitive processing of information (Hermans, 1985). Throughout the past years, I have become distanced from that idea. Learning is not something that a student does alone, and it is not something that is reduced to mental processes in the head of the learner. Learning is a shared effort in a certain practice by means of tools used in this situation (Hermans, 2003). Just to stick to the example of the hammer: an expert in the field of hammering can operate a hammer; he knows the history of operation of the hammer and can therewith understand the practice of hammering. In order to give meaning to one's own life, we also need tools that can help us in order to provide meaning to life. Without all those tools a human being cannot know how to live, also not when it comes to questions of existence (the other-than-rational, contingency).

Narrowed Knowledge

Our students only learn knowledge *about* the tools: they know what a candle is, what the meaning of Easter is, what our legal system is. However, without getting access to the experience knowledge stored in the tools, they learn nothing. The abstract knowledge (apart from the use in life) has 'pushed aside' the experience knowledge in real life. The complexity and wealth of the experience knowledge is hidden behind the abstract, de-contextualised knowing. This is also what the Schools Inspectorate wants to know from schools. For learning with regard to other-than-rational, this narrowing is 'deadly': in this way you cannot provide pupils to get access to the meaning of existence.

The pedagogue Jerome Bruner (1986) distinguishes between instrumental-explicative knowledge and interpretative-narrative knowledge. The former could also be called the knowledge of reason (the cognitive element), and the latter the knowledge the other-than-rational (the non-cognitive element). According to Bruner, all people have the capacity to learn instrumental-explicative knowledge: that is the knowledge of natural sciences, mathematics, technique, language, and reading (in as far as this is a skill). This knowledge can be tested with a multiple-choice test. With this knowledge, one can get far on the social ladder (with regard to money and esteem). But this is not the total human condition in which students need to be introduced in education; moreover, this type of knowledge does not include human dignity. The cognitive (mastering) knowledge is necessary for the production of goods (everyday living conditions) and the construction of society (houses, facilities, social care) (Arendt, 1956). However, this knowledge does not provide an answer to the 'why', the (non)sense of existence, the human dignity, the loss, and the brokenness. This 'why' is not accessible for the instrumental-explicative reason. This knowledge finds its origin where reason is interrupted, loses its control, and people are apprehended by life. The interpretative-narrative knowledge is embedded in the tools and the practices in which generations have learned to give meaning to their dealing with existential questions. It is the knowledge embodied in the special worlds set apart of religions? This knowledge cannot be tested with multiple-choice questions (*What* is? *How many? When?*). One has to test this in interaction with these tools, (also) together with others, connected with emotions, longings and attitudes, and exploring the sources of wisdom incorporated in it. Through this process, one learns to handle experiences of contingency in one's own life.

PRACTICES REGARDING EXISTENTIAL QUESTIONS

In my scientific work, I learned to understand the limits of instrumental-explicative thinking. I have discovered that I have not learned religion by reason, but by interpretative knowledge connected to deeply-human existential questions. The explicative knowledge is the highest form of knowledge in science. During my doctoral research I approached learning from religion and ethics from insights from cognitive psychology about acquiring and storing information. I developed in my PhD research explanations on the success of a certain type of construction of a curriculum in moral education, in which students learn how to assess morally (Hermans, 1985). Gradually I came to realise that interpretative-narrative knowledge is far more complex and of a different nature than can be explained and understood by means of explicative knowledge. Looking back at my doctoral research, the assumption was already latently present there. I added something to the explanatory model of cognitive psychology, namely knowledge distributed in a practice of moral formation of judgment. We made a film for the curriculum: a dramatised display of a practice of building a moral judgment. This film consisted of scenes from a trip with youngsters to the Biesbosch region. We filmed these students during their process of moral judgment on nature management. In hindsight, that approach already showed something from learning in practices in which the moral judging takes place. If I would carry out the same research now, I would create a design research aimed to understand learning practices in which pupils can develop their moral and religious judgment. I think that design research is the future of Religious Education.

Design of Practices of Meaning

In my doctoral thesis as well as in much research I have supervised, I have focussed on effect research. Effect research focuses on existing practices; the objective is to demonstrate that certain practices are effective, and why (under which conditions) they are or are not. Statements from effect research are evidence-based. You know what pupils did or did not learn, and what has stimulated the learning process (aspects of the curriculum, learning environment, teacher behavior). However, the most urgent problems with regard to moral and religious education do not lie with measuring existing learning arrangements, but with the development of new ones. We hardly know anything about the non-cognitive learning with regard to questions of meaning of life. How do pupils actually acquire virtues with regard to citizenship? If one takes it seriously that it is about a specific kind of knowledge (interpretative-narrative), one starts to realise that most insights from the pedagogic field, educational science, or learning psychology cannot just be transferred to the non-cognitive learning. Our greatest need is not to measure the effects of existing situations (what the authorities mostly want, and preferably large-scale) but to design yet unknown learning situations in which pupils can acquire the knowledge to deal with the other-than-rational experiences in human existence. The urgent question for teaching religious education is: how do I shape a practice that does not exist yet?

There is a need for the development of practices that comply with a number of criteria: the practices must connect with the existential questions of students; they must learn to deal with other-than-rational situations (or contingency); according to different stager in the development of pupils; students with different ethnic and religious backgrounds must be able to become acquainted to them; they must provide access to worlds of meaning in different traditions – meanings of life and sorrow, of grief and happiness, of me and the other person, of guilt and forgiveness; they must provide insight in how pupils can obtain access to meanings by participating in them. I experience a great urgency for the development of practice-oriented knowledge with regard to moral and religious learning. There are models for the design of a rich learning environment of practices that have a phased structure in order to provide pupils with tools for dealing with questions that are of a vital importance to them. Tools that mean a lot to them, that contain meanings that they can understand, and tools that *they* can use. Practices embodied in reading texts, practice rituals or shared actions in which students can enter a special world of meaning (set apart) in which they learn to understand what a live in fullness/ wholeness can be.

Design research aims to build knowledge about new, future learning arrangements in a scientifically responsible manner (Van den Akker et al., 2007; McKenny & Reeves, 2012). I wish to contribute to the design of new practices that foster imagination in help new generations to learn to deal with moral and religious questions. That is an exciting challenge for Religious Education in the coming years.

REFERENCES

Akker, J. van den et al. (2007). *An introduction to educational design research*. Enschede: SLO.

Arendt, H. (1956). *The human condition*, second edition (with an introduction by Margeret Canovan). Chicago: Chicago University Press.

Bruner, J. (1986). *Actual minds, possible worlds*. Cambridge: Harvard University Press.

Geertz, C. (1966). Religion as a cultural system. In M. Banton (ed.), *Anthropological approaches to the study of religion* (pp. 1-46). London: Travistock.

Geertz, C. (1973). *The interpretation of cultures*. New York: Basic Books.

Hermans, C. A. M. (1985). *Morele vorming*. Kampen: KOK.

Hermans, C. A. M. (2003). *Participerend leren. Grondslagen van religieuze vorming in een globaliserende samenleving*. Budel: Damon.

McKenny, S., &. Reeves, T. C. (2012). *Conducting educational design research*. Oxford: Routledge.

Pollefeyt, D. (2008). Difference matters. A hermeneutic-communicative concept of didactics of religion. *Journal of Religious Education, 56*(1), 9-17.

Pollefeyt, D., & Lombaerts, H. (eds.). (2004). *Hermeneutics and religious education*. Leuven: University Press Peeters.

Ricoeur, P. (1991). Life in quest of a narrative. In David Wood (ed.), *On Paul Ricoeur. Narrative and interpretation* (pp. 20-33). London: Routledge.

Tavens, A. (2009). *Religious experience reconsidered. A building-block approach to the study of religion and other special things*. Princeton: Princeton University Press.

Taylor, C. (2007). *A secular age*. Cambridge: The Bellknap Press of Harvard University Press.

Ward, K. (2004). *A case for religion*. Oxford: Oneworld.

Wuchterl, K. (2011). *Kontingenz oder das Andere der Vernunft. Zum Verhältnis von Philosophie, Natuurwissenschaft und Religion*. Stuttgart: Franz Steiner Verlag.

Wuchterl, K. (2012). Kontingenz als religionsphilosophischer Schlüsselbegriff zur Klärung von Grenzen zwischen Naturwissenschaft und Religion. In H. Müller (ed.), *Wie gewiss ist unser Wissen? Alles nur eine Mode der Zeit?* Berlin: Frank & Timme.

AFFILIATIONS

Chris Hermans
Research Fellow, Department of Theology
UNISA, Pretoria, South Africa
Professor of Empirical Theology, Department of Theology,
Radboud University, Nijmegen, The Netherlands

ROBERT JACKSON

RELIGIOUS EDUCATION AND THE ARTS OF INTERPRETATION REVISITED

INTRODUCTION

I took on influences from others
– sometimes consciously and sometimes less so –
but the sound, however limited, turned out to be personal

I was born and brought up in Derbyshire, in the English East Midlands, in a coal mining and iron making town in South Derbyshire. Many of my family were involved in iron making, and I had several vacation jobs working on the blast furnaces at Stanton Ironworks.

I went to one of the few secondary technical schools available in post-war England. Here the curriculum centred on science and technology. At school, I was lucky to have an excellent RE teacher who was interested in and knowledgeable about recent biblical criticism and it was through him that an interest in religion started. My head teacher had me down in his own mind to study zoology at Sheffield. When I told him I wanted to read theology, he more or less told me that I would be wasting my time. My interest further developed via two young curates who ran the church youth club, and whose combined interests were impressive. One of them opened the doors not only to theology, but to ancient history, the Mediterranean world, wine and cooking (I still love to cook). The other – he was a prison visitor for example – introduced us to Christian approaches to social responsibility. These two aspects, context and social responsibility, stay with me.

Home Background

Religion in my home background was experienced through my mother's involvement with the Christian Science Church. My mother's version of Christian Science was very personal, and she selected ideas and values from Mary Baker Eddy's writings that spoke to her. She certainly did not subscribe to all the beliefs and practices of Christian Science as expressed in Eddy's writings (she occasionally consulted doctors, and was not averse to a glass of sherry or a cigarette), but she remained a faithful practising member of her church. My father followed me into the Church of England (I was baptised and confirmed as an Anglican in my teens), and when my mother died, my sister, father and I organised a funeral service conducted jointly by a female Christian Science Practitioner, who my mother had consulted in difficult times, and an Anglican priest. My interest in

I. ter Avest (ed.), On the Edge: (Auto)biography and Pedagogical Theories on Religious Education, 57–68.

the beliefs and practices of individuals in relation to the doctrines and teachings of their tradition possibly originates with childhood encounter with Christian Science, but it was influenced formatively by my experience of teaching and of research.

In my mid-teens I became passionately interested in jazz. My then brother in law played me a Louis Armstrong record. This is the only time in my life I have experienced instant conversion! From then onwards I listened to and played jazz (initially on drums) whenever I could. My passion for jazz continues.

I studied in Wales – Greek (language and history), Greek philosophy (Plato and Aristotelian logic) and biblical studies for part one of the degree followed by theology, with some philosophy for part two, and I became especially interested in philosophy of religion and in what was then called Old Testament Studies, including Hebrew language. It was having my eyes opened to the pluralistic world of the Ancient Near East that spawned a later interest in the study of religious diversity. I also played drums and sang with the jazz band in Lampeter. I had some background in playing brass instruments so, when the trombonist left, I bought a trombone and taught myself how to play it well enough to join the band. I handed the drums on to someone else, but have played jazz trombone and sung jazz and blues ever since.

TEACHER TRAINING AND TEACHING

Post-theology degree I went to Cambridge University to do a Postgraduate Certificate in Education (PGCE), a one year teaching qualification. Most memories of the Cambridge part of the PGCE are to do with the Idle Hour Jazz band. However, the best thing about the PGCE course was meeting another RE student called Brian Gates. I learned more about RE informally from Brian than from our tutor, but the real learning began with the reality check of a full school term's teaching practice. Basically, you sank or swam. I was sent to Nottingham High School, situated about 8 miles from my parents' home in Derbyshire. The school itself was a shock to the system. It was a high-powered independent day school (the novelist and poet D H Lawrence's school) that also took very able students on local authority scholarships from Derbyshire and Nottinghamshire primary schools. I expected the school to be deeply traditional and old-fashioned. I actually found very innovative work going on in English and drama and a young and very talented RE teacher, Allan Hawke. I benefited from his expertise (as a practitioner and thinker about the subject), patience and capacity to see that people need to develop different teaching styles to suit their personalities; he also conveyed the perception that *learning* needs to be distinguished from teaching.

Because of my membership of Footlights (the Cambridge University review club), I was asked to teach a little drama. I explained that I had no formal academic background in the arts whatsoever, and I had no qualifications in English or drama. This made no difference, and I was 'adopted' by the English and drama team. One of the physical education teachers heard that I used to play rugby, so invited me to referee under 13s rugby matches, which I also enjoyed. There was a shortage of staff teaching biology, so I was asked to do some of that. The idea of motivating others, and nurturing confidence through sharing enthusiasm and giving encouragement to try new activities and roles has stayed with me in my own career as a teacher and leader of a research group. Towards the end of the teaching practice I was offered and accepted a job at the school for the following September.

Cambridge Again, then Teaching

Once the PGCE examinations were over we – the band – bought an old van from Addenbrooks Hospital and set off with tents and instruments for the Côte d'Azur. The one relevant story, as far as RE is concerned, is that a BBC TV news magazine programme did a feature on 'alternative' life in St Tropez. The BBC1 footage included me playing and singing with the band in a St Tropez street, a bit of publicity gleefully picked up by staff at Nottingham High School. Instead of my getting into trouble, it was regarded as pretty okay to have the new RE teacher representing Mediterranean sleaze on national television. Easily the most memorable event was playing the music of Louis Armstrong as publicity for the Louis Armstrong All-Stars' concert in St Tropez on 28 July 1967. We met Louis and the band after the concert, and I still have photographs, as well as a poster advertising the event signed by members of the Armstrong band (framed and hanging on my study wall).

I joined the school in the September and taught mainly RE.I spent a significant amount of time teaching English and drama. There was an annual Play Festival, and we wrote, produced and performed a play each year, the text produced through co-writing with the students during English lessons. I also used drama in my RE teaching and in assemblies devised and presented by students.

Through pupils in the school, I made contact with some local communities. We had a significant number of Jewish pupils in the school and I contacted the local Rabbi. This led to visits to the Nottingham Synagogue and to regular visits by the Rabbi to the school. I also invited parents to give talks, usually in assembly, and usually with questions. I remember asking a father, who was a Muslim and an engineer, to speak to the lower school about Islam in 'assembly'. He turned up looking very nervous, with a big sheaf of notes, which he proposed to read out. Fortunately, over a cup of coffee, I asked him if he could remember being 11 years old. He said that he could; he was a Palestinian from Jaffa. At Ramadan, he and his brothers would really try to keep the fast. But by midday, the sun was beating down so strongly that their will power failed, and they climbed orange trees and sank their teeth into the flesh of the juicy fruit. I said 'Do you think you could tell the children this story rather than read your notes?' Fortunately he did this very engagingly – there were many very interesting questions – and *I* learned a lesson about inviting guests into the school, as well as learning something about the representation of religions to young people, a topic that was to become more important later in my career.

Some of my favourite teaching was with a philosophy group of sixth formers (16-18). Although my group was always a mixture of people with and without religious commitments, the general and strongly held opinion of the sixth formers was that religious education should always be intellectually open and *inclusive*.

Secularity and Secularism

I have long maintained the distinction between 'secularity' and 'secularism'. In my view, in schools that are not religious foundations, religious education should be 'secular' in the same sense that the Indian Constitution is secular. That is, it should adhere to the principle of freedom of religion or belief, be methodologically impartial in relation to the truth claims of religions, and inclusive, allowing students to learn about religious diversity and to express their own views in a civil way. However, religious education should never be *secularist*; that is it should not set out to convey the view that religious claims are false or meaningless. The exploration of truth and meaning are both key elements of the subject, but the methodology of the subject should not promote a particular view of truth. Education should be towards autonomy for learners. This does not mean doing or saying anything you like, but does imply independence of thinking, reasoning and critical judgement, in a context of civility, against a background of social responsibility. I am also committed to the view that liberal education should cover all areas of human knowledge and experience, and that includes the arts and religion as well as humanities, the natural and social sciences, and physical education. Moreover, this human knowledge and experience should be seen as closely inter-related.

In 1968, I was approached by a BBC producer called Ralph Rolls who was preparing an education series for Radio 4 called 'Religion in Its Contemporary Context'. Ralph had produced some beautiful Radiovision programmes, aimed at 16-18 year olds, on the main religions of the world and he was seeking comments from potential users. Some of my sixth formers gave their responses to the trial programmes and their feedback helped to shape the series.

Outside school, I played with various Nottingham jazz bands, eventually joining Jazz Spectrum and helped to organise the jazz programme for the first Nottingham Festival in 1970, and the second in 1971.

TEACHER TRAINER, PHILOSOPHY AND 'WORLD RELIGIONS'

After 5 years in the school I felt I should move on. I didn't want to go into management in schools, so thought I might have a try at teacher training. To cut a long story short, I got a job as Lecturer in Religious Education at Coventry College of Education, with responsibility for teaching philosophy of religion and ethics and for introducing some courses on world religions. I enrolled at the nearby University of Warwick to do a part-time MA in philosophy.

At the same time as I started my MA, I was visiting schools in North Coventry to supervise students on teaching   practice. This was 1972, the year that President Idi Amin gave the South Asian population of Uganda 90 days to leave the country, leaving their possessions behind. Many held British passports and entered the UK as refugees. By a process of chain migration, many families came to Coventry and to other English cities. While Warwick University provided a course in philosophy, North Coventry provided an amazing learning environment for the study of religions and cultures. I formed a jazz group, which included some students and staff from college, called the Red Room Jazz Band, named after the startling variety of shades of red in the pub room where we played.

In 1974, I spotted an advert in the *Observer* drawing attention to Fellowships in World Religions and Education at London University School of Oriental and African Studies (SOAS). I applied and was fortunate to be offered a Fellowship and spent a term full-time learning at the feet of experts in the religions and cultures of the East and of Africa. At that time, SOAS had specialists in many Oriental and African languages, as well as historians, lawyers and social anthropologists who focused on particular regions. These scholars were often experts in the relevant religions. Instead of learning generalised accounts of religions, I was, for example, given vivid and very different pictures of Buddhism and Hinduism, and introduced to the diversity of Islamic world and its history, law, politics, and architecture.

BROADCASTING AND FIELD RESEARCH

Broadcasting

Drawing on some of the ideas gained through the Fellowship, I followed up my interest in Hindu communities and initially did some research with a Gujarati Hindu community in Coventry (Jackson, 1976). It was while I was doing this that Ralph Rolls contacted me again. He thought the work that I was doing would make innovative educational broadcasting (nothing had been done on recently arrived minority religious communities in Britain), so he invited me to make some programmes for BBC Education. Ralph was a tremendous encouragement, and sent me on a training course to learn interview technique and how to record and edit. The first of these programmes was on the Hindu Festival of Holi. I went on to make other programmes with Ralph, including Coventry's Square Mile, a Radiovision programme featuring four religious communities in North Coventry (Sikhs, Hindus, Muslims and Ukrainian Catholic Christians) (Marshall-Taylor, 2010) and a programme on a black Pentecostal church, the First United Church of Jesus Christ Apostolic.

Ralph introduced me to a new young producer called Geoff Marshall-Taylor. Geoff supported my ideas for various programmes about how festivals were actually celebrated in the lives of families from different religious backgrounds in Britain. Typically, these included recorded actuality material from the festivals themselves, some commentary and extracts from interviews with parents and children as well as religious leaders. However, the extra dimension that Geoff brought was that of drama. I really missed the drama side of my work from teaching, and Geoff gave me the opportunity to write mini-dramas again. These were usually based on versions of stories told to me by parents and children interviewed while we were preparing for the programmes.

Research

In 1978, Coventry College of Education merged with the University of Warwick. The combination of the college staff and the University's own Department of Education formed the Faculty of Educational Studies. Religious Education was placed in the Humanities Department, then for 15 years in the Arts Education Department, and then finally all the Faculty of Education departments merged to form the Warwick Institute of Education, a large, single department within the Faculty of Social Sciences. Within the ethos of the University, I had taken religious education in a research direction (initially through ethnographic research with children and young people), linking research projects to a new MA in religious education and recruiting our first research students. I also completed my own PhD at this time and, in 1994, established Warwick Religions and Education Research Unit (WRERU) within the Warwick Institute of Education, and was promoted to Professor in 1995.

Research methodology.   Around the time I was working with Ralph Rolls and Geoff Marshall-Taylor I met Eleanor Nesbitt who had been teaching in India and who was well versed in Indian religions and the Hindi language. After a short time, I managed to recruit Eleanor Nesbitt to join me in some research on Hindu communities in Britain, especially in the city of Coventry. We have worked together ever since until her early retirement in 2011, although Eleanor still contributes to WRERU's thinking and shares her beautiful poems. Initially, we did a project on the formal nurture of children in classes held at temples and community centres around the country. Then, recognising that this formal activity was but a limited part of the story, we designed a project to study children from various Hindu backgrounds in the context of their families and communities, plus some time in their schools. This research built directly on the studies I had started after my Fellowship at the School of Oriental and African Studies, and my BBC work. We focused particularly on the transmission of religious culture to young people and were fortunate to get two grants from the Leverhulme Trust to support this research (Jackson & Nesbitt, 1993).

The initial methodology we designed was essentially phenomenological. We were going back to the theory and method advocated in some of the Religious Studies departments. The idea was that the researcher should set aside his or her presuppositions, and then empathise with those being studied. I soon realised that, as a practical set of research methods, phenomenology, as understood in Religious Studies circles, was inadequate. However much you tried to set your presuppositions to one side, you could never be sure what your presuppositions *were* (Jackson, 1997, pp. 7-29). Moreover, without understanding the language and terminology used by practitioners – in other words, if you did not understand their *meaning* – how could you possibly empathise with their feelings and experiences?

I went back to the literature to look for more effective methods and, partly going back to my experience at SOAS, I turned to social anthropology and other sources (Jackson, 1997, pp. 30-48). For me, the discovery and refinement of theory and method has always been a hermeneutical process related to direct experience through fieldwork or other forms of practice, with theory and method informing and supporting empirical observation and practice, and with the fieldwork and practice informing and suggesting modifications to theory and method.

At various times, I have been criticised for using anthropological methods on the basis that they are inherently secularist. This in my view is simply not the case. There have been and are various debates within social anthropology, about the colonialist legacy of the discipline, about its evolutionary assumptions and about its inherent anti-religiousness. I have taken an interpretive and non-secularist approach to social anthropology. The theoretical and methodological version of social anthropology that most closely reverberated with my experience in the field was that developed by the American ethnographer, Clifford Geertz (e.g. Geertz, 1983), located through discussions with colleagues in the Arts Education Department at Warwick.

Essentially, Geertz saw social life as a text to be interpreted much as a literary critic might interpret a novel or a poem, or how a biographer might interpret the life of a person. Geertz's technique was to collect a mass of data in the form of observations and interviews and to reflect on these in the light of insights into the religion or culture being studied, picked up from various sources. It was the interplay between the 'parts' perceived through fieldwork (for example, the personal stories of members of Hindu communities in Coventry) and the 'whole', picked up provisionally from a number of sources (for example, in the case of my research, portrayals of 'Hinduism' in the scholarly literature), that provided insight into the nature of social reality and the key to editing a massive amount of field material into a well crafted ethnographic story. His term for moving from a mountain of data to a finished, artistic account – akin to a good history or biography – was 'textualisation'.

I then discovered the work of some of his critics, including the ethnographer and cultural historian James Clifford (Clifford, 1986), and was interested to find some of my own reservations (for example, the lack of voice given to individuals and the language of 'wholes' in relation to 'cultures') repeated and reinforced. I did not adopt the post-modernist stance of Clifford and some of his colleagues, but I did temper Geertz's approach with some of Clifford's observations. Thus, in brief, there was a methodological and theoretical shift in my own work from phenomenology to a particular approach derived partly from a particular tradition within social or cultural anthropology.

The Term 'Religion'

One of the shifts in my work centred on problems, raised in my and Eleanor Nesbitt's fieldwork, by the term 'Hinduism' and the term 'religion'. Although I was aware of diversity within religions, I had still thought of Hinduism as a 'whole', a complete religion. However, experience of meeting many so-called Hindus in the field put a question mark by the categories 'Hinduism' and 'religion'. My reading in religious studies and comparative religion didn't really help much, until I discovered the work of the Canadian scholar Wilfred Cantwell Smith, which complemented some key elements of Geertz's cultural anthropology.

> *An anecdote.* My friend and colleague John Hull, working at Birmingham University, had eventually lost his sight completely. These days he is equipped with a barrage of electronic devices to assist him in reading or hearing others' words. When he first went blind, this was not the case, and he relied on a small army of assistants to read books on to audiocassettes, which he then listened to in order to keep up with his reading. My mother-in-law did some of this reading, and I did a bit when I could fit it in. John always said that my mother-in-law was much better at this than I was. He remarked that, since my mother-in-law wasn't interested in the subject, she read everything evenly and clearly. The problem with me was that, if I got interested, I tended to slow down!

Well, I *did* get interested in Smith's book. Essentially, Smith argued that we should criticise conventional representations of religions and religion. These were shaped by Western cultural assumptions that ignored the fundamentally personal nature of religious belief in relation to accumulated tradition. In order to understand a religious position you needed to examine the interplay of the individual voice and the cumulative tradition. Smith saw close connections between all the religious traditions of the world. For me Smith's insight was the hermeneutical one, and this parallels the work of Geertz very closely in seeing the importance of the relationship between 'parts' and 'wholes'. As noted above, I have reservations about the language of 'wholes', which often need to be seen as provisional, and I sometimes refer to the relationship between individual cases and the wider context. My view is that pictures of 'whole' religions are perfectly possible, but there are competing accounts and their boundaries are contested (Jackson, 2008a).

While feeling that both Geertz and Smith provided theory that helped me to explain the complexity of my own field data, there were still questions unanswered. These, largely, had to do with human power – the power to represent one branch of the tradition as the truth, for example. In looking for helpful analyses of power, I found the work of Jürgen Habermas (1972) helpful, but drew especially on the ideas of Palestinian cultural critic Edward Said who had given a neo-modernist, humanistic interpretation to the more radical thought of Michel Foucault (Said, 1978). Said's post-colonialism has its faults, but, nevertheless, his analysis of power relations remains a highly useful tool in interpreting social relations on the ground.

Theory and practice. The perspectives of these various theoreticians reverberated with the material we collected from the field and provided a set of tools for analysing and interpreting data. At the same time, had we not collected that data, then questions would not have been raised which guided me towards a particular theoretical framework and set of practical methods. It was reflection on the hermeneutical relationship between questions raised through the practice of research and theory that shaped my ideas.

It was in interpreting our data (several years worth of field notes, interviews with children and their parents, fieldwork diaries and documents collected in the field) for an ethnographic report that I began to wonder about the potential of some of these ideas for representing religious traditions to young learners, and for devising pedagogical methods that might be used to offer more flexible ways of interpreting religious material than those offered in comparative religion and world religions textbooks to date. This was the birth of the interpretive approach to religious education which had its germ in some writings from around the late 1980s, including *Approaches to Hinduism*, an introduction for teachers which combines a provisional overview of the tradition with specific case studies of different topics, drawing on ethnographic, biographical and autobiographical sources, and a children's book called *Listening to Hindus*, written with Eleanor Nesbitt, and drawing on the direct experience of families of various Hindu backgrounds from Coventry (Jackson & Nesbitt, 1997). The interpretive approach is strongly reflected in my chapter in a book on religious education and the arts (Jackson, 1993), and in the experimental Warwick RE project materials for children and young people that appeared between 1994 and 1996. However, the ideas were first articulated at length in my 1997 book *Religious Education: an Interpretive Approach* (Jackson, 1997) and in *Rethinking Religious Education and Plurality* (Jackson, 2004).

LEARNING AND CREATIVITY

Reflecting on my own experience, much of my own learning has been concerned with following my own curiosity (fuelled often by encouragement from others), discovering general principles, and then applying them as creatively as I can in practice. For me, learning to play jazz on trombone was inspired by listening to improvising musicians and then wanting to express my own musical ideas; it consisted more in applying principles rather than in following any highly structured teaching or learning programme. I found out how the instrument worked and how to make notes, experimented with the easier keys, and tried to play the improvised music I could hear in my head, following the pattern of musicians heard on record. As with most jazz musicians, I took on influences from others – sometimes consciously and sometimes less so – but the sound, however limited, turned out to be personal. This is why the playing of so many jazz musicians is quickly recognisable to those who listen to the music closely or play it. Charlie Parker sounds like Charlie Parker; Ben Webster sounds like Ben Webster; Billie Holiday sounds like Billie Holiday; Louis Armstrong sounds like Louis Armstrong. And my learning tends to be informed by different kinds of sources, just as jazz is an eclectically influenced music. Learning to do ethnography was more structured, but there was still a strong element of trial and error, and the same kind of eclecticism that one finds in jazz. I found no problem in taking an idea or method from one

65

source (e.g. social anthropology) and combining it with ideas and techniques from other sources (e.g. hermeneutics, religious studies, social psychology, and the practice of teaching). This is essentially where creativity comes in.

I was a member of the Department of Arts Education at the University of Warwick throughout its history. I had the privilege of working with various colleagues from the arts including Ken Robinson who wrote the foreword to Dennis Starkings' edited book on *Religion and the Arts in Education* (Starkings, 1993). This is the book in which I was first able to articulate some of the ideas of the interpretive approach, emphasising the artistry (as well as the social science) of ethnography, the value of a hermeneutical approach, and writing for the first time on 'religious education and the arts of interpretation' (Jackson, 1993). In his foreword, Ken Robinson wrote:

> This is a book of explorations and connections. It might take as one of its axioms, Raymond Williams' observation that the study of culture is not of the various aspects of social life as separate processes but the connections and relationships between them: of how religion interacts with politics, with law, with economics and with the arts and how all of these interact with each other. One of the expectations of this collection of papers is that by laying bare some of the fundamental and common processes of religion, the arts and spirituality, there may be greater unity of purpose in the curriculum in general, in aiming to meet the needs and interests of the pupil as a whole. (Robinson, 1993)

At this time Ken Robinson was also engaged in work on creativity (as he has been subsequently), arguing that creativity is as important in education as literacy. His ideas included the notion of a much more holistic approach to education, involving the education of the mind and the body, the recognition and nurture of creative abilities in young people, and their capacity to make novel connections across different fields of study. This last point was totally consistent with my own approach to making connections between the practices of fieldwork/teaching and research, as well as connecting ideas from different disciplines and literatures.

PAST, PRESENT AND FUTURE

In 1980 I was invited to join the International Seminar on Religious Education and Values (ISREV) for its second meeting in Schenectady, New York. The following year I was invited to join the Shap Working Party on World Religions and Education and, as I write, ISREV has just had its 17th biennial meeting, in Turku, Finland.

In 1996, I took over the editorship of the *British Journal of Religious Education* from friend and colleague John Hull, and continued in this role for 15 years until 2011. There is much to say about these experiences, but I will save that for another occasion.

From the mid-1990s, WRERU continued to undertake a variety of qualitative research projects funded by UK research councils and charities. In 2006, WRERU undertook its first mixed methods research in the context of the REDCo Project, involving eight European countries and funded by the European Commission, my first opportunity to have an involvement with quantitative research. In 2007, with the appointment of Leslie Francis and other colleagues as quantitative specialists, WRERU consolidated its capacity to undertake large-scale mixed methods research. It has been inspiring to have a team who can combine the strengths of both qualitative and quantitative research and to see the two traditions as complementary. It has also been inspiring and highly educative to work with so many international researchers and research teams. I have a 'special relationship' with Norway, through Oslo University College, the European Wergeland Centre and colleagues across Norwegian higher education institutions. Since 2002, I have been deeply involved in the work of the Council of Europe in relation to developing ideas for introducing the study of religions into public education systems across Europe.

I will draw on my current work in the Council of Europe and at the European Wergeland Centre, in order to give a view about the future for the place of religion in public education in Europe and beyond. There should be a widespread and continuing debate about this. My own view is that, at the least, young people should be as well educated in the sphere of religion and religions as they ought to be in the arts, the humanities and sciences. The 'intrinsic' liberal education argument for this breadth in education stands. However, there are various complementary instrumental arguments for developing religious literacy among young people, including social arguments – contributions to citizenship (learning to live together) and social cohesion, and to cultural understanding, for example, and there are arguments about personal development related to identity, values education and growth towards autonomy. Developing policy ideas that could be useful discussion topics across the diverse nations of Europe, with their different histories and cultural experience, and across the wider world, is no easy task.

We do know from research on the REDCo project that many adolescents from different backgrounds want to have the opportunity for learning about each other's religious traditions and worldviews, and for doing things together (e.g. Jackson, 2012). We also know from research and policy discussion at the Council of Europe and the European Wergeland Centre that there are many issues to resolve. These include: clarifying the confusing range of technical language used in this field; the clarification of competence required to be able to understand at depth and engage with a plurality of religions and non-religious convictions; dealing with issues of the representation of religions, especially by the media; the provision of 'safe space' for student-to-student dialogue within the school; issues concerning the classification and possible incorporation of 'non religious convictions' or 'non-religious worldviews' into this field; issues and debates concerning human rights; and guidance on developing policies for linking schools to local communities and organisations, and developing contacts with other schools, including international relationships. Our present project from the Council of Europe and the European Wergeland centre aims to address such issues, and those of training religion

ROBERT JACKSON

specialist and non-specialist teachers, in ways that might be helpful to policymakers, teacher trainers and teachers at national, regional and local levels. Just as I hope to combine this work with more jazz, poetry, and observation of wildlife I hope, Siebren, that you will continue to weave a beautiful tapestry of theology, education, music and verse.

REFERENCES

Clifford, J. (1986). Introduction: Partial truths. In J. Clifford & G. Marcus (eds.), *Writing culture: The poetics and politics of ethnography* (pp. 1-26). Berkeley: University of California Press.
Geertz, C. (1983).*Local knowledge*. New York: Basic Books.
Habermas, J. (1972). *Knowledge and human interest*. London: Heinemann.
Ipgrave, J., Jackson, R., & O'Grady, K. (eds.). (2009). *Religious education research through a community of practice. Action research and the interpretive approach*. Münster: Waxmann.
Jackson, R. (1976). Holi in North India and in an English city: Some adaptations and anomalies. *New Community, 5*(3), 203-210.
Jackson, R. (1993). Religious education and the arts of interpretation. In D. Starkings (ed.), *Religion and the arts in education: Dimensions of spirituality* (pp. 157-166). London: Hodder and Stoughton.
Jackson, R. (1997). *Religious education: An interpretive approach*. London: Hodder and Stoughton.
Jackson, R. (2004). *Rethinking religious education and plurality: Issues in diversity and pedagogy*. London: RoutledgeFalmer.
Jackson, R. (2008). Contextual religious education and the interpretive approach. *British Journal of Religious Education, 30*(1), 13-24.
Jackson, R. (ed.). (2012). *Religion, education, dialogue and conflict: Perspectives on religious education research*. London: Routledge.
Jackson, R., & Nesbitt, E. (1993). *Hindu children in Britain*. Stoke on Trent: Trentham.
McKenna, U., Neill, S., & Jackson, R. (2009). Personal Worldviews, Dialogue and Tolerance: Students' Views on Religious Education in England. In P. Valk, G. Bertram-Troost, M. Friederici, & C.Beraud (eds.), *Teenagers' perspectives on the role of religion in their lives, schools and societies: A European quantitative study* (pp. 49-70). Münster: Waxmann.
Said, E. (1978). *Orientalism*. London: Routledge and Kegan Paul.

AFFILIATIONS

Robert Jackson
Warwick Religions and Education Research Unit,
Institute of Education,
University of Warwick, UK and
European Wergeland Centre
Oslo, Norway

FEDOR KOZYREV

RELIGION AS A GIFT

A Pedagogical Approach to RE in St. Petersburg

INTRODUCTION

A gift from outside
– an encounter with a colleague – awoke a gift inside:
the intuitively felt need to elaborate
the third paradigm of RE

It all started in May 2000 when I crossed the border of Russia for the first time in my adult life to participate in a seminar on religious education at Kappel (Switzerland). I was invited by Walter Sennhäuser, a leader of RE-Network – an organization active at that time in building cultural bridges between Eastern and Western academic societies. There I met John Hull who led the seminar, and who changed in a few days not only my vision of the proper ways of teaching religion but also my view on the pedagogy as a whole. He awoke the intuitively felt need to elaborate a third paradigm for RE in the Russian context. John Hull just showed me that pedagogy exists as a serious science – the fact I resisted to recognize before in spite of (or due to) lectures on pedagogy I had attended in St. Petersburg as a post-graduate university scholar ten years ago. So as a result of this crucial meeting, I stopped doing theological hermeneutics I was interested in and started doing RE studies.

The next equally important and unexpected impulse for developing a theoretical framework for RE in the Russian context came with an invitation to participate in a programme of academic exchange (Prospect-Plus Program) organized by the Institute of Eastern Christian Studies (Nijmegen, the Netherlands). There in the library of the University of Nijmegen in October-November 2003 I collected materials that allowed me to present a synopsis on the development of RE philosophy and theory that had taken place during the decades of iron curtain and state atheism in the Soviet Union. Later, this material became a basis for my first monograph on RE and for my dissertation defended in January 2007.

There was an indicative incident connected with my dissertation that I find worth to mention here. After finishing my three-year doctoral research in the Herzen State Pedagogical University in St. Petersburg, I had to present its results to the commission in order to receive permission for the defence. During my presentation, one of the influential persons in the commission suddenly asked me to repeat the theme of my dissertation. I replied: "Non-Confessional Religious

I. ter Avest (ed.), On the Edge: (Auto)biography and Pedagogical Theories on Religious
Education, 69–79.

Education in Schools Abroad". He said: "But you must change your theme. Religious education *is not* a *pedagogical* topic. It is a matter of religious bodies." As a result I was suspended for almost a year, since I refused to change the topic, and I still don't know why I was finally permitted to defend. But the idea of 'RE being not a pedagogical topic' appeared also stimulating in shaping my theoretical framework, for it was exactly opposite to what I had learned from John Hull.

THE THIRD PARADIGM

I returned from my sailing over the boundless ocean of literature, written on RE topics, I found in the Nijmegen library with a clear message that might be formulated as a disclosure of a third paradigm in RE. This message was equally challenging in the Russian context for proponents of a 'scientifically objective' study of religious history and culture as well as for those advocating the return of a catechetical approach, since both of the two parties treated RE as non-pedagogical topic. The former declined to regard the study of religion on the scientific premises as a form of RE, the latter rejected any form of RE that was non-confessional, that is, not based on theological premises and not integrated in the missionary activity of religious bodies. The idea of the third paradigm broke this customary dichotomy and demanded a radical re-conceptualization of the ways of dealing with religion in school both parties were not ready for yet. From the very beginning I recognized this dichotomy as the main hindrance for developing adequate educational practices in teaching religion and devoted a good part of my work to a critical analysis of this dichotomy and its evaluation in order to overcome it. Unfortunately I did not quite succeed. The very name of the newly introduced religious school subject – 'The Basics of Spiritual & Moral Culture of the Peoples of Russia' – shows that Russian experts and authorities in charge of the national curriculum reform have not agreed to use the concept of RE in its wide meaning common for the European context and preferred to substitute the term 'religious' by a more imprecise but apparently less problematic term 'spiritual'. For this subject the learners in the schools are divided in groups according to their religious socialization at home. And I am sure that the decision to separate children on the confessional ground for studying this subject also came as a direct result of neglecting or being unable to grasp the perspective associated with a 'third way' reconciling and combining pedagogically fruitful insights of 'objective' and 'confessional' into a new approach for the study of religions. I am sure that the still widespread vision of religion as something entirely in the competence of religious bodies contributes to an escalation of tensions regarding the presence of religion at school. In the long run this may lead to an alienation of a person from religion, even more so in cases where the political establishment around the world is inclined to look at religions through the lenses of potential hazards and benefits related to national security and social cohesion.

Opposing this trend, I find it of primary importance to emphasize the personal dimension in religious life. Without such an emphasis, RE cannot be congruent with the principal aim of general education as it has been understood since

Pestalozzi and accordingly cannot be based on pedagogical grounds. So, taking into account this consideration, the third paradigm may be defined as *humanitarian*, meaning both its humanistic orientation and its methodological affinity with humanities. The concept of a humanitarian paradigm of RE and the general scheme of paradigm changes were presented by me in a number of papers in English (Kozyrev, 2005a, 2008, 2009) and systematically described in my second monograph on RE (Kozyrev, 2010). Having no possibility to depict it here, I would like only to mention the epistemological focus of the proposed theoretical framework. The turn toward existential aspects of religious life and the enrichment of RE with a phenomenological and hermeneutical methodological approach is considered in this framework as a particular manifestation of larger changes that the epistemological situation of post-modernity imposes on science, philosophy and culture.

Among numerous descriptions and names given to the third paradigm by Western scholars, the most popular seems to be *learning from religion* coined by Grimmitt in 1981. Grimmitt fruitfully and creatively adapted and developed many aspects of Ninian Smart's phenomenological approach to RE. Apparently time was ripe for Grimmitt's triple typology of RE, since it elaborated upon what was proposed ten years earlier. In the seventies of the twentieth century a group of English scholars, with Smart among them, had proposed to distinguish between dogmatic, anti-dogmatic (meaning objectively scientific) and a-dogmatic approaches (School Council, 1971). Grimmitt's trichotomy of learning '*in*', *about*', and '*from*' religion followed the same pattern of thought but expressed it in a much more comprehensible way. Yet for Russian ears it sounded linguistically a little bit strange, so it inspired a group of scholars from the Institute of Religious Pedagogy in St. Petersburg to look for an adapted version of Grimmitt's typology. Finally we decided to distinguish between learning religion *as a law*, *as a fact* and *as a gift* (Kozyrev, 2005b)

RELIGION AS A GIFT

Since the religious subject taught in Russian schools before revolution was called 'God's Law' there was no need to explain the first concept to Russian educators. Corresponding to what was called in Western countries learning 'in', 'into' or 'for' religion, the concept of 'God's Law' aimed at initiation of students into a particular system of values, beliefs, ethical standards and epistemic assumptions, constituting together a specific religious tradition. The concept of teaching and learning religion as a fact clearly referred to a distancing and objective presentation of religious data for studying them on the scientific premises as external facts affecting in no way personal commitments of students. The third concept, teaching and learning religion as a gift, borrowed from Birmingham scholars with Grimmitt and Hull among them (Grimmitt et al., 1991), was less clear and raised more questions. As in English, 'a gift' in Russian means both the inborn talent and a given that is received from outside. We found this ambiguity of the term 'gift' precisely fitting the two-dimensional semantics of the term 'religion' as disclosed in particular by W.C. Smith in his 'The Meaning and End of Religion' (1963). While English scholars conceive gift as primarily "a possible benefit which children might derive from the encounter with this [religious] material" (Hull, 2000), one might conceive it instead as a latent sensibility of a child toward religion. Unlike the Birmingham 'Gift *to* the child' approach, our approach more focused on that second understanding of the term, which might be properly coined as a 'Gift *of* the child' approach. However, the idea of "religious education as contributing to the development of the children rather than being mainly concerned with teaching for an understanding of religion" (Grimmitt, 2000) remains central for both approaches. Indeed, if we talk about *religiously gifted* children, the demand for providing them with external stimuli to develop, refine and enrich their gift is no less urgent as it is with their literary, mathematic, physical and all other kinds of gifts. Developing our theoretical framework we found it resonating with contemplations of some Russian religious philosophers, particularly with the following words by Ilyin: "Not knowing his predestination, each man is always free to act and to live as a man predestined for living in the face, not in the absence of God. He is not able to judge whether the corresponding gift is granted to him, or not. That's why it is his task to try to find this gift inside him, to awaken it, to strengthen and to develop it" (Ilyin, 1953).

The developmental quality of RE. The developmental quality of RE, emphasized in the paradigm of 'religion as a gift', is tightly connected with its educational quality. 'Educational religious education' – this famous tautological definition of the third way offered in 1971 by another representative of the Birmingham scientific school, E. Cox (see his article of the same name), highlights the already mentioned general idea of putting RE in line with general educational aims. It presumes primacy of the teacher's educational competence and expertise over theological and scientific ones in constructing, implementing and evaluating syllabuses and programmes in the same way as it takes place with all other school subjects. The concepts of the third paradigm of humanitarian RE and of 'religion as a gift' incorporate these two meanings and add to them one more meaning connected to the humanitarian quality of education.

The humanitarian paradigm. To enter the humanitarian paradigm means to oppose both scholastic and scientific paradigms of the late Middle Ages and Modernity, since in both of them religion was present in the form of objective truths. The humanitarian approach emphasizes the fact that religious truths are essentially subjective (which does not mean that they can't have a transcendental origin). These religious truths can be shared by a community as we share other subjective things, but they can't be objectified like physical laws. The experiences of God can't be proven. One may even say that the more scientific proofs of a religious truth or of regularity of a religious experience is provided, the more doubts arise about the religious character of these experiences. The essential subjective character of religion may be approached both in a confessional and non-confessional setting. What matters is that in both cases participants deal with personal knowledge. What matters also is that they deal with this personal knowledge hermeneutically, that is they study religious phenomena neither as bare objects (religious facts) nor as statements of axiomatic beliefs (religious laws) but as elements of rich semantic and symbolic systems requiring a certain level of contextualization and responsiveness on the part of the learner to enter them, to understand them and to benefit from them. The experience of being drawn into these lines of thought is part of the game. It is not an ultimate aim, as it is when we learn into religion and not an infringement as it is when we learn about religion. It is a liable form of initiation into religious experience of humanity in which the processes of interpretation, search for meanings and reflection on these meanings in the light of personal life experiences play the key role.

PUTTING THEORY INTO PRACTICE

In 2006 the Concept of National Educational Policy in Russia made public the State's new priorities with an emphasis on the ethical and social function of education as well as on the task of 'spiritual consolidation of the multi-ethnic Russian population into one political nation'. Three years later this shift in national policy brought a new subject area into the school curricula called 'Basics of Spiritual & Moral Culture of the Peoples of Russia' (2006, 2011).

Among eight key targets of the new national curriculum for primary schools that came into force in September 2009, spiritual and moral development of children and formation of their civil identity were listed on the second place next to the guarantees of equal opportunities to get qualified primary education for all citizens of Russia. The national curriculum for secondary schools caused long controversies and its adoption was delayed for two years. The final version included a special Programme on 'Formation and socialization of students on the secondary level of education'. In particular the Programme oriented schooling toward helping students "to understand the meaning of religious ideals in personal and social life", "to give them an idea of civil ethics, faith, spirituality, human religious life and value of religious outlook on the basis of inter-confessional dialogue", and also to give them an opportunity to learn about the activity of religious bodies.

Another conceptually important part of the new legislation was 'The Concept of Spiritual and Moral Development and Upbringing of the Personality of Russian Citizen', developed by a group of experts under the leadership of A. Kondakov in 2009 and accepted as the theoretical foundation for the new subject area in Russian schools. In this document, traditional Russian religions were listed among the basic national values and sources of morality. It also stated that the teaching of the spiritual basics of religious cultures as well as of laic life may become one of educational units in state schools.

FEDOR KOZYREV

New Opportunities for RE in Russia

According to the new legislation in April 2010, a federal experiment of introducing the new subject area into school practice was launched in 19 selected regions of Russia. School children of 10-11 years old (grades 4 and 5 in the Russian school system) were offered a choice of 6 subject units: Basics of Orthodox, Islamic, Jewish, or Buddhist cultures, World Religions and Secular Ethics. For the whole teaching course 34 hours were allocated, notionally divided between the last semester of grade 4 (last grade of primary school) and the first semester of grade 5. The first and the last lessons of all 6 units are to be delivered in the joint group of students and committed to the topics of 'Russia is our common home' and 'Love for the Fatherland'. Since September 2012 the subject became an obligatory part of school curricula all over Russia.

The federally assigned approach to 'Spiritual & Moral Education' is supposed to be non-confessional regarding teacher competences and teaching methods. Still it is not clear what role religious institutions will play in the educational process and in training teachers, but this role has been quite prominent over the last years in designing syllabuses and textbooks for the new subject.

Spiritual and Moral Talks. The experiment revealed two major problems with the tested approach. First, it appeared to be hardly realistic to provide all six options in every school, so it is more likely that only the dominant religious culture (Orthodoxy or Islam in some regions) and Secular Ethics as an alternative will be provided in the majority of schools. This situation is charged with potential protests from religious minorities. Second, there is a definite lack of competence on the part of teachers. Short courses of post-diploma training provided by federal and local experts in the regions are not enough to compensate the profound lack of religious knowledge in those who graduated from state schools and universities where religion was never taught.

Facing these new opportunities and challenges, our Institute of Religious Pedagogy developed its own syllabus called 'Spiritual & Moral Talks' (SMT). The St. Petersburg Committee of Education supported our initiative and granted the status of 'city lab' to one of the state gymnasiums to test and to elaborate our model for 10-12 years old students. Three other state schools joined the experiment of testing this approach. Our approach differs from the federal one in at least two aspects.

Integration. First, it is an *integrative* approach, based on the idea of 'RE for all' as formulated by Wolfram Weisse and his colleagues from the University of Hamburg (Weisse, 2012). We decided not to separate students and to provide them a common room for discussing religious and ethical problems together during all the 2-years teaching course of SMT. The teaching content of SMT does not duplicate that of the 'World Religions' unit of the federal subject. Besides four 'traditional religions of Russia' it includes some other traditions and also pays more attention to the existing diversity within them. For instance, Christianity is presented with pieces of not only Orthodoxy but also of Roman Catholic and Protestant art and theology. Three sequential thematic units constitute the teaching course. They are 'Gospel Parables', 'The Wisdom of the East' (presenting traditions of Hinduism, Buddhism, Confucianism, Taoism, Judaism and Islam) and 'The Pearls of Virtue'. The first and the second units are based on the study of scriptural texts, and the third one presents life stories of outstanding people, including well known persons from the Russian and the world history and from different religious and non-religious traditions – Christian content occupying roughly half of the unit.

Interpretation.   Secondly, our approach is *interpretive* and it follows in several methodological aspects the framework of the Warwick Interpretative approach. For instance, following Jackson we distinguish three aspects of the educational process: representation, interpretation and reflection/edification. The micro-cycle formed by these aspects recurs each time with a new topic, first within a lesson and then on a bigger scale when a sequence of topically connected lessons ends with a special 'summing-up' lesson closing a subject sub-unit. We also focus our classroom interaction not on receptive but on interpretative activities of students. Search for meanings of texts and narratives under study are a core activity on the part of the learner. As a result, our approach acquires a *dialogical* quality, since the participation in discussions and classroom conversations becomes a natural element of sharing meanings.

We try to minimize indoctrinating and ideological influences that an encounter with religious values may produce in the child, and to ensure a certain distance that helps children to bridge their spiritual experience with religious traditions, not endangering the privacy of their personal religious life. We regard our learners as researchers interested in understanding and engaging with what they are introduced to, but not necessarily *adopting* it. Compared to catechetical approaches, these prerequisites tend to give what Jackson calls "… a looser, more personal and organic picture of religious traditions" (Jackson, 1997, p. 109).

BUILDING BRICKS FOR RE AS A GIFT

We have found two other English methodological sources useful for us in practical terms. The first is related to the phase of *representation*. The practicality of John Hull's concept of 'boot-strapping' as presented in his 'Gift to the Child' approach became evident for us in the course of selecting Gospel parables for our lessons. Indeed, some parables, while successfully translating the core message of Christianity and thus satisfying the 'phenomenological criterion' for selection, were found not satisfying the 'experiential criterion' in being too difficult or confusing for children of the specified age. The focus on the ethical dimension of religious traditions made us slightly change priorities and select parables based not on phenomenological but rather on ethical criteria of representation. Thus we chose parables delivering some clear moral message and avoid parables concerning mysteries of the Kingdom. We also found two straps not enough for our boot. The criterion of coherence was added as soon as we realized that the sequence of parables may serve as a 'staircase' of Christian ethics, starting with more simple and basic metaphors and imperatives and ascending to more sophisticate ones. Some parables, beautiful from other points of view, did not meet this criterion for example for the youngest learners and so had to give way to less complex parables which were able to 'fill up the gap' in the sequence. An additional criterion for selection was a cultural one, as we tended to choose, if possible, parables introducing concepts, images and ideas so deeply rooted in our everyday culture that their religious origin may be unclear for children (such as the concept of talents).

The second idea to be mentioned regards the phase of *interpretation*. The difficult situation of an ordinary 45 minutes lesson in a class with some 20-30 pupils, getting tired during the school day, brings limitations to discussion and conversation and sometimes makes teachers' expectations about children's receptivity and activity unrealistic. There is a need in this situation not only 'to unpack the range of concepts but also to select one or two of these to be the focus of attention in this particular unit of work', as underlined by Trevor Cooling in his description of the Concept Cracking model (Cooling, 2000, pp. 153-169). Another common point with our vision is Cooling's understanding of hermeneutical process as 'the interaction between the horizon of the student and the horizon of the text', to which I would like to add the horizon of previous readers including both representatives of canonical exegetics and representatives of secular literature and arts creatively using the text. In any case, purposeful broadening of students' horizons works very well as the guiding idea to help the teacher not to lose her/his orientation during spontaneous dialogical classroom interactions and to balance a variety of pedagogical tasks.

When the ethical dimension of religious life is central for the subject, the final stage of the cycle quite naturally takes the form of *edification*, a term completing the characteristics of Jackson's interpretive approach. It is at this stage that the task of bridging religious tradition with the personal experience of the child, as shared and expressed by all the theorists mentioned above, becomes the teacher's main concern. Edification is essentially the part of the story students should find and formulate themselves and as such it completes the cycle. Our textbooks do not contain any 'prepared' conclusions of the lessons. Instead, every lesson ends with main questions to be answered and with an invitation for students to draw their conclusion themselves about the meaning of the offered material of the RE lessons for their personal life. The second round of reflection takes place at home when children do their homework. These exercises are designed with an agenda of making links between parables. Results of these second round reflections and interpretations are discussed during summing-up lessons, completing the edification process.

THE MEANING OF THE EXPERIMENT FOR THE FUTURE OF RE

The personal participation of the authors of SMT in its approbation stimulated the development of some new ideas and visions as well as the construction of new knowledge regarding both the concept of religion as a gift and the methodology of an interpretative RE in the Russian context. In particular we found it reasonable to distinguish between two types of lessons. One type of lessons constitutes of lessons where a new topic is presented. We found out that success of these lessons highly depends on how the teacher manages to keep on an intensive pace of discussions. It's good for these lessons to be a sort of brainstorming sessions. And it is the cognitive dimension of the learners' own gifts that is employed and developed primarily at these lessons. The second type of lessons constitutes of lessons of generalization and reflection. The topic now is familiar for the students and they have already struggled with it both in the classroom and at home while doing their exercises. These lessons may be conducted in a more tranquil manner and focus more on the existential dimension of religious phenomena and their meaning for the personal life of the student. The classroom discussions in these lessons involve deeper emotional, imaginative and creative aspects of religious giftedness of students.

One of the unexpected results of the experiment was the level of children's sensitivity and openness to the metaphoric and symbolic dimension of meanings. Contrary to our expectations it was not a difficult task at all to encourage allegorical and metaphorical understanding in our students. The task was rather to restrain them from symbolic interpretation when it ceased to be relevant to the context. Having started with gospel parables, they diligently tried to transmit the allegoric language of the genre to other religious traditions and genres. When asked about the purpose of the turned up tips of Tibetan Buddhist boots, an 11-year old female student decisively answered that they symbolized the curvature of the Earth. Another example: children are asked about the meaning of a Zen-Buddhist story telling how a young man looking for wisdom came to a monastery and instead of getting spiritual revelations received an advice from an old monk to wash his plate after eating some rice. Children readily and immediately conclude that rice must symbolize sins and accordingly the old monk called for repentance. In our view this persistent intention to disclose hidden meanings may be interpreted itself as one of expressions of religious giftedness not necessary to be fed up or cultivated in the course of school education but worth to be refined and improved.

Following John Hull and his colleagues, we found out that "the gifts of religious education were not necessarily of a religious nature" (Hull, 2000, p. 118). Cultural and socio-historical aura surrounding religious texts, narratives, or symbols contain the highest manifestations of human spiritual and moral responsiveness and creativity. Religious experiences of mankind teach us not only how to believe but also how to feel and think about things we regard as sacred, priceless or primarily important in our lives and also how to express these feelings and thoughts. Perceived this way, a religious gift comes to or arises in any human being as a general educational attainment, no matter what kind of religious commitments this person is going to follow.

Among various ways of approaching this *educational* task of religious education, the involvement of children into the textual interpretation has been found by us to be practical and effective. We are thankful both to the members of the Warwick team who developed their interpretative approach and also to those who made efforts to defend this approach against criticism and doubts. Siebren Miedema is certainly a person to be mentioned in this respect. His brilliant and vigorous defence of the interpretative approach in the polemics between participants of the REDCo research rests in our memory as one of the unforgettable moments of solidarity and encouragement for pedagogical improvement.

REFERENCES

Basics of Spiritual & Moral Culture of the Peoples of Russia (2006, 2011). О Концепции национальной образовательной политики Российской Федерации (приказ Минобрнауки России от 03.08.06 № 201) // Вестник образования России. - 2006. - № 18. С.18-20; Примерная основная образовательная программа образовательного учреждения. Основная школа / [сост. Е. С. Савинов]. — М.: Просвещение, 2011 (Стандарты второго поколения)

Cooling, T. (2000). The Stapleford Project: Theology as the basis for religious education. In M. H. Grimmitt (ed.), *Pedagogies of religious education. Case studies in the research and development of good pedagogic practise in RE* (pp. 153-169). Great Wakering: McCrimmons.

Cox, E. (1971). Educational religious education. In *Learning for Living*, p. 10.

Grimmitt, M. (1981). When is commitment a problem in religious education? *British Journal of Religious Studies, 29*(1), 42-53.

Grimmitt, M., Grove, J., Hull, J., & Spencer, L. (1991). *A gift to the child: Religious education in the primary school.* Simon & Schuster Education.

Hull, J. M. (2000). Religion in the service of the child project: The gift approach to religious education. In M. Grimmitt (ed.), *Pedagogies of religious education. Case studies in the research and development of good pedagogic practise in RE* (p. 117). Great Wakering: McCrimmons.

Ильин И.А. (1993). Аксиомы религиозного опыта. – М.: Рарогъ [Ilyin, I. (1953). Axioms of religious experience],154.

Jackson, R. (2000). The Warwick Religious Education Project: The interpretive approach to religious education. In M. H. Grimmitt (ed.), *Pedagogies of religious education: Case studies in the research and development of good pedogogic practice in RE* (pp. 130-152). Great Wakering: McCrimmons.

Jackson, R. (1997, 2002). *Religious education: An interpretive approach.* London: Hodder and Stoughton.

А.Я. Данилюк, А.М. Кондаков, В.А. Тишков (2009). Концепция духовно-нравственного развития и воспитания личности гражданина России. – М.: Просвещение.

Kozyrev, F. N. (2005a). Humanitarian religious education – A concept for Russian schools. In J. Lähnemann (ed.), *Bewahrung – Entwicklung – Versöhnung. Religiöse Erziehung in globaler Verantwortung*, Referate und Ergebnisse des Nürnberger Forums 2003 (pp. 219-225). Hamburg: EB-Verlag.

Козырев Ф.Н. (2005b). Религиозное образование в светской школе. Теория и международный опыт в отечественной перспективе: Монография (СПб: Апостольский город) [Kozyrev F. N. (2005). Religious education in public schools: Theory and international experience in Russian perspective], 56.

Kozyrev, F. N. (2008). Two concepts of religious education in postmodern age: 'Humanitarian' versus 'holistic'. In B. J. Hilberath, I. Noble, & P. De Mey (eds.), *Ecumenism of life as a challenge for academic theology: Proceedings of the 14ᵗʰ Academic Consultation of the Societas Oecumenica* (pp. 77-92). Frankfurt am Main: Verlag Otto Lembeck.

Kozyrev, F. N. (2009). Towards a new paradigm of RE in Eastern Europe. In W. A. J. Meijer, S. Miedema, A. Lanser-van der Velde (eds.), *Religious education in a world of religious diversity* (pp. 21-39). Münster/New York/München/Berlin: Waxmann.

Козырев Ф.Н. (2010). Гуманитарное религиозное образование: Книга для учителей и методистов (СПб: РХГА) [Kozyrev F. N. (2010). Religious education as one of the humanities].

School Council (1971). Religious education in secondary schools (School Council Working Paper 36) (Evans/Methuen Educational).

Weisse, W. (ed.). (2008). *Dialogischer Religionsunterricht in Hamburg: Positionen, Analysen und Perspektiven im Kontext Europas*. Münster/New York/München/Berlin: Waxmann.

AFFILIATIONS

Fedor Kozyrev
Director of the Centre for Religious Pedagogy
St. Petersburg, Russia

HENK KUINDERSMA

INNOVATION OF RELIGIOUS EDUCATION

Innovation of RE in Primary Education as a Lifelong Challenge

INTRODUCTION

Let's talk with children about the question 'What do you think of this story?'

I was born (1946) and raised in Joure in the province of Friesland, one of the most northern provinces of the Netherlands. People from various backgrounds were always welcomed in our home. My father (1912-1989) came from a liberal Protestant tradition. My mother (1915-1991) belonged to a pietist movement in the Protestant Churches.

During my early childhood my mother would sing hymns which would nowadays be considered as related to the evangelical movement. She was a talented singer as was illustrated by the fact that she became a member of one of the best choirs in the region. Whether it was a song by Mozart, Händel, Bach or Fauré, she could switch between genres with ease. She loved it and enjoyed singing along to the hymns that we, my two brothers, my sister and I, brought home from school. She was also keen on transferring this passion for singing to us. In my case my mother succeeded. Like her, I have loved to sing all of my life. And thanks to her, teaching children to sing songs became an important topic in my later religious education (RE) work.

My father loved reading aloud and telling stories. At the dinner table he always read the Children's Bible *De weg naar het licht* (Renes-Boldingh, 1950). aloud to us. According to a critical study into children's bibles, it was these children's bible that 'allowed the child room for own images and imagination'.[1]

My father guided our lives with stories. These stories were inspired by his own experiences and history, as well the numerous books and stories he read. He liked to tell the following story:

> A dog, even if it starts to stray, will never forget its owner, who gave him what he needed: food, love and, if necessary, punishment. A good owner will always keep hoping that his stray dog will return. He will keep looking for him. Call him the moment he sees him. And when his dog returns to him, he will be very pleased. That is also how God acts towards people.

Besides being an avid storyteller, my father was also someone who could easily have conversations with us and our friends.[2] And always posing that inviting and familiar question: What do you think, personally?

I. ter Avest (ed.), On the Edge: (Auto)biography and Pedagogical Theories on Religious Education, 81–91.

And he would listen to the answers that followed with great dedication.

Sunday School

It must have been 1956. I was about ten years old. With some twenty children I attended Sunday School. My dad was the teacher. That morning he told us about Adam and Eve and Paradise. Adam and Eve ate from the tree that God had forbidden them. And He punished them by sending them away from this beautiful Paradise. It was typical of him to conclude his story by asking the question:

What do you think of this story?

Jacob was the first to respond and raise his finger: "Sir, if Adam and Eve had not eaten from that tree, would we then still be living in Paradise?" The question was met with another question: "What do you think, Jacob, would there not have been a fair chance that you or I would have made mischief?" Jacob, with a great sense of self, burst into laughter and immediately answered: "Yes, I'm afraid you're right". But straight after he asked: "Did this really happen to Adam and Eve like you said?" "Is there any way we can know this?" my father replied. Jacob shook his head: "Maybe we should just think about ourselves, as you just did, and ask ourselves: what would I have done if I had been Adam or Eve?"

Interpretation

What was it that led my father to religious guidance of children in this way? Was this just who he was? "We resemble the people in the Biblical narratives", was one of his convictions.[3] Whether these stories were true accounts or not was not all that important. They could have happened ... It appeared to be real: the people in our time often behaved in the same ways as people in the Bible did. Was it his liberal upbringing, free of dogmatism, which led him? Perhaps. But there was more to it than that. He enjoyed taking inspiration from educated people, such as Jan Ligthart (1859-1916) and his book *Jeugdherinneringen* (Lighart, 1954), which was filled with wisdom on (educational) upbringing:

Children should feel safe with their educators and those who are charged with their upbringing. Otherwise they will fly away from you like sparrows is one example of such a piece of wisdom. (p. 116)

Every year my father attended meetings for Sunday School leadership in Amsterdam. And this meant quite a long journey from the north of the country. I remember on one occasion how he returned, brimming with enthusiasm. He had attended a lecture by Professor Johan W. van Hulst of the VU University Amsterdam. This pedagogue was someone, he felt, who truly understood the times we were living in and recognised what inspired children and educators. On Sunday the 29th of January 2012 I watched an elderly Van Hulst (101 years old) on TV in the most famous talk-show on Dutch television.[4] He was still as sparkling and wise as my father had once spoken of him.

CHOICE FOR EDUCATION AND PEDAGOGY

In my father's footsteps, his love for children and the ways in which he educated them, I began to develop a particular interest in children. I decided to become a primary school teacher, which turned out to be the right choice. I was fascinated by what I learned at the Teacher Training College in Sneek. Inspirational teachers shaped me and fellow classmates by means of themes from history, theology, sociology, art and literature. This opened up a whole new world to me.

In our final year, Marinus Baaijens,[5] teacher of pedagogy and educational innovator, discussed *Beknopte theoretische pedagogiek* (Bos, 2011, pp. 214-219) by Martinus J. Langeveld (1905-1989), one of the founding fathers of Dutch pedagogy. Pedagogy and educational innovation became my favourite fields of study. Langeveld led me to the understanding of everyday togetherness between educator and child, which can turn into – intentional – education/rearing at any moment. Langeveld appropriately called the 'togetherness of educator and child' a pedagogically pre-formed field. In this field, those concerned with upbringing and education could only act correctly if they understood that the child is dependent on them and on the education. At the same time the child yearns to be an individual and develop its individuality. The child is a person and it wants to be a person, is Langeveld's basic statement (Bos, 2011, p. 219). And this is how it should be. The child needs to come of age. These insights and convictions – which I, to this day, firmly believe to be true – were thoroughly in line with my own upbringing.[6]

Practice and Theory

After finishing my teacher training, I started work as primary school teacher in 1968, which I very much enjoyed. Five years later I took equal pleasure in my new position as managing director of an innovative school for primary education in Drachten[7], a medium-sized town in the east of Friesland.

Driven by my educational ideals to give children opportunities to develop themselves in relation to others and in the context of their cultural backgrounds, I decided to take up pedagogy and educational studies at Groningen University next to my work.

At our school in Drachten, my colleagues and I were idealistic and purpose-driven in the spirit of Leon van Gelder (1913-1981). Theory and practice were connected organically. For example, his theory of language and model of Didactic Analysis (DA) was linked to our school practices; much emphasis was placed on the relationship between language and thinking (Evers & van Gelder, 1968). I felt at home in that place; on the hinge of theory and practice, and it was to remain my permanent home.

However, quite remarkably, RE was not involved in any of the innovative activities at our school. And our school was no exception in this respect. In the whole country RE remained stuck in teacher-centred approaches of didactic transfer: preaching rather than teaching.[8] Vision and didactic innovation attuned to children was lacking. And despite the varied approach, which I myself practiced, including all sorts of activities, discussions and lot of singing, this status quo, in which children were not challenged to ask questions, to come to discoveries and an own understanding of religion began to have quite a negative effect on me.

New Choices

After ten years of primary school teaching and studies at Groningen University,[9] I became general advisor for innovative primary education in the north of Friesland. During this period, in the early eighties, I met the pedagogue Jan Dirk Imelman during a teacher exam session. He appeared to be most interested in my questions on the stagnation of innovation of RE in primary education: the reflecting of a theoretical foundation of RE and a practical approach in which children got opportunities to deserve an own meaning about religion.

Imelman proposed a joint RE investigation, a cooperation of the two faculties of pedagogy and theology. Within that programme I particularly studied the foundations of pedagogy of religion so as to (further) develop my vision of RE with an open mind and with the ecumenical interest which my parents had passed on to me. My most important reference in this study was Karl Ernst Nipkow (1928), who offered guidelines for practices of RE at home, in church and at school. After my graduation Karl Ernst Nipkow has remained a permanent source of reference in my aims to develop an ecumenical RE.

Doctoral Dissertation 'Symbol Didactics'

In the mid-eighties I was asked to be advisor for RE for the entire province of Friesland. In this I saw that a 'proclaiming didactics of transfer' makes children sit still, listen and imitate. I recognized that my studies in pedagogy of religion were insufficient to contribute to the solution of the problem that I observed.

In the mid-eighties I met Hans-Günter Heimbrock, who was briefly professor of pedagogy of religion in Groningen. In answer to my questions on the stagnation of RE, Heimbrock guided me towards the concept of symbol didactics

Authors on the subject symbol didactics take as their starting point the language of religious traditions, notably the Christian tradition. They convinced me that religious language should be understood as narrative language, storytelling language, poetic language, as a language of symbols and metaphors. It is in this language that people express their religious experiences. With religious language as symbolic-metaphoric starting-point, pedagogues of religion, both catholic and protestant, are able to create a varied, activating approach to RE. An approach that suits children in an intercultural, secularizing culture. Symbol didactics starts off with everyday universal symbolic themes, easily accessible to any child, such as road, water, house, light, hand, tree, star.

In line with Peter Biehl, one of the most prominent scholars in symbol didactics, I proposed to have religious conversations with children about their learning experiences in an environment that is rich in symbols, to give meaning to symbols in dialogue and to find answers to questions of life as these are raised by RE.[10]

To achieve this I used the philosophizing-with-children approach, introduced in the Netherlands by the children's philosopher Berry Heesen (see Kuindersma, 1998, p. 228; Valstar & Kuindersma, 2008, p. 154) and the work of the British pedagogue of religion John Hull (1991).

Many were enthusiastic about the varied didactic approach and the children's personal activities. But in practice symbol didactics turned out to be too complex for everyday educational practice. I was challenged to look for a simpler and more manageable alternative, embedded within the educational innovation as a whole. And this line of thought would present itself by means of the work of Prof. dr. Siebren Miedema.

TOWARDS A PEDAGOGICAL FRAMEWORK

I knew Siebren Miedema through his publications. After obtaining my doctor's degree in 1998, I became extensively acquainted and involved with his theory on school and curriculum development. The identity of a school, as Miedema perceives it, should not be developed in terms of the legal framework of the 1981 Act on Primary Education. Neither does a Protestant, Catholic, or Islamic view on life constitute the framework to characterize a school. Schools need to achieve an identity-in-practice by giving meaning to three interactive dimensions. These three dimensions are:

– The dimension of the view on life: broadly indicated as the area of religion and existential questions on sense and purpose of life; values and norms and opinions on mankind and society.
– The educational dimension: this dimension reflects on concrete acts in the school, acts that relate in some sense or other to the pupils' learning, their acquisition of knowledge and skills.
– The dimension of pedagogical and organizational aspects: this entails all aspects concerned with didactic approaches that are directly related to the content of the curriculum and to the pupil's education and development (Miedema, 1999, 67).

This clear-cut cognitive offered tangible guidelines for the integration of RE. Next to that it also challenges schools to develop RE in cohesion with other curricular elements in accordance with identical principles.[11]

Miedema convincingly argued that these three dimensions seamlessly combine with the concept of Developmental Education as had been developed in the Netherlands based on the theories of Russian educational psychologist and pedagogue, Lev Semennovič Vygotsky (1996-1934) (van Oers & Wardekker, 2000, pp. 71-213).

The main characteristic of Developmental Education is that its point of departure is not the content of the lessons, but the actions of the child. The child must be given the opportunity to grow into the historically developed language system as well as into the cognitive and systems of a culture. It must be challenged to critically question these systems and where it sees fit, to adjust them. This in order to transform acquired knowledge and meaning to a continuously developing self-awareness and personal knowledge base.

The social aspect of learning plays an important part in Developmental Education. First of all in relation to the teacher, who, according to Vygotsky, should observe the pupil carefully to be able to observe the zone of current development and then needs to answer the question if the child can achieve the zone of proximal development on its own or with focused guidelines (scaffolding). Secondly, the social aspect of learning in relation to pupils amongst each other; pupils can help one another by offering a helping hand and direct insights, to progress in their thinking and in acquiring knowledge and meaning.

Inspiration and Personal Tracks

In the meantime I was employed as pedagogue of religion by the protestant Theological University in Kampen. Inspired by Siebren Miedema, I found that the concept of Developmental Education took up an increasingly important position in my thinking. And not only in my thinking, but especially in the mind of my closest colleague and co-author Johan Valstar, of the neighbouring Windesheim, School of Education in Zwolle. Together we began writing a textbook RE for primary education called *Verwonderen en Ontdekken* (*Marvel and Discover*) (Valstar & Kuidersma, 2008). In this book in close cooperation we attempted to answer our questions about 'good RE' by means of a threefold theoretical basis: first of all through the concept of developmentally-oriented education; secondly, a model of 'elementarising', in essence a theoretically designed educational model of preparation inspired by the work of the German pedagogues Karl Ernst Nipkow en Friedrich Schweitzer,[12] and thirdly, the concept of 'Theologising with children'.[13]

In accordance with their level of development, and in carefully measured dosages, generally shared, elementary information and meaningful notions from theology and science of religion information are introduced. This method is open and non-dogmatic manner, just as I was familiar with at home with my parents, and later on in my own educational experiences, in ecumenism and didactics of symbolism.

The approach methodically uses the experiences of 'Philosophizing with children' (see Kuindersma, 1998, p. 228; Valstar & Kuindersma, 2008, p. 154).

On the basis of our studies of the abundantly available empirical material, we came to the conclusion that 'Theologising with children' offered many opportunities to explore religious themes with children and to attach meaning to their experiences.[14] We are concerned with the relation between the pupils' experiences and questions and the religious domain: primarily expressed in the Biblical stories in relation to stories from the Quran and other holy writings.

The original Elementarization model (Nipkow & Schweitzer) focuses on the theological conversations with children, using five interrelated components or Perspectives from which a learning environment can be created.
− Elementary structures of the instructional content;
− Elementary experiences, as involved in the worlds of the past and the present
− Elementary accesses to understanding in developmental and biographical terms;

- Elementary truths or meaning of life, resulting from different perspectives, and finally,
- Elementary learning activities, which may support meaningful religious learning.[15]

Based on experimental research, explorations and experiences with prospective teachers in Windesheim School of Education (Valstar 2006-2007) the Tübinger Model (Nipkow & Schweitzer) was dynamically modified and extended.

A remarkable new extension in the model elementarization is the component: Elementary Incentives & Media colleague Johan Valstar added to the origin model. As we know, theological conversations do not just happen out of the blue. They are dependent on incentives, which evoke a certain kind of intrinsic motivation, by which the children/students as if by magic begin to experience a strong sense of involvement with their learning process.

Verwonderen en Ontdekken, has led to experiences, from which may tentatively concludes we have made progress with the integration of innovative RE in primary education.

However, this does not hold true with respect to my love for 'singing with children'. *Verwonderen en ontdekken* contains a well-written chapter on children's songs Thea Endedijk-Griffioen, teacher music at Iselinge School of Education, Doetinchem (Valstar & Kuindersma, 2008, pp. 262-304). But children's songs in RE have not yet received the attention they unequivocally deserve.[16]

Challenge and Progress

How do the principles of '*Verwonderen en Ontdekken*' work in practice? We give some examples:

A teacher asks the children to draw a picture for each fragment in the Joseph story: Joseph in his multi-coloured coat, Joseph in the pit, Joseph at Potiphar's, Joseph in the Round Tower where the king's prisoners are kept and Joseph as viceroy. These drawings are then looked at with each other and compared. The children immediately recognized the contrasting situations in which Joseph found himself.

On the whiteboard the teacher then drew a zigzag: drawing up and down and then up again and down, and he asked: "What kind of line is this?" The children saw it straight away: "That's what Joseph's life looks like". He then asked if someone could write down what had happened on each of the angles. On the top angles, Greetje accurately wrote: 'Joseph the dreamer' and 'Joseph at Potiphar's' and 'Joseph as viceroy'. And on the bottom angles: 'In the pit' and 'In the Round Tower'.

After this, the teacher introduced the highs and lows in the lives of the children themselves to the conversation. The children had absolutely no problem in giving all sorts of examples. Highs, such as "my mother was very ill, but she has now completely recovered". And lows, such as "my granddad passed away last month".

A teacher with a mixed group of Christian and Muslim pupils told them Quran stories on Yusuf after the Biblical stories on Joseph. The children already knew that Joseph is called Yusuf in the Quran. But the fact that the pharaoh is called firaun; that sounded different. And when talking with each other, the children noticed more differences. By the end of the conversation the children showed curiosity when it comes to learning more about stories in both the Bible and the Quran. They were actually surprised to discover so many similarities.

Another teacher read aloud the part by the narrator in the Joseph stories: "And the Lord was with Joseph".[17] But Joseph never even noticed until later. So the teacher posed the question: "Is it possible that God is also hidden but present in us in this way?" This question catches the children unawares. They hesitate and think. "Maybe", Mieke finally says. Others nod: "Maybe". The teacher left it at this. Just thinking about the question is enough.

These and other examples lead me to the insight that the Bible and the Quran and other holy books are always concerned with biographies or fragments of biographies, in which people are able to recognize their own lives.

In 'Theologising with children', biographies of children and biographies from the Bible or other holy books are continuously interchanging. The model of 'elementarising' and theologising with children aims at a double disclosure: the disclosure of one's personal existence and disclosure of the religious domain.[18]

FUTURE DEVELOPMENTS IN RE

I find it poignant and special to observe that my father more or less had the same approach at home and at Sunday School. Where he got his precise inspiration from, we will never know. But it can be said with certainty that having a background in theology or science of religion is essential for teachers who lead children onto certain paths.

Vygotsky strongly emphasizes the role of teachers when it comes to content:

There are moments when children cannot proceed on their own accord. Scaffolding, social and instructional support, will be necessary.[19]

And this is precisely what happens in children's theology, where theological information and insights are introduced openly and proportionally. In terms of content the central question is the 'question about God', the question about 'the mystery of the hidden God'.

For the future of RE I would like to further explore this theme, both within the Christian tradition and between faiths: just like the teachers in their conversations with the children on the stories of Joseph and Yusuf.

I was lucky enough to experience in practice how interested children are in comparing stories and how special they find it to discover that many stories, both in the Bible and the Quran, relate to the lives of the same persons like Joseph and Yusuf. I therefore expect to find, based on these first experiences, that listening to each other responding to the question 'What do you think of this story?', and reflecting together on the stories and the variety of answers will bring about mutual respect and will consequently bring them closer together than informative projects about festivals, places of worship, holy writings or anthropological projects, in which children from various religious traditions tell each other how they experience their faiths. No matter how much these projects are supported by excursions and authentic meetings with members of the various religions, they remain peripheral; the world of another person, who does not really enter into your world.

I made a first attempt at working with interreligious narration, by studying the project *Samenleesverhalen* (Clijnk, 2011) from Bible and Quran for children in the lower years of primary education. A project, in which the compiler, the religious scientist and the teacher engage in conversation with children on religious questions like the question 'What do you think of this story?', including the question 'What do you think about God?' Again, exciting times lie ahead of us.

NOTES

1. Rapport (1975), 85.
2. The conversations I had experienced during this time were later repeated when it came to our own children. My wife, my girlfriend from early schooldays, and from an accepting family as I myself has, actively engaged in this as well. Her interest in education has substantially contributed to my work. I wrote about all this in 1998 in the preface to my doctoral thesis (Kuindersma, 1998, p. 16).
3. This opinion reminds us of Nico ter Linden, the former minister and storyteller of the Westerkerk Church in the centre of Amsterdam: 'A Biblical story is about myself. If it is not about me, it is about nothing' (ter Linden, 1997, p. 66).
4. Ivo Niehe's television show airing for over thirty years, in which prominent artists, politicians, sportsmen and women from all across the world have been interviewed.
5. Marinus Baaijens has become known in particular as the expert who managed the innovation of primary education of children aged 4-12 in the Netherlands, as regulated in the 1981 Act on Primary Education.
6. My later studies of Langeveld's work, confirmed this. It was striking that the mennonite Langeveld held religious conversations with his children, just like my father used to do (Langeveld, 1964, pp. 92-93).
7. The innovative school in Drachten took part in the national project 'Geleide Vernieuwing' ('Guided Innovation') of which my former teacher Marinus Baaijens was in charge.
8. In my doctoral dissertation I attempted to analyze and interpret the backgrounds of this practice with the title From initial stages to points of attention for further study (Kuindersma, 1998, chapter 4, pp. 55-66). There I reach the conclusion that didactic publications have led to a new understanding of the Bible, but not to didactic innovation. The teacher-centered didactics of transferring information has remained the central concept until well into the nineties.
9. Here I obtained the A diploma in pedagogy and the B diploma in educational studies.
10. Peter Biehl talks about critical knowledge and understanding of symbols. See Kuindersma (1998, p. 228).
11. In my working situations in the north of the Netherlands we have transformed these three dimensions in terms of a course proposal with a working group (Kuindersma, 2002).
12. Most recently explained in Schweitzer (2011).
13. Friedrich Schweitzer recently put 'theologising with children' and 'elementarising' together in Schweitzer (2011). It strengthened us in our choice for the coherence of 'elementarising and theologising' in Valstar and Kuindersma (2008).

¹⁴ I refer here to the 'Jahrbücher Kindertheologie', which have appeared annually since 2002 (Bucher, Büttner, Freudenberger-Lötz, & Schreiner, 2002, 2003, 2004).

¹⁵ Recently explained in Friedrich Schweitzer (2011).

¹⁶ Educational boards and managers of teacher training colleges hardly pay attention to children's songs despite repeated pleas.

¹⁷ Genesis 39: 21-23.

¹⁸ According to Klafki (1946).

¹⁹ The application of the theory of scaffolding is based on Vygotsky (1978, p. 86) and is used in many publications. Also by us in Valstar and Kuindersma (2008, p. 142). Vygotsky himself however did not introduce the term scaffolding.

REFERENCES

Bos, J. (2011). M. J. Langeveld. *Pedagoog aan de hand van het kind* [Pedagogue at the hand of a child]. Amsterdam: Boom Publishing.

Bucher, A. A, Büttner, G., Freudenberger-Lötz, P., & Schreiner, M. (eds.). (2002, 2003, 2004). Jahrbücher Kindertheologie: Band 1: *Mittendrin ist Gott. Kinder denken nach über Gott, Leben und Tod*; Band 2: *Im Himmelreich ist keiner Sauer. Kinder als Exegeten*; Band 3: *Zeit ist immer da. Wie Kinder Hoch-Zeiten und Festtage erleben*. Stuttgart: Calwer Verlag.

Clijnk, I. (2011). *Samenleesverhalen* [Stories to read together] (Bible and Koran, H.K). Amersfoort Kwintessens Publishing.

Evers, E., & Gelder, L. van (1968). *Nederlandse taal. Didactische aanwijzingen voor het lager onderwijs* [Dutch language, Didactic directions for primary education]. Groningen Wolters-Noordhoff Publishing.

Hull, J. (1991). *God-talk with young children. Notes for parents and teachers*. Derby Christian Education Movement.

Kuindersma, H. (1998). *Godsdienstige communicatie met kinderen door symbooltaal* [Religious communication with children through symbolic language]. Kampen: Kok Publishing.

Kuindersma, H. (ed.). (2002). *Elke school een eigen gezicht. Een samenwerkingsproject van CHN, Metrium en GCO Fryslân* [Each school a face of its own. Cooperation project of CHN, Metrium and GCO Fryslân]. Leeuwarden: GCO Fryslân.

Langeveld, M. J. (1964). De religie en het wereldbeeld van het kind [Religion and the child's world view]. *Rondom het kind. Pedagogische etherleergang van de NCRV, 1*(4), 90-93

Lighart, J. (1954). *Jeugdherinneringen* [Memories of youth], 14th impression. Groningen: Wolters Publishing.

Linden, N. ter (1997). Bijbelverhalen vertellen vereist de beheersing van twee talen [Telling Biblical stories requires command of two languages]. In T. Kroon (ed.), *Kleuren van de toekomst. Christelijk onderwijs en schoolcultuur* [Colours of the future. Christian education and school culture]. Hilversum: NZV Publishing.

Miedema, S. (1999). Vorming en identiteit in drievoud: Een ontwikkelings-gerichte visie [Threefold educational development and identity: a developmental vision]. In S. Miedema & H. Klifman (eds.), *Christelijk onderwijs in ontwikkeling* [Christian education in development]. Kampen: Kok Publishing.

Klafki, W. (1964). *Das pädagogische Problem des Elementaren und die Theorie der kategorialen Bildung*. Weinheim: Belz Verlag.

Oers, B. Van, & Wardekker, W. L. (2000). De cultuurhistorische school in de pedagogiek [The cultural-historical school in pedagogy]. In S. Miedema (ed.), *Pedagogiek in meervoud. Wegen en denken over opvoeding en onderwijs* [Pedagogy in the plural. Ways and thinking about raising children and education] (pp. 71-213). Houten/Diegem: Bohn Stafleu Van Loghum Publishing.

Rapport van een onderzoek naar kinderbijbels [Report of an investigation into Children's Bibles] (1972). Haarlem/'s-Hertogenbosch: NBG/KBS Publishing.

Renes-Boldingh, M. A. M. (1950). *De weg naar het licht, Jeugdbijbel* [The way to the light, Youth Bible]. Nijkerk: Callenbach Publishing.

Valstar, J., & Kuindersma, H. (2008). *Verwonderen en ontdekken. Vakdidactiek godsdienst primair onderwijs* [Marvel and discover. Didactics of religion for primary education]. Amersfoort: NZV Publishing.

Vygotsky, L. S. (1978). *Mind in society; The development of higher psycholigical processes.* Cambridge, MA: Harvard University Press.

AFFILIATIONS

Henk Kuindersma
Protestant University in Kampen
The Netherlands

ALMA LANSER

DOING AND UNDERGOING

Learning to Believe as Algorithm and as Heuristic

INTRODUCTION

A heuristic is a strategy for problem solving.
We don't know where it will take us,
but with an open mind we set off,
hoping to discover new perspectives.

My faith started with my mother. My pleasure in thinking with my father, who used to teach us mathematics over our Sunday lunches. One day, my father wanted to make us understand that counting with letters was a quicker and much smarter way of counting than counting with figures. I don't remember my exact age, but I was still in primary school. Instead of adding, subtracting, multiplying and dividing numbers, my daily exercise at school, one could use letters – and open new worlds! My father chose no less than Pythagoras' theorem to illustrate this. The lengths of the legs of a right-angled triangle, he said, were a and b and one could calculate the length of the hypotenuse, c, by adding the squares of a and b and then extracting the root of that third square and … voilà. My father was a bit of a prig, but a didactically skilled one: next Sunday he asked us what we remembered to check whether we had really understood his teaching. Later on he added algebra and stereometry, but this explanation of Pythagoras' theorem is one of my finest memories.

FAITH AND THINKING

The memory is multilayered. First, there's the methodical aspect of my father's approach, his use of algorithms. With his mathematical explanations he showed us the usefulness and efficiency of algorithms. Algebra is, in its essence, a set of rules with which certain problems can be solved. The rules offer the possibility to make calculations one could not have done with numbers exclusively. The algorithms contain extra, but invisible data and assumptions which go back to agreements that precede the rules. For example, one should know that Pythagoras' theorem only applies to right-angled triangles. Algebra, of course, is very procedural. Once you understand the premises and procedures, know the formula with which to solve problems, and see which type of issues that specific formula is applicable to, you're almost done. A well defined problem calls for a specific formula which will provide a necessary outcome.

I. ter Avest (ed.), On the Edge: (Auto)biography and Pedagogical Theories on Religious Education, 93–102.

The second layer in this memory is my father literally radiating with pleasure while explaining all that to us, and his enthusiasm about the possibilities of mathematics. It offered wonderful tricks, he said, and enabled people to develop another concept of reality. The combination of pleasure in thinking, the kick one gets out of understanding, and an approach of reality that creates new spaces, that was the real learning. I can still see it in my brothers, who were at that same Sunday lunch table, and are gifted with practical skills, brainpower and creativity, a different proportion in every one of them.

The pleasure in thinking, and in discovering and designing new possibilities is the backbone of science, and this also goes for Religious Education as a science. Heuristics can function as passwords for entering the creative space of science, they enable the search for new possibilities. A heuristic is a strategy for problem solving. We don't know where it will take us, but with an open mind we set off, hoping to discover new perspectives.

My contribution to this Liber Amicorum for Siebren Miedema is about algorithms and heuristics in the theory about religious learning. I will explore the relationship between these two epistemological concepts and the way they function both in Religious Education and in religious learning.

EXPERIENCE

After years of coaching local 'Women and Faith'-courses within the project 'Women and Faith Noord-Holland', and many discussions, courses and coachings I did as a Youth Consultant, I am convinced that faith flourishes when it can be connected to people's everyday lives – a conviction that has grown to be my passion. Faith is not just a book, not just the story from the pulpit, faith has to do with our here and now, with our choice to act or not to act, with experiences that inspire us and make us suffer. The term *Lived Religion*, as it is used nowadays by many of my fellow practical theologians, is tailor-made for me.

I share my conviction with the people who in the last decades of the previous century developed so-called 'genitive theologies' (because they were theologies 'of' a particular group, both *by* that community and *for* that community, such as the South American liberation theology and the feminist theology). The term 'genitive theology' seems to have been chosen with some hesitation (Heitink, 1988), but I think they had an important point. In feminist theology, which has inspired and encouraged me very much, women changed their position from being the object of men's theologizing to being the subjects of their own thought. They also claimed the experiences of women as a theological topic. In their criticism of the dominant academic theology female theologians showed that what was meant as theology-for-all was in fact colored by the male gaze and thus biased. Nobody expressed this criticism better than Mary Daly (1973) did in her aphorism *If God is male, then the male is God.*

The inclusion of these then new theologies in academic reflection was all but a matter of course. For years there were discussions about the relationship between revelation and experience. Wouldn't the upgrading of the human voice automatically lead to the decrease of the authority of God's speech (Biezeveld, 2008)? Not only do these theological questions challenge us to take position, they also invite us, perhaps even more urgently, to find an explanation for this contrast. How can engaged religious people think so differently?

My Own Experience with Learning

Understanding and applying algebra is one thing. Things get even more interesting when one succeeds in 'transcending' algebra as a discipline, and recognizes the procedural nature of algebra in, for example, philosophy and methodology. My fascination for understanding and learning started at that Sunday lunch table, and it has accompanied me since then, as I was formed and educated by my experiences. What is happening in the interaction between people and between people and the world? What makes things 'click' in their brains? And why does this 'click' sometimes fail to happen, in what situation, to whom? We are still very uncertain as to what happens in our brain. Unfortunately, 'black box' is still the most appropriate metaphor for our head. The only basis for statements about the process of learning and understanding is the behavior of people who are learning. Observing them allows us to design heuristics with which we set off into our scientific research, testing them in the reality of people's daily lives.

The questions raised by all of my professional and personal experiences all boil down to this one leitmotiv: What precisely is learning? What exactly brings about a learning experience? Among those questions certainly this one: whether learning to believe is something different from learning mathematics.

LINES MEETING IN PRAGMTISM

As a 'second chance' theologian I obtained my master's degree at the Faculty of Theology of the Free University in Amsterdam, after ten years of studying part time. That was in the first half of the 1990s. A year after that joyful day I got a job as a lecturer in Religious Education at the same Faculty, because of that degree *and* because of my work experience as a Youth Consultant. A university teacher is expected to continue studying, and eventually write a dissertation. During my PhD I tried to figure out how experience as a theological concept could be connected to the process of learning to believe. Did all those involved in the various genitive theologies have a point or were they on the wrong track? Then I found an article that opened a new world: Biesta, Miedema and Berding (in their contribution to *Pedagogiek in meervoud*, see Miedema, 1994) explained the word *experience* as *doing and undergoing*. Under the heading 'Pragmatic Pedagogy' they describe *pragmatism* as a philosophical and pedagogical school. Central concepts in Dewey's pragmatism are *'upbringing as coordination of individual and social factors'*, *'ongoing reconstruction of experience'* and *'the experience as doing and undergoing'*. In pragmatism the experience and the thinking about the experience are not presented as opposites, but as aspects of a process, as simultaneously occurring phenomena.

As a philosopher and an educationist, Dewey reflects about the way we know and learn. He analyses how Plato and Aristotle described their worldview and deduced from that how man arrives at knowledge about reality. Dewey proposed another theory on the construction of knowledge (Dewey, 1929). The classical Greeks said that one can only gain real knowledge by stepping back from a subject and observe reality from a distance. Thinking was placed between the observer and the world. The outcome of the process (taking distance, observing and thinking about what was perceived), was called true knowledge. From that moment on the scientist finds himself in a subject-object ratio with the world. To gain true knowledge one must step back from the object one wants to investigate. Objectivity becomes the dominant standard for true science. This scientific attitude has yielded spectacular results, our Western science, technology and prosperity developed thanks to this way of thinking. But the objectification of the world has its price, and a high price it is: we will have to deal with the exploitation of nature, negative aspects of class society, alleged differences between races and peoples and a paradigm in which everything is divided into high and low. The primacy of rational, objective knowledge over all other forms of knowledge narrows the view on the wealth of the world and on everything that is of equally great value in life. Faith in particular should remain a private activity, and theology is, according to many, still no a real science.

Dewey developed an epistemology in which intersubjectivity, not the subject-object relation, was the starting point. People are an integral part of the world surrounding them. Even if we try to observe objectively and study science in a objective way, we cannot place ourselves outside the world we observe. Materially, we continue depending on air and food, clothing and shelter. And as humans we would be lost without our parents, without the people around us that have made us what we are and who taught us everything (Lanser & van der Velde, 2000).

With intersubjectivity as a starting point of an epistemology, we can conceive learning as a continuing process in which rationality and irrationality, theory and practice are all modes of experience. In the experience, embedded in the world and in social relationships, we undergo reality and because we exist, we do something to reality. Our being-in-the-world changes the world as we are in it. Our changing, growing and learning is at the same time changing the world and creating something new, together with our fellow man (Dewey, 1934).

If we want to distinguish the elements of this process, such as the daily experience and thinking about it, we can only do that in retrospect. Looking back we can distinguish experiences, see what previous experience (habit) was present in the process and how the new experience has brought us knowledge, however provisional. In the process, it was a matter of doing and undergoing, resulting in 'warranted assertions' about the situation. Giving meaning and in doing so, learning is an ongoing process in which, on the one hand, one is bound to time and context and one's fellow men, and on the other hand one can continue to create, think and design. This description, however short, shows that everything that has been developed later on as social constructivism has included the elements of Dewey's pragmatism.

My introduction to Dewey's epistemology and pedagogy allowed me to see that the alleged contradiction between revelation and experience, thinking and doing, scientific and common knowledge was non-existent. This felt like pure gain. Thinking in opposites comes with the Greek-Western subject-object view on the construction of knowledge. The problems arising from this way of thinking will disappear once we've chosen a different way of thinking. In an intersubjective paradigm the distinction between higher and lower no longer exists. In my dissertation, I elaborated on the significance of this new way of thinking for the theological, empirical and religious educational field. This matter is most dear to me in Religious Education: this epistemology offers us the firm ground on which to contend that a religious experience is as real as everything else. Claims to the irrationality of religion no longer have any authority. Religion and religious education is as rational and irrational as any other field.

Learning as algorithm and heuristic

For this argument, the backbone of which is formed by the concepts *algorithm* and *heuristic*, it is important to distinguish religious learning following algorithms from heuristic religious learning. I will expose them briefly. Often, learning begins with trying to understand a theory, uncomplicated as it may seem. Even learning in primary schools is in fact the acquisition of hidden theories. The theory then functions as an algorithm, i.e. as a set of rules for the solution of a problem. A good theory organizes reality. The theory reduces the complex, sometimes chaotic reality to a few clear concepts or a nice framework. What was confusing, can then be seen in categories, in a neat ordering. Counting, calculating, writing, a geographical map, algebra, Habermas' *Theorie des kommunikativen Handelns*, Dewey's pragmatism and Berkouwers *Dogmatische Studiën* – all are abstractions that function as a pair of glasses providing a clear view. Let me elaborate an example.

When we read the Gospel of Matthew from the beginning to the end facts, sentences, stories and events romp over one another. If we read it, using the theory 'the Gospel of Matthew is a textbook for new converts preparing them for their baptism in the Easter night' we suddenly see a structure (Lanser & van der Velde, 2004). The book turns out to consist of five Discourses and a lot of quotes from the Old Testament. It constitutes a coherent whole of teaching, preaching and healing and as a particular stylistic device the Gospel pays special attention to the small and nonentities . The theory 'textbook for new converts' organizes the multitude of data in Matthew, it solves our chaos. We hover over the subject and no longer risk to drown in it. Applying a theory algorithmically to a problem will free the structure and yield insights, thanks to the reduction of the multitude.

Learning can also take place along the heuristic path. For religious learning, in which in my opinion and following the genitive theologies, the connection with everyday life and the dynamics between religious tradition and experience is of the utmost importance, the heuristic met-hodos even is preferable (Lanser, 2006). In contemporary educational science and (religious) didactics methods in which

97

education is realized by activating students, is seen as the best and most effective approach. Learning activities carried out by the students themselves lead to better and more sustainable study results. Here too, an example may be illustrative.

At the course 'Didactics of religion' in the Master *Religious Education* the students get the assignment to create a concept map. A concept map is a structured overview, a picture of existing knowledge and the relationships between the different concepts. It is the schematization of what the student already knows, their starting point. The assignment is intended as an impetus to the formulation of a research question. The research question is the starting point of an article that counts as the test for this course. In carrying out this assignment (creating a concept map about the three types of religious education, according to Grimmitt, 1987) students detect the gaps in their knowledge. Generally, the moment they fail to describe the relationship between two topics, for example 'church and youth', they realize they've got a gap in their knowledge. Experiencing the absence of knowledge provides the subject about which they are going to collect information and will eventually write their paper. The search for an answer to a religious educational question is a heuristic process. There is a conjecture, but no more than that. It is searching for what you don't know yet.

Religious learning as algorithmic and heuristic process

A theory of religious learning that is modeled like an algorithm differs considerably from a theory that presents religious learning as a heuristic process. I will briefly sketch the characteristics of the two routes, and will go into some detail in the following two paragraphs. In reality both views often co-exist. It is only for the sake of making explicit the differences between the methods and their consequences, that in this contribution I present them as opposites or extremes. As I've explained, the distinction goes back to two epistemological positions, but epistemology is meta-theory (van Peursen, 1984) and not reality. In reality things are more mixed up and we use the way of thinking that is most obvious to us or seems the most plausible.

On the first route, religious learning as an algorithm, learners use a set of rules to solve a problem. They will reach the fixed outcome relatively fast. This is the transfer model of religious learning. It is extremely useful and efficient. When knowledge is transferred to them, pupils, students and catechesists can pick up a lot of data, theories and insights in a short period of time. In transfer learning large quantities of cultural knowledge (accumulated in centuries) can be passed on in a relatively short time. When it comes to collecting factual knowledge, for example dates, names from history and unquestioned religious truths, transfer is the appropriate method.

Second, there's the route of heuristic learning. Synonyms for this form of learning are reciprocal learning, learning as transformation or learning according to constructivism. Unlike the transfer model, basically boiling down to 'applying the rules', this form of religious learning mainly consists of a process, a joint search for possible answers. Some problem has arisen, someone's got an idea, turns it into a design for searching and sets off with others, looking for meanings. Heuristic learning is an option when one is triggered by a religious experience, or an existential question. Looking for Bible texts or stories that can shine a light on your question fits into this model. Heuristic religious learning is a search for wisdom rather than for factual knowledge. In other words: in a situation in which open questions prevail, meanings are created together, this echoes Dewey's words: 'making things in common'.

The Algorithm: The Transfer Model of Religious Learning

The epistemological starting point of the algorithmic transfer model is the subject-object relationship of people. Students are the object of the activities of the teacher, children the object of their parents' actions and church community members of the minister's. Consciously or unconsciously they use a cognitive learning theory: learning is acquiring cognitions. Thus you learn chiefly with the head. Rational arguments count and the logic is that of the natural sciences. A consequence of the subject-object ratio is a separation between theory and practice, with the usually hushed up qualification of theory as higher, and more valuable than practice: *cogito ergo sum*. As indicated earlier, this mindset is dominant in Western society. Results of a study are displayed in figures as the ultimate truth and a statistic in the newspaper radiates the authority that is ascribed to real science. Along the same lines thinkers are thought to be worth more than people who work with their hands. Their social rating is higher and they are better paid than the workers in the vineyard. University teachers earn more than university cleaners, although they are both indispensable.

In a transfer model we create separation between thinking and doing. Rationality is paramount and morality, feelings, beliefs and opinions are banned to the domain of personal taste. We discern between real knowledge and individual beliefs. In this context religion is banned from the public domain and the only space it has a right to exist in is 'behind the front door'. The background of this seemingly reasonable attitude is the hidden practice of the separation between the logic of science and daily learning processes. Science has its own domain, in which learning differs from the learning processes in daily life. Only what is incontestably true, applies to all – and science suggests to know what is true.

The transfer model includes the opinion that theological contents do not change. The contents of theological knowledge must be transferred as they are (and always have been and will be). Knowledge is passed on without the original context and without the questions to which it was an answer in earlier days. Paolo Freire called this *the banking concept*: knowledge is seen as money lodged in a bank, stowed away safely, not wearing out and passed on without changes.

When used for the learning process in schools and universities, the transfer model leads to passive students, whereas teachers have to be very active. They are the initiator and the owner of the learning process. The teacher selects the content of the course, the topics and the working method. As if the students haven't learned that much yet, and as if what they know is not that relevant. Content and method of education are two different things. Or more precisely, it is assumed that the method of teaching does not affect the content of the knowledge. The 'how' and the 'what' of a learning process are separated. Summarizing: in the transfer model – learning as algorithm – learning is a linear event. Knowledge is transferred hierarchically and knowledge is, basically, something you have.

Heuristics: The Reciprocal or the Transactional Religious Learning

In this paradigm, the epistemological starting point is intersubjectivity. The paradigm has immediate consequences for the educational acting: teachers and students depend on each other and cooperate. A teacher can't be a teacher if there are no students and vice versa. They need each other to be who they are. The constructivist learning theory is developed out of this intersubjectivity-based epistemology. Students construct their own knowledge, collaborating with others and the learning process is contextually bound. Using what they already know and with an open mind for each new experience, for uncertainty and questions, they give meaning to what they are experiencing and they develop new lines of thought and creative options for action. This theory on learning contains a continuum between theory and practice. Every (theological) theory is developed out of practical questions and returns to daily life when the theory is applied. For example, students can learn something about homiletics, but they will only know whether the theory is fruitful and inspiring when they will sit down to make a sermon. If things don't work out as they hoped they would, the students will have to start looking for a new theory which incites to devise new homiletic options for action.

In each experience doing and undergoing go hand in hand. Knowledge cannot be separated from acting, from feelings, morals and faith. New knowledge must be integrated into knowledge that is already present. A teacher should know the level of departure of the students and let new knowledge blend with what the students had already collected and constructed. The level of departure is a factor in the learning process, and it is more than just a starting point of learning. The logic of science is the same as the logic of the daily learning processes. There is no watertight separation between the two. In the world of science you have more time to think about questions and read everything that others have said about your topic, but the nature of the learning process is the same.

There is one characteristic in the process of religious learning that, in discussions, causes many reactions. If religious learning follows the heuristic method, both the knowledge content and the participants will change in the learning process. For example, students pick up a certain theological content. In this process of 'appropriation' knowledge is re-contextualized in their lives, connected to the reality of this person and of this person's everyday life. In this process of re-contextualization the content knowledge becomes topical and relevant for their present time. That is only possible if a topical, contextual meaning is added to the already known, to the tradition. In this process of creative actualization, learners construct new meanings.

100

The subjects or participants in the learning process also change. Learning processes, at school as well as elsewhere, imply the development of identity. Knowledge is 'filed' in the head, but at the same time the individual as a whole changes in the learning process. This development is stimulated by reflection on the learning process ('learning to learn'): what did I know when I started this course, what steps did I take in the learning process and how – thanks to what activities – did my knowledge change? This process of reflection integrates skills, theological knowledge and personal identity and this integration entails a developmental step.

The subjects, the participants in the learning process, it was already said, cooperate. Participants in a process of religious learning are involved in the same practice, but their roles, tasks and responsibilities differ. Teachers and coaches are active in the preparation of a course. It is their task to create an environment fit for learning so that pupils and students may undergo learning experiences. Students are active in collecting and developing their knowledge. They are the owners of the learning process and responsible for what they want to learn (Dewey, 1938).

Content knowledge and teaching method influence one another. The 'how' and the 'what' of a learning process are internally connected. Students who are only welcome to listen to lectures receive the implicit message that speaking theologically is only allowed if you're in the position to speak *ex cathedra*.

Teachers who are working within the intersubjectivity paradigm will choose their teaching methods in such a way that students may develop both theological contents and academic skills. An important consequence of heuristic religious learning is a conversion to activating didactics. All participants in the process of searching and learning simultaneously develop knowledge and skills. They learn to think critically, develop their own theological questions, objectives and goals, and learn how they can tackle questions concerning life and faith heuristically. They learn the quest for knowledge and they learn how they can carry out this quest.

Summarizing: in the heuristic process of religious learning students become independent (but socially connected) and creative people. Every age requires new and contemporary theological and religious insights. Believers must therefore acquire the skill to continue learning long after religion is explained to them in transfer. Learning to believe is a lifelong, ongoing process.

THE FUTURE OF RELIGIOUS EDUCATION

The theme we discussed in this contribution allows us to say a few words about Religious Education as a field – keeping away from easy generalizations. The entire educational field has to deal with an increase in pressure of time and an ever growing emphasis on efficiency. Students must complete their studies within a certain time, programmes must offer demonstrably effective and affordable curricula, and diplomas and degrees must be awarded on time. The emphasis on efficiency and control leads to a preference for the algorithmic model of learning. I do hope that Master's programmes and PhD trajectories will keep reserving time and space for heuristics. Yes, a heuristic trajectory takes time, but it is obvious that, if parents, teachers, lecturers and pastors are aware of the differences between algorithms and heuristics, and know when to choose one or the other method, this will benefit the whole process of religious learning. If religious learning doesn't go beyond transfer and algorithm, it will miss the association with the questions of today's life.

Searching and learning together we may experience the wisdom of the religious tradition shining its light over our daily life and learning. Siebren Miedema's efforts for Religious Education and for the dissemination of knowledge about pragmatism, and his constant plea to keep connecting scientific and daily religious practices – all this constitutes a firm and inspiring basis on which many people can build creatively, cooperating with him.

REFERENCES/BIBLIOGRAPHY

Biezeveld, K. (2008). *Als scherven spreken. Over God in het leven van alledag* [When splinters speak. God in everyday life]. Zoetermeer: Meinema.

Dewey, J. (1929). *Experience and nature*, p. xiv. New York: Dover Publications.

Dewey, J. (1934). *Art as experience*. New York: Berkley Publishing Group.

Dewey, J. (1938). *Experience and education*. New York: Macmillan Publishing Company.

Daly, M. (1973). *Beyond God the Father. Toward a philosophy of women's liberation*. Boston: Beacon Press.

Grimmitt, M. (1987). *Religious education and human development. The relation between studying religion and personal, social and moral education*. Great Wakering: McCrimmon.

Heitink, G. (1988). *Om raad verlegen, doch niet radeloos. Ervaringen van aporie bij de beoefening der praktische theologie* [At a loss for advice, but not lost. Experiences of aporia in the practice of practical theology]. Kampen: Kok.

Lanser, A. (2006). De actualisatie van de traditie. Over de dynamiek van oude teksten en moderne levens [Actualising tradition. The dynamics of old texts and modern lives]. In S. Miedema & G. Bertram-Troost (eds.), *Levensbeschouwelijk leren samenleven, Opvoeding, identiteit & ontmoeting* [Philosophy of Life and Learning to live together. Education, identity and encounter] (pp. 93-104). Zoetermeer: Meinema.

Lanser, A., & Velde, van der (2000). *Geloven leren. Een theoretisch en empirisch onderzoek naar wederkerig geloofsleren* [Learning to believe. A theoretical and empirical study in reciprocal religious learning] (esp. chapter 2, pp. 27-65). Kampen: Kok.

Lanser, A., & Velde, van der (2004). Leraar en leerling, Het evangelie volgens Matteüs [Teacher and student. The gospel of Matthew]. In F. Maas, J. Maas, & K. Spronk (eds.), *De Bijbel spiritueel. Bronnen van geestelijk leven in de Bijbelse geschriften* [Sources of spiritual life in the Scriptures] (pp. 527-534). Zoetermeer: Meinema.

Miedema, S. (ed.). (1994). *Pedagogiek in meervoud* [Pedagogy in plural], 4th revised version (esp. chapter 8, pp. 315-336). Houten/Zavethem" Bohn Stafleu Van Loghum.

Peursen, C. A. van (1984). *De opbouw van de wetenschap. Een inleiding in de wetenschapleer* [The construction of science. An introduction to epistemology]. Meppel: Boom.

AFFILIATIONS

Alma Lanser
Faculty of Theology, VU University
Amsterdam, The Netherlands

WILNA MEIJER

REASON AND RELIGION: A LIFE-TIME CURRICULUM

INTRODUCTION

I retrospect,
I can see how Protestant in nature
my explicit farewell to the religion of my forefathers was:
it was itself actually a confession

In her mid-thirties, Ayaan Hirsi Ali wrote the autobiography, *Mijn vrijheid* (2006). The title refers to the individual freedom she gained vis-à-vis the traditional Islamic background of her youth. The contrast between, on the one hand, her life at that time as an, intellectually as well as politically very important person in Dutch public life, and, on the other, the life of her grandmother, a Muslim woman in rather primitive circumstances in Africa, is indeed massive. The autobiography ends at the point that her time in the Netherlands is drawing to a dramatic close. Death threats have followed her short movie *Submission*, a fierce criticism of the position of women in Muslim communities, that she presented on Dutch television in the summer of 2004. In November that year, Theo van Gogh, producer of the movie, was in actual fact murdered, and Hirsi Ali is forced to go into hiding. She is soon to decide to move to the US where, once more, her career goes uphill in no time.

I admired Hirsi Ali – for her courage, her independence, her intellectual vigour, her brilliant public performance, her impeccable Dutch, for the way in which she, after arriving at the age of 23 in the Netherlands, lived the far from easy life of a migrant and reached in about 10 years, with hard work and inimitable input, the top of Dutch political life. And yet, reading the autobiography, I felt the desire to read her future autobiography. The one that actually appeared in the meantime (2010), is once more highly critical of Islam and of multiculturalism in Western societies. Will the future autobiography I hope she will write after another 20 or 30 years of life, show new developments? I am curious whether she will in time change her attitude towards religion in general, and especially towards her original religion. I changed in this respect, in the course of my life, as I will try to show in this article. The development over the years of my thinking in my discipline, philosophy of education, has been of influence in my personal relation to religion; probably this holds vice versa as well.

I. ter Avest (ed.), On the Edge: (Auto)biography and Pedagogical Theories on Religious Education, 103–113.

DISTANCING FROM RELIGION

Although I can certainly in most respects not compare myself to Hirsi Ali, I do personally recognize the way she criticized and distanced herself from the religion of her forefathers and explicitly developed her own, individual position regarding that heritage. A logical, analytical criticism of religion, concentrating on arguments for and against the existence of God, as developed by the Dutch philosopher Herman Philipse in his 'Atheist Manifesto' (2004) inspired her to leave Islam behind, or at least gave her arguments to justify that decision. Hirsi Ali wrote an interesting foreword for a revised edition to this manifest of Philipse, in which she expresses the hope that it will function as a 'short-cut to enlightenment' for other Muslims, as it did for her personally. This is what she says:

When I was confronted with the *Atheïstisch manifest* by the philosopher Herman Philipse for the first time in 1998, I didn't even look inside. My boyfriend at the time gave it to me, because our discussions on religion always ended in an argument. At the moment I saw the title on the orange-brown cover, I screamed 'haram!' and threw it into a corner of the room, me, a virtuous Muslim woman. But in 2002, our relationship had broken up long before, I asked him if I might borrow it. I can hardly think of a book that has had a more liberating effect on me. (...)

The turnabout was caused by the September 11, 2001. I read the letter, written by Muhammad Atta in which he requests the help of Allah in order to be able to accomplish his terrible deed. I thought, yes indeed, if one is a Muslim one has to be able to do something like this, if Allah so wishes, because one must obey Allah always. But how could Allah wish for something so horrific? Can a good god really exist that drives Muslims to such a monstrous crime? (...) After a few months of indecision I asked my ex-boyfriend if I could borrow the *Atheïstisch manifest* by Herman Philipse.

How simple and clear is the argument of that book, and how guiltless the world became for me after reading it! Allah doesn't exist, other gods don't exist either, or hell! When I had finished it, the heavens did not cave in on me and I didn't become paralysed or insane for invoking the wrath of Allah. And so, all those threats were sheer nonsense. It was an immense relief and instead of damned I was enlightened. No doubt erudite philosophers raise many clever objections to Philipse's argument, but I am convinced that he is right on the whole. I want all 1.2 billion Muslims to read the booklet and I tried to persuade the author to write a much simpler version for export. Unfortunately he refuses because he believes he has already watered down the philosophical wine too much with popularising water. Sometimes intelligent people can be incredibly short-sighted!' (Hirsi Ali, in: Philipse, 2004, pp. 9, 11-12)

I too concentrated on the relation of reason and religion, when I made the explicit decision to leave my ancestral religion behind – in the next section I will tell this part of the story of my life. And, as Hirsi Ali, I too experienced it as enlightenment and a kind of liberation. That enlightenment and personal autonomy are the aims written into proper education, was one of the tenets of the philosophy of education that I had come to embrace during my studies in teacher training and the subsequent years at university. My explicit recognition of that ideal may indeed have influenced my personal decision to leave religion behind. The days of my very first publication, 1979, written shortly before I ended my graduate studies in history and philosophy of education at the University of Groningen, in which Siebren Miedema was just a few years my senior, were also the days of my explicit farewell to the *gereformeerde kerk*, one of the Dutch Protestant churches at the time. My religious beliefs had, however, already been dwindling for years.

PERSONAL AUTONOMY

In the 1970s, Siebren and I both studied philosophy of education with Jan Dirk Imelman at the University of Groningen. At that time there was a lively debate in Continental philosophy of education between three schools of meta-theoretical and educational thought: the hermeneutical and cultural educational theory of the *geisteswissenschaftliche* tradition, the empirical school intending to turn speculative educational thought into a genuine scientific, empirical discipline, and the critical-educational theory inspired by the philosophy of Habermas, that gave social criticism from the angle of a Neo-Marxist ideal of social equality a central position in each and every social science, the educational discipline included. Students in theory of education in Groningen were immersed into this debate. We were expected to read the works of representatives of the three schools of thought, and often felt the need to choose sides explicitly and to participate, in class, amongst ourselves and in presentations and papers, in lively, often fierce debates as to what position was the most sound and promising for philosophy of education.

Whereas I sided with the Continental educational school of thought that our teacher was representing, e.g., in his PhD-thesis (Imelman 1973), in my own PhD-thesis (1983) I looked into the possibilities of combining it with the Anglo-Saxon linguistic philosophy of education of, e.g., Richard Peters and Israel Scheffler, an approach that was also rising at the time, Siebren Miedema rather opposed it and defended the critical-educational position. Although the differences regarding the way to realize freedom and autonomy in education were considerable, both positions shared the idea that personal autonomy (German: *Mündigkeit*, Dutch: *mondigheid*) is the proper aim of education. One of the high-profile representatives of the empirical school of thought, Wolfgang Brezinka, explicitly abolished that value, both in the science of education (because as a science it should be value-free), and in his 'praktische Pädagogik', the normative practical educational theory complementing the empirical educational science. Here, Brezinka pursued the idea that humans are not capable of realising the ideal of individual autonomy – that this is an unrealistic illusion, a myth.

My first publication, an article in a Dutch educational journal, gave an analysis and critique of the dichotomy of religion and reason in Brezinka's educational and meta-theoretical thought (Meijer, 1979). Brezinka advocated an empirical

105

educational science along the lines of Popper's critical rationalism. Popper emphasized the importance of the use of reason and critical thinking in more areas of life than the scientific and academic (think of his famous *The Open Society and Its Enemies*). Brezinka, however, very unlike Popper in this respect, downplays the importance of critical rationality for human beings in their personal and social lives – and in upbringing and education, for that matter. He is convinced of the necessity of a normative theory, in addition to educational science, to guide educational practice, to support parents and educators, strengthen them in their world-views and morals, so that they will raise their children by immersing them into these ideas and values, without any doubt and hesitation as to their validity. According to Brezinka, individuals are lost without the support of a religion and a religious community. Without a faith community as a social spine, they would be entirely at the mercy of the whims and fashions of the day and of ever-changing arbitrary impulses.

The meta-theoretical distinction of science and normative theory illustrates the dichotomy of fact and value and of rationality and religion, that is fundamental to Brezinka's thought: the empirical, educational science that is fully rational, is opposed to essentially irrational, normative educational theories grounded in faith. The knowledge produced by educational science is universally valid, but there is essentially a plurality of normative educational theories. A distinctive practice-guiding normative theory can be developed for each and every different religion and life-stance, and it should according to Brezinka: educators, parents should not be left to fend for themselves in upbringing and education. The same dichotomy surfaces in Brezinka's substantive educational ideas, and it were the latter that really provoked me. Brezinka denied the very possibility of personal autonomy, the aim and value that I endorsed, personally as well as professionally, as an educational thinker.

I was vehemently critical about Brezinka's idea that children should be immersed in the religion of their parents and the religious community they belong to, to grow roots, whereas the role of reason and reflection in religious education was at most secondary, rather inessential, and anyway should be postponed until teenage or adolescent years. Only when fully socialised, rooted in a community, having internalised its world-view or religion, i.e., in their adolescent years, can our offspring according to Brezinka be trusted to face today's cultural and religious plurality, because then it will no longer bring them to lose their certainty and grip on life, their sense of footing and identity. Only then will they be able to make a positive use of reason to defend and strengthen their own tradition as opposed to other traditions in the context of religious diversity, and to stick to it. Brezinka acknowledges only the negative aspect of doubt and critical reflection: it's being uprooting and destructive, creating uncertainty and inconstancy, instead of strong, solid characters, capable to act and build an existence.

It follows that Brezinka's understanding of the multi-cultural, multi-religious society can only be an image of apartheid: a plurality of closed religious and world view communities, each group closed into itself, protecting their offspring from outside influences. Again, I was appalled, and so Brezinka triggered me to explicitly defend the exact opposite as educationally worthwhile: being open to difference, learning about and from other worlds and lives, thus also being provoked to really think about and reconsider one's own ideas and values, truisms and prejudices – to be stimulated to consider one's own individual position, rather than to share the community's faith position self-evidently and unreflectively.

BROADENING HORIZONS

In retrospect, it is clear that my interest in the theme of the relation between religion and education was there right from the start, in that very first publication of 1979. Since then, I regularly contributed thoughts on religious education for the present context of cultural and religious diversity in books and in articles. In the first years, this happened mainly in the context of a religious education research group, the 'Werkgroep godsdienstpedagogiek' at the University of Groningen, in which educationalists, theologians and religious studies researchers co-operated. It came into existence in 1983, following my PhD thesis of that year, in the final chapter of which religious education appeared as one of the examples of an education aiming at reason and reflection, knowledge and critical thinking. In 1986, the research group published a critical study on religious education textbooks in use in Dutch Catholic and Protestant schools (Imelman et al., 1986), which fuelled a lively debate in the Dutch religious education scene. British developments in religious education were an inspiration for our research group. In those years, I started to attend the International Seminar of Religious Education and Values (my first session was Kemptville, Canada 1984). There I met the initiators of the British developments, whose publications our research group was already familiar with, Edwin Cox (1983), Michael Grimmitt (1973), John Hull (1982) and Robert Jackson (1982). They have been a true and lasting inspiration in the development of my thoughts on religious education; the bi-annual ISREV sessions that I attended religiously have also been quite inspirational.

Non-confessional Religious Education

In the initial stages of the development of a new, non-confessional form of religious education, oppositions between, e.g., commitment and neutrality, preaching and teaching, religious nurture and religious education, were used to develop the contours and contents of this new religious education, one not aiming at fostering faith, but at understanding religions (in the plural, indeed). Perhaps there was a parallel between my personal development and this development of a new type of religious education: in order to move from a more or less habitual confessional religious stance to a post- and non-confessional phase, one is looking for the demarcation of a new position, in order to make room for an alternative to come into being and further develop. The conceptual distinctions, the clarification by opposing traditional, confessional ideas on religion and religious upbringing and education, may have served that purpose just right. However, they carry the risk of reinforcing the very dichotomy of reason versus religion that I criticized in Brezinka's conception.

In his introduction to *New Directions in Religious Education*, Hull, overseeing recent British developments, emphasizes the merits of the new approach, but also discerns this imminent danger.

> The best was the ideal of a truly educational enterprise, appropriate to the common schools of a pluralist and freedom-loving democracy in which a wide variety of beliefs and values exist, a religious education which would not seek to mould the mind along sectarian lines or even in conformity with the wishes of a powerful majority, but would be informative and rational, enabling pupils to express and defend their positions, making them 'worth attending to' and thus raising the level of general intelligent participation in matters which are controversial precisely because they are so important. The worst was a religious education which was afraid of controversy, one which sought in fact to avoid the direct teaching of religion, one which was insufficiently vibrant, consisting of inert facts unrelated to pupils' lives, one which became falsely academic instead of truly liberating, and which failed to confront pupils with the rich religious experience of humanity. (Hull, 1982, p. xiii)

Although it was quite understandable that teachers, coming from the 'faith-fostering period' and now facing the job to teach the new religious education, were apprehensive of possible unconscious tendencies to convert pupils and would therefore emphasize factual knowledge and try to present it objectively and impartially, the stakes of the new approach were higher.

So it was right from the start that Hull identified the Achilles heel of the new religious education. I would like to draw attention to the fact that he emphasises educational reasons in his critique of 'arid factuality': 'Pupils are not being stimulated to think' when 'too much religious education teaching remains at the level of information giving' (1982, p. 157). That is remarkable – against the background of the recurring debate on the role of commitment in religious education in Great Britain as much as in other multicultural and multireligious societies of Europe. I myself was involved in this debate in the Netherlands in the 1980s and often experienced discussions having the following course.

Debate on Commitment in Religious Education

Contributing to the debate as a philosopher of education I was identified and just as much identified myself as a non-religious person, interested in religious education in common schools from an educational perspective. The non-confessionalist type of religious education that I advocated in the Dutch context was indeed often criticized for its assumed purely informative, factual, external, arid, superficial character – and for that very reason missing out on the essential, inward, warm, living, real, authentic, etc. etc. true nature of religion, which was then identified with the commitment of religious believers. The immediate effect of this argument is, that non-religious persons are 'excommunicated', shut out from the debate as outsiders. Relevant considerations can only come from the insiders of religion because their religious commitment is made into the prerequisite for understanding what religion is about. In a discussion thus polarised educational considerations and religious or theological considerations as to the subject of religious education have fallen apart.

I have had a few rather odd experiences in this connection. Once, for example, I was invited to give a talk about my educational ideas on religious education (why the aim should be understanding of religions instead of the fostering of religious faith) for members of the board and the parent council of a group of Protestant schools in Groningen. They were very kind, listened with intense interest, then there was a break. I was invited to have a cup of coffee with them, but it was also made clear that I was expected to leave after that. The meeting was to continue with a discussion that I was not supposed to further contribute to. I had been invited to start it up, I had given them something to think about, but now it was up to them to assess and determine for themselves what to think about it and to make up their own minds about their own religious education in their own religious schools. I was literally shut out as an outsider. This happened somewhere in the 1980s.

REREADING AND REFLECTION

Meanwhile, a couple of decades later, in the Netherlands as in many other European countries the new pluralist religious education is well established and its relevance for the pluralist democracies of the present broadly accepted (Jackson, 2010, cf. Meijer, 2011). It fits this present, that the earlier justification of this type of religious education, which was of a logical-analytical nature, has developed into a more historical-hermeneutical style of justification. The latter is less concerned with oppositions and demarcations, and more with meaningful patterns, contexts and historical developments, with all the relativity coming with that.

In Retrospect

In retrospect, I can see how Protestant in nature my explicit farewell to the religion of my forefathers was: it was itself actually a confession, and indeed approximately at the age that my Protestant church considered suitable for individual confession. It was a goodbye then, but now I also see how much I nevertheless inherited from that religious tradition and carried with me up to the present. Certainly, I am not a religious believer and when it comes to logical-analytical arguments in matters of philosophy of religion, I yet embrace agnosticism. With the Dutch literary author Nicolaas Matsier, I can really say that the churchgoer inside has long gone. But of course there is so much more to religion than a church. There is also, in my case, e.g., the protestant work ethic, the love of reading, texts and books, and the taste for liturgical music (though the Renaissance polyphony that I have recently come to enjoy so much is Catholic rather than Protestant in nature). This is why I am curious of the future autobiography of Hirsi Ali, and why I can, at the present point in my life, identify more readily with the mentioned author Matsier, who started to reread the Bible at middle age and recognized his roots in the curiosity for and preoccupation with texts and interpretations, for 'the Protestant is the true Bible reader'. He wrote two books, on his rereading the Old and the New Testament respectively (Matsier, 2003, 2011).

> A Christian youth, with all that goes with it, includes the burden of an inheritance. At first, one isn't very happy with this. But with time, I have come to appreciate it, e.g. simply having an understanding of Christianity. That I don't need explanations when I listen to or look at Christian art when entering a church. That is an advantage of a Christian upbringing. And further, precisely when the churchgoer inside has long gone, one can become very curious to read the Bible once again with one's own eyes. (...) Coming from a Protestant tradition, to me the text comes first. I read and reread the text as closely and curiously as possible. (Matsier, 2011a)

Broadening of Horizons

Education is often a matter of overcoming one's horizons of expectation, in other words, it is about broadening of horizons. This is not a once-and-for-all matter; rather, it continues throughout life. The following example from my own biography may not be as striking as Matsier's return to reading the Bible, but it is at least culturally related to Christianity. From early childhood on Bach's Matthew Passion was familiar to me, as part of my parent's household. The recordings that my father used to listen to, and that he tried to draw our attention to when his enthusiasm brimmed over ('Listen, the boys' choir is coming in!'), were of the romantic large-scale performances in the line of Mendelssohn's rediscovery of Bach – they may have been Eugen Jochum's or Mengelberg's. It constituted my horizon of expectation as to Bach and choirs and the singing of classical music. As a teenager, I turned away from that old-fashioned stuff for old people and I probably needed the new 'authentic' performances in small ensembles of the 1970s to overcome my prejudice. A defamiliarizing of Bach's Matthew Passion was occasioned by these performances that had an 'ear-cleaning effect' (as a Dutch music critic once put it), in order to rediscover its beauty and the truth of that famous tragic story set to music so expressively and affectively. And to discover the joy of singing in choirs, for that matter.

Religion and Diversity

Academically speaking, my position on the topic of religious education has also changed over the years. I started out, some decades ago, with a position that very much opposed reason to religion; in the meantime, I have come to appreciate the diversity, the contextual and historical flexibility, and also the multifaceted character of religions. I am quite convinced today, that logical-analytical analyses of arguments for and against the existence of God, however clever, can hardly count as the essence of religion, on the contrary. People that would call themselves religious are as a rule occupied with quite different matters, and very diverging ones at that. My research on Islamic education, that I started in the 1990s, has been very helpful in gaining insight into the historical and cultural pluriformity of this religion, Islam, and, mutatis mutandis, any other religion. It was the black-and-white Dutch Islam-debate, in which Hirsi Ali played such a prominent and indeed polarising role, that motivated me to enter into these studies and to write the book *Tradition and Future of Islamic Education* (2009). Thirty years ago, I might have sided with Hirsi Ali in a debate on reason and religion, but now I felt the need to fight her position.

Thirty years ago I couldn't have pictured myself arguing that Islamic schools do have a place in the present pluralist Dutch context and that Islamic religious education is appropriate in these schools, albeit alongside pluralist religious education, and both up to educational standards. The same holds, I would say today, for Christian schools and Christian religious education. Unaltered, however, is my educational philosophy that education should initiate into knowledge and understanding, further and stimulate critical thinking and broaden horizons, religious education not excepted. Schools should do what school are good at, as John Goodlad (1979) rightly advocated, and that also extends to the subject of religion. What schools can do well is a different thing as compared to what families and churches or mosques can do well.

First, for today's context, I would advocate that everybody should learn in school about the diversity of religions that exist and are influential in our shared world. A religious education geared towards learning about religions deserves a place in the general education curriculum, possibly integrated into another subject such as, e.g., history. Secondly, a more 'mono-religious' education is in place in religious schools of whatever nomination. It should, however, likewise aim at knowledge and understanding, critical reflection and the broadening of horizons. There is always more to learn about one's own religious tradition, a lot more than what one is already familiar with when one enters school. Only a religious education that aims at enlightening and broadening of the mind deserves a place in schools.

TEACHING, LEARNING AND SOCIALIZATION

In closing, I will present a few comments on the relation between school education on the one hand and the learning and socialization that takes place outside schools on the other.

Wherever generations live together, cultural transmission from one generation to the other takes place. Tradition, from the Latin verb *tradere* or transmission, is the sine qua non of the educational phenomenon. The fact that it is often predominantly an unintentional and unconscious, self-evident process certainly does not make the fact of tradition less real. From birth onwards, children are participating in daily life, in the culture and life style of their parents. Reproducing custom and habit is unmistakably part of growing up. And so is the reproduction of unchallenged beliefs on what is healthy and appropriate, beautiful or ugly, on what constitutes order and chaos, within the home or outside, in life in the private and the public sphere. In the context of a pluralist society, however, the acquired cultural self-evidences will be eroded sooner or later. How should educators handle this?

There are yet advocates of the 'mono-cultural' education that Brezinka advocated a few decennia ago: bringing children up within a single culture and world-view, thereby giving them the opportunity to take root within this one culture. In this case the school, for instance, is considered an extension of the upbringing within the family. School education is then supposed to consolidate the culture and philosophy of life acquired within the home. Those who take inspiration from modern Western educational thought, as I did and still do, will want to conceive the relationship between the family and school in a different way, and do not envisage the task of education as a mere extension of primary cultural transmission.

The hermeneutical dialectic of self-evidence and reflexivity is inspiring at this point. Education should stimulate reflexivity: thinking things through, again and again, from new perspectives, critically rethinking that which was familiar and has been taken for granted. It is the central task of a general or liberal education, i.e. of an education aimed at broadening horizons, to let one learn about new worlds. This does not mean that general, liberal education is dominated by the Enlightenment in the sense of renouncing all (religious) tradition, as Hirsi Ali seemed to assume when she called for a short-cut to Enlightenment for Muslims in the present context. It is possible to criticise the 'mono-cultural' tendency to only see the conservative side to cultural transmission, without falling into the other extreme of identifying critical reflection with liberation by rejection of tradition.

The balance of tradition and enlightenment lies in the idea of *reflexivity*. Education should certainly stimulate critical reflection, but that is not a merely negative matter. It is obviously the task of education to initiate pupils into all sorts of new knowledge and insight which they would not learn at home, and therefore to broaden horizons. Furthermore, it is the task of education to stimulate reflection on one's own familiar tradition, to cultivate a reflexive attitude towards one's own tradition.

REFERENCES

Cox, E. (1983). *Problems and possibilities for religious education*. London: Hodder and Stoughton.
Goodlad, J. I. (1979). *What schools are for*. Bloomington, IN: Phi Delta Kappa.
Grimmitt, M. (1973). *What can I do in RE?* Great Wakering: Mayhew-McCrimmon.
Hirsi Ali, A. (2006). *Mijn vrijheid*. Amsterdam: Augustus (English translation: Infidel, 2007).
Hirsi Ali, A. (2010). *Nomad. From Islam to America*. New York: Free Press.
Hull, J. (ed.). (1982). *New directions in religious education*. Lewes: The Falmer Press.
Imelman, J. D. (1973). *Plaats en inhoud van een personale pedagogiek*. Groningen: Tjeenk Willink.
Imelman, J. D. et al. (1986). *Tussen leuren en leren*. Kampen: Kok.
Jackson, R. (ed.). (1982). *Approaching world religions*. London: John Murray.

Jackson, R. (2010). Religious diversity and education for democratic citizenship. In K. Engebretson et al. (eds.), *International handbook of inter-religious education*. Dordrecht: Springer.

Matsier, N. (2003). *De bijbel volgens*. Amsterdam: De Bezige Bij.

Matsier, N. (2011). *Het Evangelie volgens*. Amsterdam: De Bezige Bij.

Meijer, W. A. J. (1979). De dichotomie van geloof en rede bij Brezinka. *Pedagogisch Tijdschrift, 4*, 413-421.

Meijer, W. A. J. (1983). *Leren in opvoeding en communicatie*. Nijkerk: Intro.

Meijer, W. A. J. (2009). *Tradition and future of Islamic education*. Münster: Waxmann.

Meijer, W. A. J. (2011). *Religious education, citizenship education, liberal education*. In D. De Ruyter & S. Miedema (eds.), *Moral education and development*. Rotterdam: Sense.

Philipse, H. (2004). *Atheïstisch manifest*. Amsterdam: Bert Bakker.

Popper, K. (1945). *The open society and its enemies*. London: Routledge.

AFFILIATIONS

Wilna A.J. Meijer
Philosophy of Education, Faculty of Social and Behavioral Sciences
University of Groningen
The Netherlands

MARY ELIZABETH MOORE

CONVERSATION THAT MATTERS

Life Transforming Dialogue

INTRODUCTION

Conversation is a way of being and engaging in community,
in which all parties pour out their perspectives, knowledge, and passions,
thus allowing a mult-faceted way of being together
and turning thought and action together

Siebren Miedema has joined with others in making conversation a centre for educational research and practice. Genç, ter Avest, Miedema, and Westerman (2012) utilize a research method of 'conversational analysis' in their recent article 'A conversational Analysis of Developments in Religious Education in Europe and Turkey'. They explore education in Europe and Turkey by engaging with one another from the distinct perspectives of their European and Turkish 'tinted lenses'. In this work, conversation is formalized as a self-conscious research method designed to explore complex religious education perspectives and practices. Their approach represents what is important in any conversation, namely that the conversation partners adopt an open, respectful approach to inquiry, recognizing that all partners have observations and insights to share and receive from one another, and that mutual learning requires cognizance and respect for difference.

The invitation to conversation in Siebren Miedema's work resonates with my own pedagogical values, which I will analyze here in an autobiographical way. The title 'Conversation that Matters' summarizes my analysis. I propose that *conversation lies at the heart of religious education and that conversation can be evaluated by its positive influence on educational participants and also on the religious, social, and ecological fabric of the world*. In its roots, conversation can be translated as: 'turning together', 'associating with', 'pondering', or 'turning around'. The Middle English word derives from Latin forms of conversári (to associate with) and conversō (to turn around or ponder). Though common connotations and formal definitions of conversation often refer to oral interchange, the word in its origins refers to multi-sensory, multi-faceted communication that shapes human lives. The prefix 'con' suggests a communal act, and the root 'versāre' or 'versari' suggests turning, pouring, discovering, and being. Even without a full word study, one can appreciate the complex meanings of 'conversation'. The word itself embodies *a way of being and engaging in community, in which all parties pour out their perspectives, knowledge, and*

I. ter Avest (ed.), On the Edge: (Auto)biography and Pedagogical Theories on Religious Education, 115–125.

passions, thus allowing a multi-faceted way of being together and turning thought and action together. I begin by sharing some of my own story and then developing diverse dimensions of conversational pedagogy.

A LIFE SHAPED BY CONVERSATION

I entered this world as an introvert, shaped in early years by robust internal conversations. I can remember sorting out the different messages that I received from my very different parents, both of whom loved me and I them. My father was quiet and serious, always pondering big questions and asking questions about human life that defied popular perspectives. He often saw the good in people who were being maligned. When one of his acquaintances was caught in a lie, my father critiqued the action but tried to understand the feelings of desperation that had led the man into lying. On the other hand, my father sometimes worried about the destructive tendencies of people lauded as heroes, saying of one such lauded man that he wished the man were gentler with his family. My mother, on the other hand, was more conventional in her thinking. She was a gregarious presence in most public places and in parties and family gatherings, though she privately expressed self-doubts about her abilities and questioned others' acceptance of her. These brief portraits are sufficient to reveal that my parents were engaged in their own internal conversations, wrestling with conflicting values and perspectives. The differences between them made me aware of conflicts within myself that I would have to mediate internally as well. Was I to be shy in relationships or step out as a leader? Was I to be like my quiet, serious father or my sociable mother? From my father, I learned to spend time thinking through issues before acting; from my mother, I learned to process questions and conflicting emotions with others. From both, I learned the value of internal conversations and intimate familial conversation; they created a home where we could talk about hopes, doubts, and (most) hard questions.

I also grew up in a world that was alive with social difference. It was a segregated world and, as a white Southern woman, I was especially aware of the sharp social distinctions made between black and white. I have written elsewhere about how my perspectives on justice and peace were shaped by those early experiences of being a privileged white, middle-class woman in the segregated United States South (Moore, 2012). Privilege came to me in educational opportunities, freedom to roam without being attacked for my color with words or fists, and a sense of wide-ranging vocational options.

My world was nearly void of honest, equal, cross-racial conversation under the social structures of segregation. Black and white folk interacted in public places but, under Jim Crow laws, those places were segregated. 'White only' and 'colored only' signs designated different restrooms, water fountains, seats on the bus, and sections in train stations. Southern schools and churches were segregated also, eliminating the possibility of cross-racial conversation about God, faith, life experiences, social values, or even about literature, science, history, and geography. The landscape of learning was divided. As a white child, I had no idea

116

of how insulting the 'colored only' signs were for African Americans, though I knew the 'colored' water fountains and facilities were not maintained as well as those marked 'white'. I criticized the injustice, but did not grasp the full weight of the inequities; I did not hear African Americans describe their experiences of insult and violence until later in my life.

The conversations that did take place were mostly in homes where black domestic workers worked for white families, often with considerable intimacy but without equality. Mary, the African American woman who worked in our home, was one of the most important people in my life, but her life – economically and socially – was more difficult than ours, even though we were not wealthy ourselves. The other conversations that took place in those days were political debates where people spoke in generalities and perpetuated prejudices. The lack of honest, communal conversation re-inscribed inequality. The lack of multi-faceted conversation in diverse venues for diverse purposes and in diverse forms meant that people could not share their faith or teach and learn together or engage as equal citizens in a shared society. The lack of conversation worked against human understanding. People could know people of other races in abstract and limited ways, but they could not know them as complex, beautiful human beings worthy of deep respect. My relationship with Mary counteracted these experiences in some ways, opening me to respect and love through the conversations she and I had every day. Only later did I realize that those conversations were limited by our disparate, unequal circumstances. I needed more conversations in more equitable venues to learn that lesson.

Readers will note that my description of race and ethnicity has thus far been in the language of black and white, which was my dominant early experience. In my first twenty years, cultural difference was conceptualized in highly generalized, sometimes oppositional, terms, with the focus on two stereotyped human communities, black and white. This conceptualization persisted until, as a young adult, I lived on the Texas border with Mexico and later in California with its multi-ethnic and multi-cultural diversity. I began to learn in a more grounded way that the world is populated by far more than two 'races' of people and that ethnic, cultural, and other forms of diversity are marked by multiplicity and never by *two* groups simplistically understood (Moore, 2010). I learned this when I encountered the complex cultures and peoples of Mexico; I learned it when I engaged in deep conversations with people whose origins were in Korea, Japan, China, the Philippines, Native America and the Pacific Islands. These experiences led me to philosophical and theological critiques of dualistic thinking in educational theories and conversations. Every religious or social issue involves more than two groups and has more than two sides. Thus, religious education through conversation needs to open people to multiplicity and not lock them into a debate style with two sides of every 'argument'. Multiplicity involves many groups with diverse, sometimes competing, perspectives, values, and patterns of action.

This discussion leads to another aspect of conversation that is embedded in my life, namely my encounters with religious difference. When I was a child, the religious differences that I knew were largely Christian. The world of southern

Louisiana was mostly Christian, with about half Roman Catholic and half Protestant, though half of the Protestants were Southern Baptist. These Christian communities were robust and were deeply engaged in conversations with one another, but the conversations were often grounded in stereotypes. For example, I assumed that my Roman Catholic friends had an easy way to deal with guilt because they could go to confession every Saturday and begin the new week with a clean slate. The Roman Catholics and Protestants related very well in social interchange, and they shared in high religious moments, such as baptisms, weddings, and funerals; however, they held their differences tightly. My mother worried that I would marry a Roman Catholic man and would then rear my children as Roman Catholic because of the strictly held practices in the Catholic Church at that time. I knew that, if I ever left the Protestant Church, my mother would be distraught, though she could accept my selecting another church in the Protestant range. On the other hand, my uncle thought that the Baptist Church was the only 'true church', and he once publicly accused my mother of leaving the Baptist 'truth' when she married my father and became a Methodist.

These formal, somewhat distant, and occasionally accusatory relationships among religious communities in my youth were modulated by moments of great intimacy. When I spent the night with my Roman Catholic friends, we prayed the rosary before going to bed. When I went to church with my Southern Baptist friends on Sunday evenings, we did Bible games that characterized their tradition. When I went to church with my Presbyterian friend, we passed the bread and grape juice down the pews instead of going to the altar. The differences between Presbyterians and Methodists seemed particularly odd to me. I was able to receive the bread and grape juice, but my friend was not. I had been baptized as an infant and she was not baptized until she was twelve. These religious differences were part of our normal world, and they revealed the strong presence of religion in the culture and in individual and communal lives. They also revealed the intensity of religious value for people. People cared about their religious identities, and they shared them generously, inviting others to join in their religious rituals and symbols; however, they did not explore the complexities in depth with one another. The situation might have been somewhat like pillarization in the Netherlands; we lived together but also apart. People in our community shared practices and important existential moments, but continued to understand other traditions in over-generalized ways.

These life stories reveal the bounties and complexities of conversation. Conversation is personal, communal, and marked by hospitality and eagerness to understand one another. On the other hand, it can be unconsciously limiting, oddly between generalities and intimacy. In my childhood, the religious issues were not as visible as the racial ones, but the patterns were somewhat similar. Religious conversation opened the door for deep sharing of perspectives and practices, and even deeper sharing of existential realities. When people in my childhood experienced traumatic deaths or moments of great joy, they expected and hoped that religious rituals and symbols would imbue the moments with meaning and connect people with what was important in their lives. One group might be curious, and sometimes judgmental, about what another group believed or practiced, but they generally appreciated and respected their religious lives and meanings. People would be moved by a friend's wedding or funeral, even if they did not fully understand the ritual. At the same time, they did not always want their own families to become entangled in another tradition, and they sometimes reflected on other traditions in distant, stereotypical ways, as my mother expressed in her urging that I not marry a Catholic. Even so, the depth of sharing and respect were the overriding message for me as a child, and I still delight in the rituals and practices of other traditions.

This pattern of intimacy and distance was even evident in my experience of traditions other than Christianity. We rarely studied other religions in school because of the strict separation of religion and state, a separation that thwarted even the study of diverse religious traditions. I had to wait until college to explore the vast interreligious world that opened to me in classes and human relationships there. Even in my childhood, however, we studied other religions somewhat in my Methodist church, and we continually discussed whether Christianity was the only way. People had differing opinions on this subject, but I never believed that Christianity could possibly be the only way. In my own Protestant congregation, I was continually faced with awe-inspiring diversity, and diversity seemed to me to be one of God's gifts. I remember my curiosity and enjoyment of the vastly different people in our congregation, where one Sunday School teacher described his frequent conversations with God, another described his desire not to be 'too religious', and another explained why his faith required him to work with the poor. I saw from my early years that people in one faith tradition could be quite diverse, but still live together in one faith family.

I share this complicated story because my experience of diversity within Christianity, curiosity about other traditions, and reflections on Christianity and other faiths prepared me for deeper interfaith relationships later in life. I believe the robust conversations *within and across* the Christian traditions of my youth prepared me to accept religious difference *beyond* Christianity. Only in retrospect do I realize how much the experience of intra-Christian conversation prepared me for the interfaith conversations that were to come. As a child, I could not conceive of a world in which some would be saved and some would not. I could not conceive that a God of Love could possibly save some and not others. Differences seemed more interesting than divisive; they intensified and deepened a continuing conversation.

Such a view was reinforced in me by two life experiences, one as a youth and one as a young adult. The first was getting to know a Jewish neighbor, who was deeply respected in our community. I interviewed this amazing woman for a school project, asking her about her life experiences and sources of strength. She spoke at length about her Jewish faith. I then asked her why she had agreed to serve as President of the Young Women's Christian Association in our city. She gave a simple reply: "This is a wonderful organization that brings people together to contribute to the community; I share the YWCA's deepest values". She was able to see that a person or community can align with a group other than 'her own' for the

119

sake of shared values and common action. I have not forgotten that lesson, and I still believe that people yearn for solidarity in community values and actions. People yearn for conversations that matter for themselves and their world. Even today, I seek to stir intra-faith and interfaith conversations that help people identify and join in common values, marked most recently in my work on an interfaith conference in interfaith peacebuilding. I also seek to stir conversations that engage people in points of difference and difficulty, as on sexual orientation or race, so people can discover one another with respect and engage the complexities of others' perspectives.

The second interreligious experience of import to me was my friendship during graduate school with Tom and Lois, a Jewish couple who lived in the same apartment building with my husband and me. We usually shared two meals a week, celebrating Shabbat in their apartment and sharing a Saturday night meal in ours. We engaged in robust conversation, often talking faith, confessing our most embarrassing actions and attitudes, expressing our deepest worries, and laughing loudly about the oddities of life. We grew so close that we grieved when the time came for Tom and Lois to graduate and move into the next era of their lives while we stayed behind to complete our degree programs. I have reflected extensively on this friendship because both families have invested heavily in interreligious relationships since that time, nourished as we were by a friendship that was permeated with faith practice and faith talk.

I suggest that the multi-faceted conversations that we shared around our dinner tables – marked implicitly by the holiness of meals in both our traditions – transformed us into people of shared faiths. Our multi-layered conversations made each of us more deeply committed to our own faith traditions and influenced by the other. We even acknowledged that my husband and I could claim to be Jewish-shaped Christians without expecting the parallel for our Jewish friends, who already lived in a culture so permeated by Christianity that they needed to be self-conscious in preserving their uniquely Jewish identity. Our lives were marked by an enduring friendship that has public and religious significance, as one might find in Hannah Arendt (1968, p. 141; cf. 1996), who was concerned with "the elementary problems of human living-together", or Elisabeth Moltmann-Wendel, who was concerned with the oft-neglected influence of human friendships (2001). Our conversations led us to build interreligious conversations and actions throughout our lives, and to do so with alertness to the complexities in individual lives and social structures. They also awakened us to structural complexities in our respective religions. My friends had to worry about the dominance of public Christmas practices when their children were young, as when their oldest child looked longingly at the festivities and gifts that permeated Christmas for his Christian school friends. At the same time, our *interreligious* spirits were nurtured by our shared lives, and we have continued to engage in conversation, including hard talk about hurtful topics, as we have entered diverse life roles. Our shared experiences, and the consequences of those experiences, have called my attention to the power of conversation as a central goal in religious study and religious education.

120

RELIGIOUS EDUCATION SHAPED BY CONVERSATION

These autobiographical ruminations point the way to religious education by conversation. To center on conversation is to take seriously the dynamic, interactive, difference-engaging, and open-ended quality of religious education. The complex character of such education opens people to a future that is not yet fully formed, while teachers and learners persistently seek a *telos* of common good. To cultivate conversation that matters, I propose six significant practices. Others could be added.

Internal Conversation

Internal conversation is self-reflection that allows a person to engage the multiple 'voices' within the self. As already suggested in my biographical ruminations, internal conversation transforms human lives. Recent research on this topic is based on longitudinal studies with adults, and it reveals the power of 'internal voices' and internal conversation for adult development, and the value of conversation partners in cultivating the internal voice (Magolda, 2009, pp. xii, 6-12). Siebren Miedema similarly recognizes the importance of 'self-edification' as people respond to the 'burden of uncertainty' in a religiously plural world (Miedema, 2009, p. 195). The practice of self-edification requires what he describes as personal and collective experiences. I suggest that such experiences are important, in part, because they stir internal conversation.

Internal conversation requires people to be present to themselves. In my autobiographical excursus, I discovered that much of my own learning about otherness arose from my encounter with others and the internal conversations that such encounters inspired. This reinforces bell hooks' link between knowing self and others through a holistic, engaged pedagogy (hooks, 1994, pp. 13-22). Such a view encourages people to see themselves in relation to a complex whole, thus to foster the wellbeing of the self *and* the whole.

Internal conversation requires teachers and learners to be at least partially vulnerable and present to themselves and one another in the learning community. Specific to religion, it encourages students to engage in religious identity formation from an interfaith perspective (Miedema, 2009). Internal conversation is intensified as people encounter the diversity of the world, and it is critical for making sense of that world. Oddly, this kind of conversation is easy to neglect in formal education, often dismissed as lacking rigor. In actuality, it is frighteningly rigorous, inviting people to probe intensely into the depths of what they believe, value, understand to be fact, and practice. It is life-transforming.

Boundary-Crossing

Another dimension of conversation that emerges from my autobiographical reflections is boundary-crossing. Encountering difference is a stimulus for learning. Even within one tradition, people cross boundaries of geography and time to

121

comprehend the fullness of the tradition, and these boundaries can be challenging to negotiate, especially when people assume sameness and are not prepared for the radical differences they encounter in the perspectives and practices of others in their tradition. This challenge escalates when people cross religious and ethnic-cultural boundaries.

A book honoring Siebren Miedema will surely feature boundary-crossing because he has featured such crossing in his own life work. Not only has he participated in academic guilds across the world, but he has participated in a major study of religion and education in Europe (Jackson, Miedema, Weisse, & Willaime, 2007), and has been Visiting Professor in the Faculty of Sociology of Saint Petersburg State University, Russia. The European study particularly exemplifies Miedema's agility in crossing boundaries, surveying the landscape of religion and education in eight European countries, attending to the complex historical and socio-political phenomena, while analyzing the multicultural, pedagogical, and globalizing shifts of the last decade. Such research documents boundary-crossings on a shared continent, while also enhancing it. It provides empirical data and conceptual tools for religious citizenship education, suggesting future approaches to pedagogy that can enrich religious and interreligious learning while contributing to a more just and peaceful society.

Two primary features of boundary-crossing emerge from my autobiography in dialogue with religious education research. Boundary-crossing at its best fosters equity among the partners in dialogue and is multi-faceted. Exchanging intellectual ideas is not sufficient. Learning across boundaries, if it is to be meaningful and life-enhancing for the people involved, needs to provide opportunities for people to share hopes, beliefs, values, and practices. My own childhood opened me to diversity in a society of active religious sharing, even while it limited my purview. The early experiences of difference helped me to develop a habitus of engaging difference with curiosity and respect. A similar approach to curiosity and respect is engendered in Miedema's work, characterized by the study of boundary-crossings on the European continent, between countries, and within schools. The challenge remaining, however, is to identify how such boundary-crossing can be grounded in and conducive to equity in human relationships and depth in the sharing of life in its complex beauty. Not all religious education can be grounded in equity and multi-faceted sharing, but some education needs to approach these high standards if it is to contribute to a more humane world.

Relationship-Building

This discussion leads naturally to another critical quality of educational conversations – the building of relationships. As I reviewed my life journey, I became aware of intimate relationships that shaped my orientation with others, whether sharing life concerns with people of another ethnicity or sitting at the Shabbat table with my Jewish friends. Friendship is often understood as a co-curricular additive to education. I propose that relationship building and conversation around shared interests should be an intentional part of education, as it has been in philosophical and theological inquiry (Arendt, 1968, 1996; Moltmann-Wendel, 2001). For many people, this aspect of education does not emerge easily, and for some it does not arise at all. Many adults do not feel safe to speak honestly, and young people often experience even more fear as they negotiate their formative years and face the possibility of being teased or bullied. Bullying, whether subtle or egregious, denies people the opportunity for authentic relationships that nourish their well-being. On the other hand, respectful conversation can foster empathy among people who are quite different from one another. Such conversation can cultivate the ground for far-reaching social harmony that is grounded in honesty and justice.

Question-Posing

This discussion leads naturally to another form of conversation, question-posing, by which people discover, identify, and probe existential, social, and religious questions of import. Questions arise from encounters with life situations and encounters with peoples and cultures that are different from what one knows. These encounters are often the places where questions emerge and where conversation is vital. Building on the work of John Hull, Siebren Miedema and his colleagues have identified encounter as a vital theme in religious education, especially in relation to religious and cultural diversity (Miedema, Bakker, Heimbrock, & Jackson, 2009). Similarly, Paulo Freire identifies dialogical problem-posing as the central method of education because it engages people in heightened consciousness and cultural interventions (Freire, 1994, p. 62). Problem-posing education sharpens people's ability to perceive the world critically and to view reality as a process to which they can contribute (ibid., p. 64). Such education resonates with the critical-pragmatic perspective that marks much of Miedema's work – a perspective that invites questions as people engage critically with the lived world. I use the term 'question-posing' here to include the problem-posing of Freire and the critical pragmatic approach of Miedema, but also to include questions of wonder, interpretation, or theoretical construction that may or may not be problem-related. In all of its forms, question-posing is an essential form of religious education conversation.

Meaning-Making

When people gather at high and low moments of their lives, and when they share their existential questions and hopes, they probe existential meaning. Sometimes they set out on a quest to discover meaning, and sometimes life's questions confront them unexpectedly. In either case, the challenge of meaning-making is another conversational challenge: to create conversations in which people integrate internal conversation, boundary-crossing, relationship-building, and question-posing in such a way that the parts make a whole.

Meaning-making is critical to all of religious education, but at no time more important than when people are forging, critiquing, or re-forging their religious identities. Consider, for example, the intensive meaning-making time of young adulthood and the important role of mentoring in that process (Nash & Murray, 2010, esp. pp. 87-160). Mentoring is a form of conversation in which one person or community has special roles in listening to and guiding another person or community. Such presence with one another has a shaping influence on meaning-making and development. Nelle Morton, writing in the second wave of the feminist movement in the United States, spoke to a passionate time when she and other women were seeking to be heard. She made a case for the urgency of "hearing others into speech", a pathway to human liberation and growth (Morton, 1985). Such listening is also important in the preparation of people for leadership and vocations (Parks, 2005, esp. pp. 73-120). All of these forms of teaching and mentoring represent meaning-making conversation.

Justice- and Peace-Building

I conclude with one further act of religious education conversation; this is conversation bent toward justice and peace. These goals have already been referenced, particularly in the problem-posing work of Paulo Freire and the holistic, engaged pedagogy of bell hooks. Miedema also shares this passion. He has emphasized the importance of *religious citizenship education*, recognizing the value of his critical approach to contribute to a world made whole. Even the language for such goals varies from religion to religion and community to community; however, most religions of the world have some vision of the common good: tikkun olam, or repairing the world, in the Jewish community; justice and peace in many Christian, theistic, and secular communities; and compassion in Buddhist communities.

I am oversimplifying the goals in my attempt to underscore this final form of educational conversation. What is important to communicate is that critique and critical pedagogy are critical moments in larger educational conversations. The movement toward action is an important outcome of critique, and the action is itself part of conversation. When people work side by side in service or advocacy, they participate in a living conversation. The actions of Civil Rights activists were essential outcomes of the tough conversations of the 1960s in the United States, and those actions were themselves *part of* the conversations. People's lives were changed by marching side by side for justice, as my life has been changed in advocating for Jews or Muslims in Christian majorities, for people of color in white majorities, or for people isolated from the church or culture because of sexual orientation. My own activism for justice has been an outcome of my lifelong conversations about race, class, gender, sexuality, and religious diversity; however, that activist activity has continually transformed me, awakening me to hidden prejudices in my own soul or hidden discrimination in our society.

In conclusion, conversations that matter must be multifaceted, and conversations need to take multiple forms. The quality of those conversations is also critical. As my decades of conversations with close Jewish friends have taught me, deep conversations include empathetic embrace, wrestling with hard questions, social critique, and common work for justice and peace. No element of the conversations can be lost if conversations are to be transformative and to make contributions to human flourishing.

In this chapter I took the opportunity to reflect on the contributions of Siebren Miedema and to reflect autobiographically on pedagogy. Siebren has been generative for me and for religious education worldwide as he combines analytic, empirical, and constructive approaches. He has stirred communication across disciplines, continents, and areas of inquiry. The autobiographical dimension of this publication enabled me to highlight the conversational dimension of pedagogy – an accent that emerges from my life history and is critical for communities and societies that I know best, including my personal communities and those I have studied. Conversation is also an accent in Siebren's work, and hopefully will be in his future work, as in the practices of many educators worldwide.

REFERENCES

Arendt, H. (1968). *Between Past and Future*. New York: Viking, 1968.

Arendt, H., McCarthy, M., & Brightman, C. (1996). *Between friends: The correspondence of Hannah Arendt and Mary McCarthy, 1949-1975*. Eugene, OR: Harvest Books.

Freire, P. (1974/1994). *Pedagogy of the oppressed*. New York: Continuum.

Genç, F., ter Avest, I., Miedema, S., & Westerman, W. (2012). A conversational analysis of developments in Religious Education in Europe and Turkey. *British Journal of Religious Education*, *34*(2), 1-17.

bell hooks (1994). *Teaching to transgress: Education as the practice of freedom*. New York: Routledge.

Jackson, R., Miedema, S., Weisse, W., & Willaime, J.-P. (eds.). (2007). *Religion and education in Europe: Developments, contexts and debates*. Munster: Waxmann Verlag.

Magolda, M. B. (2009). *Authoring your life: Developing an internal voice to meet life's challenges*. Sterling, VA: Stylus.

Miedema, S., Bakker, C., Heimbrock, H.-G. & Jackson, R. (eds.). (2009). *Religious education as encounter: A tribute to John M. Hull*. Münster: Waxmann Verlag.

Miedema, S. (2009). Religious education between certainty and uncertainty: Toward a pedagogy of diversity. In W. A. J. Meijer, S. Miedema, & A. L. van der Velde (eds.), *Religious education in a world of religious diversity* (pp. 195-206). Münster: Waxmann Verlag.

Moltmann-Wendel, E. (2001). *Rediscovering friendship: Awakening to the power and promise of women's friendships*. Minneapolis: Fortress.

Moore, M. E. (2010). Education for peace: Exploring the margins of human rights and religion. In K. Engebretson, M. de Souza, G. Durka, & L. Gearon (eds.), *International handbook of inter-religious education* (pp. 1087-1104). The Netherlands: Springer Academic Publishers.

Moore, M. E. (2012). Let freedom ring: Let peace reign! *Religious Education, 107*(3), 236-240.

Morton, N. (1985). *The journey is home*. Boston: Beacon.

Nash, R. J., & Murray, M. C. (2010). *Helping college students find purpose: The campus guide to meaning-making*. San Francisco: Jossey-Bass.

Parks, S. D. (2005). *Leadership can be taught*. Boston: Harvard Business School.

AFFILIATIONS

Mary Elizabeth Moore
Dean and Professor of Theology and Education
Boston University School of Theology, Boston, USA

BRAM DE MUYNCK

JONAH WAS MY RELIGIOUS TEACHER

*The Paradoxical Character of the Gospel Challenges a Transformative and
Transmission Pedagogical Approach to Go Hand in Hand*

INTRODUCTION

*I was participating in a religious practice,
not only in a passive way,
but active restructuring my mental images of God,
of Jonah and of people in the church.*

As a young boy of about 9 years old I used to accompany my mother in weekly
Wednesday-evening services in our church. In summertime, the pastor of a
neighbouring congregation, preached every week about the prophet Jonah. I
remember the devoted atmosphere in the church building that summer. Imagine a
church building in a small village, the doors being opened because of the quiet
warm summer temperature. I remember myself looking to my mother supposing
she was eager to hear the message and then looking to the preacher's warm and
inviting exposition about Jonah in the fish. It impressed me that reluctant Jonah
was saved by staying in the fish, although this was a terrible place to be. He prayed
to God and the fish deposited him on the shore. It puzzled me what was happening
in the story. Not because I wondered about the physical impossibilities of living in
the belly of a fish, but because of the paradox in the story. Jonah was reluctant to
fulfil his task and fled from the presence of the Lord, and nevertheless he was
saved in a miraculous way. I remember the joy I felt that God saved Jonah but also
feeling awe and wonder about the way God was at work in this story: suffering
caused by own fault, can be followed by deliverance, even after three days and
three nights being in a place of death. During his stay in the belly he was able to
pray to and trust in God. Interpreting 40 years later, the story of Jonah seems to
have triggered basic senses about the paradoxical character of the gospel and
appears to have evoked a spiritual sensitivity.

The congregation in which I grew up belonged to an orthodox reformed
denomination, one of the many Dutch churches rooted in the non-conformist,
pietistic movement in the 19th century. I attended a church school of the same
congregation and in that place many other events triggered my spiritual sensitivity.
The educational tradition in those circles are generally seen as having a strong
socialising and even indoctrinating climate in which critical dispositions might be
suppressed. That elicits the question whether an open formation process in an

*I. ter Avest (ed.), On the Edge: (Auto)biography and Pedagogical Theories on Religious
Education, 127–136.*

orthodox educational climate is possible or not. In one of his volumes with studies about religion and education Siebren Miedema suggests that an educational tradition of transmission can be opposed to a tradition of transformation. Each tradition represents a certain consistent and uniforming but fundamentally different way of thinking, feeling and acting' (Miedema, 2002, pp. 74-75). When *transmission* is adhered to, an objective world of meaning is presupposed. In the classroom the acquisition of cognitions and skills are emphasised, while values and norms are supposed not to belong to the curriculum. Repetition, imitation and reproductions are main characteristics of the teaching method. Successful reproduction of well-defined knowledge and skills is a criterion of evaluation. In a *transformative* tradition meaning giving of reality is a matter of individual construction in collective settings. Learning content is not the purpose but the start of learning. The teacher is seen as a partner in a participative process. Criterion of success is whether the individual is able to make individual choices and can create his individual worldview. Everyone knowing Siebren Miedema recognises his preference for the second position. His view on education is in line with what he learned from great educators like Kohnstamm (Miedema, 2005) and probably most of all Dewey (Biesta, Miedema, & Berding, 1997).

In this contribution I would like to discuss whether an orthodox theological view will definitely determine educational practices in church and school as adhering to a transmission-approach. Or is it possible, or even desirable to practice a transformative tradition in orthodox Christian schools? By using the adjective 'orthodox' in this context I simply refer to the Christian movement in churches that cherish purity of basic assumptions about the truth in Christianity, usually opposed to more open and fluid positions in which credo or dogmatic assumptions are not seen as basic characteristics of the church (De Muynck, 2008, pp. 90-92). 'Orthodox' is neither the same as conservatism intending to preserve conventions nor it is an equivalent to 'fundamentalist', which is connected to a critical attitude towards modernization society, to militant activism and to equating messages from the Scriptures with traceable and historical events. In this article I will summarize the sound orthodox voice of the Dutch theologian Bram van de Beek, who I perceive to be one of the most erudite and original reformed scholars of the last decade, because he is able to make firm and consistent statements, that are broadly and deeply founded in dogmatics and church history and about which he doesn't hesitate to oppose to mainstream life philosophy in society. I have followed his thinking since I was a university student. In the eighties I was impressed by his theological insights about suffering. On the one hand in his writings my childish fear of God was echoed and on the other hand it changed my image of God. We cannot reason about causes of suffering related to God in human terms. God is totally unlike mankind and yet is ready to come very close to mankind. While his thinking has influenced my theological thinking, I have until now not drawn consequences for education.

Before starting my quest into the relation of an orthodox theological position to the formation process of young people I would like to make one remark about orthodox schools. In the Netherlands these schools are well located in reformed communities (De Muynck, 2008, pp. 88-123; De Wolff, De Ruyter, & Miedema, 2002) where there is a strong relationship between family, church and school. This relationship is not always institutional, but mostly students, staff and board belong to the mental orthodox population. De Ruyter and Miedema (1997, p. 120) call those schools 'pillar-schools' referring to the strong relationship of the schools with the confessional structures in society (in the Netherlands mentioned as 'pillars'). In Catholic communities we may find orthodox schools as well, but generally they are not organised separately. Sometimes they are called 'monologue-schools'.

I will start with a brief exposition about what can be seen as an orthodox view of Christian faith and what this probably might mean for religious education. Next I will sketch what can be seen as decisive for a formation or transformative process in education. In the discussion I will consider the two positions and consider on which issues they concord or conflict. In the concluding paragraph I will try to summarize the answer to the problem, raised in this article.

AN ORTHODOX THEOLOGICAL POSITION

Van de Beeks thinking is mainly based on core texts in the Bible about the character of Jesus and on theologians in the first centuries like Irenaeus, Justin Martyr, Ignatius, Origen, Tertullian, Clement of Alexandria and Augustine. The basis of Christian thinking is the confession that Jesus is Lord (*Kyrios*) (Van de Beek, 1998). Since the apostles, people have been attracted by the message about the strange and unbelievable news that God presented himself in an earthly human being. The message contends that God made himself similar to mankind, including sin. God presents Himself not as glorious and powerful, but as a weak, disdainful being who humiliated Himself on the cross. Having died on the cross means that God himself has bared the curse that rested on mankind. The cross however is the most grating element in Christian thinking, because people generally prefer to identify themselves with mighty and influential powers and not by vulnerability. Nevertheless or therefore the idea of this *Kyrios* is the most crucial element which people experience as setting them free from anger and evil powers. Faith gives them a new identity and means being united in a new eternal life that already has begun. The core business of the church and church members is celebrating this new life in the Eucharist and proclaim this new reality to others. The new identity puts the believers in a new reality, and at the same time makes them foreigners in this earthly world. By the coming of Christ the old world is judged and condemned (Van de Beek, 2008, pp. 109-129). Believers live in an eschatological reality of deliverance in unity with Jesus Christ, but on the other hand they fight an unavoidable struggle during their life-time that cannot be solved (Van de Beek, 2012, pp. 413-415). Nothing is to be expected from this earthly world anymore, and therefore believers are longing for the heavenly world. Christian theology should not aim for Kingdom-aspirations in this immanent world, because this means a denying of the fact that the world is already condemned and a new Creation is realized in Christ. The Church-community is not meant to be a forerunner or a facilitator of the Kingdom of God to come, but is the Kingdom itself. Christian theologians should be critical about theology that promotes an active and prophetic role for the church, because activities suggests that peace and justice can be acquired, which in history has proved not to be a valid position and this never will be (Van de Beek, 2012, pp. 100-145). This radical position is in contrast with mainstream evangelical thinking and with 20th and 21st century critical or liberal theological thinking. Both are expecting that theology and Christian religion might have an impact on society.

What does this position mean for Religious Education? Because Van de Beek has hardly written about this issue, I have to argue from his work and I will try to retrieve conclusions myself. What follows are a few educational ideals that refer to desirable educational situations. The first is that RE must be equated to church education. Since (infant) baptism signifies that God starts His work in His chosen people, the church has to teach its members to know deeply and broadly what their position is in the world. Church members have a new identity and are alienates in this word. RE aims to socialize young Christians in a strong image of the Church being a community of foreigners. To educate in Christian religion means evoking a specific self-image, which is not a matter of 'feel good' or of 'self-confirmation' that is strongly being promoted in the Western world, even in the church (Van de Beek, 2012, p. 36). The ideal of self-realisation will in the extreme lead to power and abuse of influence, either by individuals or by groups, because there is no transcendent criterion by which one can be restricted (Van de Beek, 2012, pp. 144-145). Identity formation is not promoting personal flourishing or personal wellbeing but developing a self-image of being 'the possession of another' (Van de Beek, 2012, p. 20). The second consequence is that RE intends for young people to see themselves as belonging to a world-wide community. Being a Christian is not narrow-mindedness in the sense of defending group-interests. According to Galatians 3:28, in Christ there are no borders between race, socio-economic status and gender. The self-image of a Christian is intercultural and oecumenical (Van de Beek, 2012, pp. 70-92). Seeing the Credo as basis of every expression of the Christian church, one cannot hold its own denomination – be it Catholic, Protestant, Charismatic – as the true or the pure one. Although Church-unity is not a visible reality, it is an unavoidable demand for the Church. The next generation should be taught that there is no Church without unity in credo (Van de Beek, 2012, pp. 184-194). The third consequence is about citizenship. Believers, having a new identity in Christ, will consequently experience themselves not at ease in this world. In terms of citizenship RE intends for a two-sided position. On the one hand children will be taught to be critical members of society. They feel the serious problems of this world, are worried about, and should not hesitate to appoint abuse and sin. They might not accept certain norms and values of this world, especially when they could elicit violence (Van de Beek, 2012, p. 472). Criticism however intends not to blame, because one knows of one's own sin. Neither does it intend to transform society, because Christians are mere strangers in this world. On the other hand they will practice ultimate solidarity and charity with this world (Van de Beek, 2012, pp. 26, 124, 132-135). They distinguish themselves by showing unconditional love to each other and to non-believers (Van de Beek, 2012, pp. 244-145). They express themselves not by taking a polemic position, but by mere living in the position they have. The fourth consequence is that thorough knowledge of the Bible and the credo must be instructed. When a church neglects to instruct the transmission of confessional core issues, this institution is to blame because it doesn't take its core message serious (Van de Beek, 2012, p. 345).

Observing these four characteristics it is fully clear that the school, carrying out this education, must be placed in a tradition of transmission. This type of education can be experienced as outdated, because positions that claim and promote absolute truth are not very popular in Western culture. Taylor, conceptualising secularisation, holds that a core characteristic of modern society is that faith has become a choice. This era is the period of authenticity, he says, in which the basic social imaginaries prescribe life to be a matter of choice (Taylor, 2007, pp. 3, 473). Consequently, teachers in a post-enlightenment era should be reserved in presenting religious ideas in the classroom (Van Crombrugge, 2008, p. 44). Raising children in families might be acceptable but Wardekker for example puts quite clear: 'the aim of religious education *at school* cannot be that students are made members of a specific religious community' (Wardekker, 2002, p. 208 – italics in original). If students participate in religious practices, it is a demand to exercise distance and critical reflection on that experience (Wardekker, 2002, p. 209).

THE FORMATION PROCES

How children and teenagers grew up in orthodox communities can be described like they would develop in any other community, at least when it is seen from a helicopter view. To explain in what happens in the development of children I like the conceptualisation of the word 'Formation' or in German *Bildung* (De Muynck & Vos, 2006). The word is not necessarily and strictly connected to the enlightenment-philosophy in which the formation-process is viewed as self-cultivation, as a 'higher-order' activity of the mind and mainly a matter of breathing in cultural expressions of the true, the beauty and the good. Yet it can be used in a broader sense of describing what is happening when we see young people develop to maturity.

Firstly the formation process can be seen as a two sided process in which the subject is being influenced and at the same time selects what is valuable for his individual development. Independent of the religious, cultural or socio-economic background, one can always observe that process. Secondly the factors and actors that are influencing the subject create a complicated and difficult to disentangle cluster of events, that post facto can be told in the narrative by the subject himself. An educator in the 21st century is aware that he is mere one of the influencing actors, next to parents, the peer-group and not forgetting the social media. In this process the individual person has a key role in how the cultural heritage is becoming part of his identity. The interwoven process of reciprocal influencing of individual and context can also be connected to the pragmatic thinking of John Dewey that was highly respected by Siebren Miedema. Though he concluded at the end of his dissertation that Dewey 'has got unsuitable little attention in the Dutch educational sciences' (Miedema, 1986, p. 242; e.g. Biesta, Miedema & Berding, 1997, p. 345), the scholar maintained to play a role in his work. Therefore – considering the character of this volume – it seems fitting to recap briefly what the formation process means in terms of a Deweyan perspective. In doing so, I mainly will refer to Biesta, Miedema, and Berding (1997). Later on I will use the characteristics to reflect about the possibility to educate from an orthodox theological view.

In the pragmatic view on education individual and social aspects go hand in hand. The formation process is not a matter of an individual psychological process that might be suggested by the *Bildung*-theory summarized above. Education is not child centred, nor is it curriculum centred. The connection between cultural environment or the curriculum and the individual is made by experiences. Education is viewed as a continuous process of reconstructing experiences. An experience is not just a mental rendering of what is seen, heard or felt, but an interaction with the environment in which the whole person with mind, heart and senses is involved. By participating in social practices the person can form so called 'habits', patterns that equip a person to act and improve has actions in communication with the environment. Incidentally, experience is closely connected to action and to communication. The child will form meaning while he is acting and communicating. The point of impact of the educator is 'which things, persons or events, draw his [the child's] attention or have meaning and value' (Biesta, Miedema, & Berding, 1997, p. 326). The focus of education is future directed: knowledge is only valuable as far as the child can use it for actions to come. Because education is an interactive process, Dewey prefers to speak about 'growth' instead of 'development'. Growth is defined as 'a cumulative movement of action toward a later result' (Dewey quoted in Biesta, Miedema, & Berding, 1997, p. 330). Therefore one cannot conclude about the moment where growth stops. Because experiencing and acting remain a continuing interactive process, education just enables persons to continue their education. To make sure that learning is not a matter of trial and error a person has to learn how to act in a reflective way. Thinking is essential to reorganise experiences in order to act as intelligent as possible. Reflection will be triggered once there are many opinions and problems. A rich environment of stimuli will evoke the wish to inquire the background of events.

DISCUSSION

In this section I will discuss whether transformative education from an orthodox theological perspective is possible or not. At a first glance theology and education seem to represent totally different domains. Miedema's assumption that a transmission approach does not concord with a transformation approach seems to be correct. How one could accomplish the first two orthodox ideals that I have identified above (learning to view oneself as having a new identity and as belonging to a worldwide community) cannot be explained by formation-theory.

Yet when considering the two positions more carefully there is more to say. Let me first remind you of my Jonah-experience. My presence in the church can be seen as an experience in the sense of Deweys conception. I was participating in a religious practice, not only in a passive way, but active restructuring my mental images of God, of Jonah and of people in the church. In a descriptive way – given in the beginning of the previous section - all children are supposed to have this kind of experiences, whether they are positively or negatively evaluated later on. So also when individuality or self-actualisation is not used as the core value in education, and when from an orthodox perspective a Christian is exchanging his own natural identity with the Identity of Christ, psychologically speaking, the process of inhaling and selecting influences is at stake. In one way or the other my spiritual formation is being influenced by the pastor during the Wednesday-evening services, by my mother, devotedly listening to the pastor, but also by the joyful singing of spiritual songs in the living room, and the 6th grade teacher who challenged us to learn Isaiah 53 by heart. However, this reasoning can indeed be seen as much too easy. Considering the two domains seriously I can discover matching points but there are also tensions. Let me highlight seven issues.

The first remark is about the anti-teleological position in pragmatic education. The aim of education is facilitating growth. There is no specific purpose in the process of individual development. Reconstruction of experiences remains during lifetime. An orthodox theological stance claims as *telos* the self-awareness of belonging to Christ. Once educators have this ideal of their students, there is no thinkable harmony with an open formation process. This is also true for the second issue. From a Deweyan perspective the result of the reciprocal process between the individual person and the environment is open. The content of experiences might diverge in unpredictable directions. A satisfying religious feeling or an aesthetic experience might in this opinion be seen as a successful result of religious education. According to an orthodox position this is undesirable. 'There cannot exist a subjective faith, without content. Faith is not a mere psychological or emotional state, but exactly on the subjective side relation and by the way involvement with Christ' (Van de Beek, 2012, p. 451). This brings me to a third remark about cognitive reflective attitude which is promoted by pragmatic education. The orthodox ideal of a Christian is someone who is devoted to the Holy Scriptures that one will experience as a life-giving source. Studying and meditating presupposes as well as furthers an attitude of critical reflection about religious experiences. This is extremely important for young believers, taken into account their position in society, belonging to a minority (De Muynck, 2010). By active reflection on their experiences they will restructure the own narrative by the authority of the scripture. Be it that the truth itself remains presupposed and by the way non-transformable, the transformation process at the side of the believer has pragmatic features. They have to be able to explain what they believe and why. They learn by rationalizing when confronted by a changing environment, on which they might have an impact as well. This leads to a vulnerable issue at the side of a strong orthodox position, my fourth remark. Emphasising citizenship of a Kingdom that has no relation with the current reality might evoke feelings of indifference or even apathy about culture and society. This is for sure not what is strived for, but could be an undesirable effect. A fifth issue of both harmony and tension has to do with participation and reconstructing experiences. The need for participation would make it necessary to have liturgical aspects in the classroom. Participating in singing, praying, Bible stories students can reconstruct their experiences like me, while hearing expositions about Jonah. At the same time one should realize that experiencing the love of God is a mystery. What the Holy Spirit is doing by experiencing remains a secret for outsiders, but even for the subject himself (Van de Beek, 2012, p. 452: 'becoming a believer cannot be grasped'). In this sense the process of religious growth is open like from a Deweyan perspective. Sixth, an attractive aspect in the Deweyan perspective is the principle of lifelong learning. The life of a Christian remains a struggle through life-time (Van de Beek, 2012, pp. 410-415). Participating in the liturgy, living with the scriptures is a constant matter of reconstructing owns understanding of being loved by God. In this way I can explain as an adult how the story of Jonah – the three days and the three nights in the fish – opens a similar meaning as the crucifixion and resurrection of Jesus Christ. A seventh more problematic theme in a pragmatic stance is that participation often is explained as meaningful if students themselves have problems (e.g. Wardekker, 2002, pp. 208-209). Participation like attending a church service however, means putting children in a context in which the secret of being chained by the shocking stories about God of the message of love can happen. Thinking from a confession concerning God and Jesus, and its claim, orthodox Christianity cannot avoid bringing children into these situations. Experience need not be meaningful by intention but will become meaningful by consequence.

CONCLUSION

In his essay about the transmission versus the transformation approach Siebren Miedema concludes that, although impossible conceptually, in practice these approaches are not always easy to distinguish. This is especially true for the protestant school he evaluates in the mentioned article. From the curriculum perspective a transmission view is claimed because one presents exclusively Biblical stories and religious practices. From the students perspective a transformational position is cherished: there is much space for the personal adoption process (Miedema, 2002, pp. 92-95). The same is concluded in the research into the ideal Christian school (Dijkstra & Miedema, 2003, p. 90). The authors conclude that there is an unsolvable tension between the linking of absolute claims of truth and an inclusivistic pedagogical practice. In my opinion this tension *must* not be solved and *cannot* be solved because it has to do with the paradoxical content from which the Christian inspired school starts. The Flemish philosopher Piet Raes (2009) has made clear that the very nature of the gospel is paradoxical, the crucified Jesus being the ultimate paradox (Raes, 2009, p. 16). Transforming the mind and lives of human beings by this message is paradoxical as well. There is a firm transcendental focus, which for human beings is unbelievable, but yet it is the faith that changes life. "Paradoxes do not deny reflection, but stimulate reflection" (Raes, 2009, p. 15). This is the reason that I prefer an orthodox position for RE more than making RE a matter of exploring religious experiences as such. The answer to the problem I have raised is that an orthodox theological position can and must go hand in hand with a transformative pedagogical approach. The message can be well-defined, but yet leaves the adoption process to occur undefined, open and unpredictable. For religious teachers this means that they should be competent to endure this tense position. On the one hand they need to have a thorough knowledge of the faith-content and its unobvious character. They must be ready to teach about it and meanwhile let children participate in religious practices. This is not easy, not because of religious diversity, but because students are less and less familiar with religious language. The competences of storytelling and explanation of the basics of Christian belief will be of great importance in the future. On the other hand RE teachers should be aware of the restrictions of their impact. RE teachers are not able to structure experiences to a well-defined outcome, except knowledge, which can be instructed and measured. There are many actors and factors besides the school. Not least the faith content itself is a factor with impact. For me, next to my mother, the preacher and numerous others, Jonah was one of my religious teachers.

REFERENCES

Biesta, G. J. J., Miedema, S., & Berding, J. W. A. (1997). Pragmatische pedagogiek [Pragmatic pedagogy]. In S. Miedema (ed.), *Pedagogiek in meervoud* [Plural pedagogy] (pp. 313-353). Houten: Bohn Stafleu Van Loghum.

Beek, A. van de (1998). *Jezus Kurios. De Christologie als hart van de theologie* [Jesus Kyrios: Christology as the Heart of Theology. English Translation 2002]. Zoetermeer: Meinema.

Beek, A. van de (2008). *God doet recht. Eschatologie als Christologie.* [God does justice: Eschatology as Christology]. Zoetermeer: Meinema.

Beek, A. van de (2012). *Lichaam en Geest van Christus. De theologie van de kerk en de Heilige Geest.* [Life and Spirit of Christ. The theology of the Church and the Holy Spirit]. Zoetermeer: Meinema.

Crombrugge, H. van (2008). Voorbij gezag en authenticiteit: Of over geloofwaardigheid [Beyond authority and authenticity: Or about credibility]. In L. Braeckmans (ed), *Niets nieuws onder de zon. De competentie van de levensbeschouwelijke pedagoog.* [Nothing new under the sun. The competency of the philosophical educationalist]. Antwerpen: Universitair Centrum Sint Ignatius.

Miedema, S. (1986). *Kennen en handelen. Bijdragen aan het theorie-praktijk-debat in de opvoedingswetenschap* [Knowing and action. Contributions to the theory-practice debate in philosophy of education]. Leuven/Amersfoort: Acco.

Miedema, S. (2002). Overdracht of toe-eigening? Over wat je kinderen wilt meegeven. [Transmission or adoption? About what you would like to give to children]. In S. Miedema & H. Vroom (eds.), *Alle onderwijs bijzonder. Levensbeschouwelijke waarden in het onderwijs.* [All education is special. Philosophical values in education]. Zoetermeer: Meinema.

Miedema, S. (2005). De actualiteit van Philip Abraham Kohnstamm (1875-1951). [The actuality of Philip Abraham Kohnstamm (1875-1951)]. In A.de Muynck & B. Kalkman (eds.), *Perspectief op leren. Verkenningen naar onderwijs en leren vanuit de christelijke traditie* [Perspectives on learning. Exploring education and learning from the Christian tradition] (pp. 113-129). Kampen: De Groot Goudriaan.

Miedema, S., & Ruyter, D. de (1997). Traditie of vernieuwing? [Tradition or renewal?] In D. de Ruyter & S. Miedema (eds.), *Tussen traditie en vernieuwing. Over de ideale protestants christelijke school* [Between tradition and reform. About the ideal protestant Christian school]. Kampen: Kok.

Muynck, A. de (2008). *Een goddelijk beroep. Spiritualiteit in de beroepspraktijk van leraren in het orthodox-protestantse basisonderwijs* [A Godly vocation. Spirituality in vocational practice of teachers in Orthodox Protestant primary education]. Heerenveen: Groen.

Muynck, A. de, & Vos, P. H. (eds.). (2006). *Leren voor het leven. Vorming en christelijk onderwijs* [Learning for life. Progress and Christian education] Amsterdam: Buijten & Schipperheijn

Raes, P. (2009). *Geloven in katholiek onderwijs. Over opvoeden en onderwijzen in christelijk perspectief* [Belief in catholic education. About pedogagy and education from a Christian perspective]. Kapellen: Pelckmans.

Taylor, C. (2007). *A secular age.* Cambridge, MA/ London: The Belknap Press of Harvard Press.

Wardekker, W. (2002). Religieuze vorming via participatie: Deelname en reflectie. [Religious formation through participation]. In C. A. M. Hermans (ed.), *Participerend leren in debat* [Debating participative learning] (pp. 197-212). Budel: Damon.

Wolff, A. C. J. de, Ruyter D. J., & Miedema, S. (2002). Identity of a Christian school: Conceptions and practical significance. *Educational Review, 54*(3), 239-247.

AFFILIATIONS

Bram de Muynck
Driestar University for Teacher Education
Gouda, The Netherlands

CORNELIA ROUX

CONFLICT OR COHESION?

A Critical Discourse on Religion in Education (RiE) and Religion and Education (RaE)

INTRODUCTION

The problems we have in the world today will not be solved by the level of thinking that create them.
Albert Einstein

In this contribution, I want to celebrate our South African diversity and the freedom of thought after 1994. I want to share my thoughts on the journey from being raised and educated in the pre-democratic (apartheid) white Christian National dispensation. I was however since 1982, exposed to the complexities of diversity during study visits abroad. In the 1990s, when I became a lecturer and researcher in post-apartheid South Africa, I experienced the complexity of being a lecturer and researcher in religion in education (RiE). The development and dissemination of the paradigmatic approach for research in RiE was to me a challenge. The one-sided fundamentalist pedagogical approach to education during the previous three decades whilst conducting research mainly in the context of phenomenology and positivism, did not fit in my hermeneutical paradigmatic stance.

My own grand narrative and interest in religion starts in my upbringing in a multi-denominational family. The different denominations in my extended family gave me the scope to "... see myself as an individual with a personal narrative, liberated from preconceived ideas and intolerant religious perceptions" (Roux & Van der Walt, 2011, p. 225). My journey started in education as a learner educated in segregated schools and universities (both for whites only and Afrikaans as the only medium of instruction). I was trained as a teacher in a segregated university and became a teacher, teaching in the frame of traditional behaviorist pedagogy. In this pedagogy the goal was/is to produce behaviorist results and correct answers to questions put as a proof of success. One can also describe this as conditioning correct answers to complex issues. Issues pre-1994, on religious diversity and RiE seem to have well-structured and 'correct answers' given to deal with social justice issues.

I started my research journey in 1978 as a part-time lecturer at the University of Stellenbosch, which allowed its academics to explore other paradigmatic stances. The Faculty of Education's curriculum was then still in line with the education

I. ter Avest (ed.), On the Edge: (Auto)biography and Pedagogical Theories on Religious Education, 137–149.
© 2012 Sense Publishers. All rights reserved.

policy of the government of the day. Pre-scribed curricula were positivistic, behaviorist and supported by a pragmatic approach, where the constellation of different voices for and on teacher training was silenced. Students of neighbouring universities (English-speaking, interracial and intercultural), with their opposition to the apartheid education system, were more open in their discourses and deliberated on the "education of the oppressed, transformative curriculum development and other education paradigms. Interaction with these students was limited, however their voices were heard at different academic platforms which I often attended as guest.

With my experiences in classroom praxis, I found myself re-evaluating my teacher-training and trying to connect my discipline (Religious Studies) within RiE. During my post-graduate studies, following academic debates locally and internationally on RiE, urged me to explore new and different trends in RiE. This lead to a series of empirical research projects in schools at the dawn of our new democracy. For example in 1993: *The development of innovative didactics in Religious Studies in the primary school;* 1994: *The development and evaluation of multi-religious content for pupils in the secondary school*; 1996: *Multi-religious education in schools for children with special educational needs* and in 1997: *Redefining of the role of religious education teachers in a multicultural and multi-religious school environment.* I could no longer adhere to the constricted religious and cultural perspectives taught to student-teachers, with their inability to understand an unjust society, where political interference in societal interactions destroyed social harmony with consequences for years and generations to come. I perceived then my lecturing task, firstly, to assist student-teachers to function as citizens in a diverse society and secondly to train them to become skilled teachers in religion in education, with the task to educate and inform the next generation growing up in an open and democratic society.

It was clear that after the democratic elections in 1994, the traditional role and function of teaching religion education within the prevailing doctrine of Christian National Education (CNE) would inevitably change. The perceived idea that CNE was the sole bearer of beliefs and values of an open and democratic society could no longer meet the needs, realities and challenges of the multi-religious South African society. Knowledge of different beliefs and values became a prerequisite for facilitating learners within the open school system. This was however a daunting task. The political and educational environments where religion had publically been politicized, prevented teachers from acting "professionally" and to respect the beliefs of learners from diverse religious and cultural backgrounds. In the pre-democratic dispensation religion as private space was extended it many spheres into public space. Specific Christian Protestant denominations extended their private space into the public domain in schools and tertiary education institutions, supported by the government of the day. This meant that student-teachers' cultural and religious backgrounds and their pre-conceived worldviews, beliefs, perceptions and attitudes influenced their ability to develop critical thinking skills on diversity and multi-religious education and also influenced their research skills. (cf. Roux & Du Preez, 2006).

I explored these issues in many research projects, and thus it was then that I embarked on a new avenue by introducing the next level in the discourses on Religion in Education (RiE).

In this chapter I will concentrate on:
- The epistemological positions of Religion in Education (RiE) and Religion and Education (RaE);
- Religion in public space and RaE;

and then present a case study on the position of RaE in tourism education relating to religious public spaces and as example for future discourses.

The Paradigmatic Stance of RiE and RaE

Research in Religion in Education (RiE) and Religion and Education (RaE) also led me through my own journey to articulate my paradigmatic position and scholarship. The paradigmatic position I took, started in exploring hermeneutics in deconstructing religious texts, combining hermeneutics and social constructivist curriculum theory. I further drew upon an action-hermeneutical principle (Roux, 2007) as a means to ascertain a double hermeneutic principle. I utilized curriculum theories of Cornbleth (1990) and Gergen and Gergen (2003) and linked these to the 'hermeneutical circle' as posed by Slattery (2009, p. 115) in post-modern curriculum development (Roux, 2009). This stance indicates especially the importance of 'lived experiences' of teachers in their appreciation and understanding of the 'other'.

The epistemology of RiE developed from the notion that a democratic and open society needs to have a knowledgeable construct of religions, world views and belief systems that will support democracy and different value systems. RiE further manifest into praxis and it was imperative that knowledge of and about different worldviews and belief systems needed to be part of the curriculum in schools, as well as the curriculum in teacher-training. The latter is not an unrealistic option, as tertiary institutions can re-assess their curricula in order to fulfill the needs of the knowledge economy, and in this particular case, teacher-training in religion education and religious studies (Roux, 2009). The implementation and approach for religion education[1] in public schools brought thus an area for innovative research opportunities. Structured curricula and the *Policy document on Religion and Education* (DoE, 2003) were developed to enhance opportunities to explore religious diversity, and to improve and celebrate respect for diversity. The cooperation approach preferred by the policy document gave RiE a new, interesting scope. RiE became the bearer for understanding different belief systems, gaining religious content and adhering to moral obligations in public and private schools. Phenomenology and reflection on the subject became the vehicle for understanding the other. In the same breath RiE also deals with religion in private space as themes on studying worship, concepts of deities, spirituality and issues important to the believers of the particular religion are dealt with as well as religious observances that form an integral part of the discourses in RiE.

In reality the policy document on RiE enhanced explicitly multi-religious subject knowledge. However, the important question for RiE was to bridge the gap between curriculum development, subject knowledge and classroom praxis within a social constructivist and hermeneutical approach. Furthermore a teaching-learning paradigm fits well into RiE with a dialogical-reflective approach and phenomenological notions, towards gaining knowledge of different religions (Roux, 2006, p. 1296). This teaching-learning strategy was based on empirical research with student-teachers (cf. Roux & Du Preez, 2006) and brought new perspectives to teaching-learning strategies in the developing democracy. It also questioned the previous applications of religious education in South Africa. In order to study or learn about religions is not a subjective exercise, but intensely knowledge-based, and if one needs to understand the paradigmatic stance and purpose of RiE; religions' content should be studied as an integrated system of beliefs, actions and experiences (Roux, 2006, p. 1297). The organization and understanding of RiE is a construction of the teacher's own frame of reference with an interpretation of the religious content, its morality and spirituality. This position in RiE might bring teachers in conflict with the insider/outsider position of facilitating RiE (Roux, 2007). RiE is therefore in the position to be an integrated dimension of students' perceptions, experiences and reflections that need to form part of discussions, with the notion of conversations, which allow explorations of new content as well as dialogue where differences and contrasting ideas are deliberated.

There is however also the concern that RiE can isolate content and religious backgrounds as the only variables for discussions, whereas conversations and dialogue might influence reflection on the humanness of religion's role in society. A well-informed RiE curriculum has the propensity to transform a developing democratic society which aims at respect and tolerance. Potgieter (2011:402) defines RiE and especially religion studies as a school subject, which includes religion in the Life Orientation curriculum, as: "… an academic subject in which students (neutrally, formally and objectively) contrive to come to grips with the generics and commonalities of religion as a phenomenon" and the position which regards RiE as providing "equitable observation of religious practices."

I can agree that RiE's paradigmatic stance is mainly to construct knowledge, infuse teaching-learning, capacitating students to engage in transformative curriculum and development research initiatives. When engage responsibly, RiE assists students to understand hermeneutically the knowledge construction, explore religion as a philosophical and epistemological phenomenon and understand its position as a core subject in pedagogy. One can affirm that RiE is not only part of the curriculum, underpinned by a policy document (2003) with an academic and paradigmatic stance, but also a research area that explores human interaction and understanding of religion. RiE should not be, and I argue that it is not, as put by Potgieter, (2011, p. 398), "the intimidation of the silent mass" not taking social justice issues into consideration, but is rather a cohesion of negotiations and processes that include all stakeholders. It is imperative that professional educators, academics in religion education and religious studies direct RiE into its responsible professional stance. It needs to serve the education system and the religious and culturally diverse post-democratic society. Taking also the ever-changing curriculum policies in South Africa into consideration, and the prolonged professional approach of teachers towards RiE, it became necessary to explore a new avenue to assure religion in and around the curriculum and to expand its possibilities in education.

Religion and Education (RaE) – A New Direction?

Education and pedagogy is not a static process because education outcomes and models change, and positions of subjects and/or core disciplines in teacher training and professional development are questioned continuously. Experience in RiE research (be it conceptual or empirical) and the notion of becoming a scholar means to seek answers to these basic and complex questions. RiE is no exception and new curriculum developments and documents urge one to continuously revisit the position of RiE. This situation has the propensity for religious knowledge in many cases to become part of a discourse on the position of RiE. New opportunities are opened up to contribute to knowledge development. The peripheral position of religion in education processes in, for example the South African school curricula, opens this new position for RiE. A fresh paradigmatic stance to RiE was explored, especially when the hidden and null curricula are becoming forces in a different paradigmatic stance to RiE. *Religion and Education* (RaE) can open up broader understandings of and possibilities for religion in public spaces and it includes the current position of religion in education as outlined in new curriculum documents (CAPS, 2012).

RaE contributes to countering misinformation and/or limited information on religious issues in private and public space. We should widen the understanding of religion in public space and not only concentrate on facilitating the meaning of places of worship and/or festivals in religion education through different approaches. The meaning and core notions of many religious issues, morals, values and perceptions visible to society in other subjects and disciplines must be explored. The RaE paradigmatic stance will therefore concentrate more on the inputs religion can make towards other subjects or disciplines where values, respect, morality, citizenship, ethics and social justice are main concerns, strengthening and supporting the notion of a religiously just society. The expansion of RaE from pedagogy to society can only contribute towards a concerned society with respect for diversity. In this regard I want to argue that Potgieter's (2011, p. 396) notion that "religion continuously serves as an important reinforcement mechanism for morality" needs to be expanded beyond arguments of religious observances and RiE in classrooms. If one positions RaE as part of the peripheral circle of religion in schools or teachers' education at tertiary level, the curricula content with reflection on and from religion become more important to the broader societal understanding of respect towards the other (Roux, 2010). The humanized landscape is always changing, as well as processes of understanding diversity, and it is in this regard that RaE can contribute to a better understanding of religion in society.

Religion in Public Space and Religion and Education (RaE)

Religion in public space has been politicized in South African society through its diverse histories of many centuries. Many visitors came as merchants to the shores of Southern Africa in pre-colonization times and brought their belief systems (Hinduism and Ancient Judaism) in contact with the inhabitants of the continent (cf. Le Roux, 2004). The colonization of the Cape (since 1652) by European nations, bearers of mainly Christianity, imported slaves from Indonesia, individuals from Islamic decent and made in many instances contact with the first inhabitants (Khoi and San and African Religions). All these contacts reflect the conflicts and the development of an unjust religious societal struggle.

Religion has always been part of the public domain and societal spaces. Histories of religions throughout the ages defined religion as a human activity in public space. Since ancient times and in many religions and societies, religious rituals and practices were part of the public domain. This means that it is also part of the collective understanding of the religious space and practices. In, for example, ancient Greece, sacrifices to the gods took place in the public market space. Chidester (2004) defines this ritual in a city as "*the middle space of humanity*" and it was further "*defined by those who shared the cooked meat of the sacrificial ritual*". In pre-Christian times, the Pan-Hellenic religious feasts were held at Olympia and Delphi. Today these two sites are also famous outside Greece as religious and tourist attractions. In ancient Greek times the oracle at Delphi drew a large number of religious pilgrims. History books described the many journeys taken by pilgrimages to holy places during the Middle-Ages. In Christianity a journey to Rome is seen as a religious act and a journey to Mecca is seen as the fulfillment of one of the five pillars of Islam. One recalls the joy at airports when Muslim pilgrims are returning home and welcomed with admiration. The belief that this pilgrimage is a step further in the spiritual growth as a devotee remains an important aspect of the religion.

For many communities and cultures, the market place is still where religious rituals and/or cultural activities take place. One can plot churches, mosques, temples and other religious public spaces and places of worship in city centers as well as rural environments throughout the world. History books and tourist guides inform or promote a society's history or beauty which are in its cities or small villages. In our country, for example, in African Religions (AR) climbing a mountain or visiting a river is often a sacred journey.

Chidester and Linenthal (1996:9-16) argue that even a "*city itself, therefore, operates as a certain kind of sacred space, as an intensively interpreted, regularly ritualized, but also intensely contested zone of religious significance*". If one argues that from the beginning religion was 'the middle space of humanity' it is obvious that religion was never only part of a private space. Chidester (2004) argues that if we define our humanity by the symbolic resource strategies deployed in negotiating a human identity, orientation and habitation, then religion has *"increasingly been situated in urban environments"*. Habibul Haque Khondker (2009, p. 132) reported that in his research in Bangladesh, *"Once a space is designated as a religious space, especially as a space for prayer, it is impossible, in the context of Bangladesh, to undo that space as a secular, civic one"*. Thus it seems that the understanding of religion in public space will differ from place to place, region to region and religion to religion. Even in countries with more or less the same democratic values, legislation can differ regarding the understanding of religion in public space. Bowen (2007) points out that people organize their society and it tells one about their own. He refers to the ban of the headscarf in public space which is an intriguing factor, especially if one regards French society as democratic, multi-cultural and multi-religious.

In his paper *"Consuming a Cathedral: Commodification of Religious Places in Late Modernity"*, Tuomas Martikainen explores the relationship between religion and a consumer society. He argues that *"contemporary cities are laboratories of religious experimentation, cultural creativity and change"* (2006, p. 127). The diversity of people from the religiously orthodox to agnostics and the expanding number of atheists in a modern city *"are all part of the religious life of that city's diversity"*. One can picture different religious landscapes, places of worship, cemeteries, religious artifacts and tourist attractions in European, Middle East and Far Eastern cities which bring forth panoramas of great cathedrals, temples, mosques and synagogues that dominate the city's landscape. Although many of the churches in Europe are still servicing a religious community, they have increasingly became multifunctional buildings as concert halls, art exhibition centres, shelters when natural disasters strike and religious sanctuaries for the members of that specific denomination.

Traditions, their narratives, understandings and appreciations are not static. They develop and change as society puts new ideas into practice where new cultures (in the broader sense of the word) and philosophies transpire. The former are products of deliberation, arguments and critique, and the best deliberations are in dialogue, which brings into being the give-and-take situation where the ideal is to meet one another in the middle and in the end deconstruct the meaning of the process and the knowledge construction. However it is important to maintain a balance between one's openness and commitment. As mentioned before, the politicization of religion in pre-democratic South African schools has urged the democratic government and academics to develop policy documents and curricula that reflect diversity of different denominations and religions (DoE, 2003). This politicizing still has an influence on the development of world views, perceptions of one another on curricula and praxis in religion teaching and learning in schools and at tertiary institutions (Potgieter, 2010).

Religion in Education (RiE) deals explicitly with the policy on religion in education, pedagogy and a curriculum for religion education, whilst RaE deals with broader concepts of religion, such as religion in public space. RaE explores issues on and the influences of religion in society, it includes the appreciation of diversity where students can experience the meaning-making of a religion to its follower(s).

RaE can also contribute to understanding social justice issues; it can foster and create an awareness during research excursions, where an understanding of religious diversity is significant. Human rights education and religion is a good example of a contribution of RaE and Human Rights (cf. Roux, 2012). RaE brings in tourism education (as demonstrated in the case study), the content-related components of the subject in relation to the interpretation on what is expected. In this case professional agents in tourism need to adhere to the meaning and values when religious observances, rituals or customs become part of public space.

In order to illustrate RaE a question from the above outline and arguments can be posed as: *Can RaE counter contrasting views in public society on how religion in public spaces can assist respect for diversity?*

Case Study and Interview on Tourism Education to Explore RaE

This part of the chapter will explore tourism education as an avenue for RaE. The reason for choosing tourism education as a case study was because the outcomes in these modules are mainly to gain knowledge on tourist attractions and provide information to the public. There are also many examples where tourist guides are trained to explore tourist sites. This case study concentrated on tourism education and research excursions for students and agents in tourism. In a lengthy unstructured interview with the lecturer in tourism education, it was clear that in most destinations religious sites, places of worship and visits to religious artifacts are main attractions. In most instances the religious sites are visited by tourists without any prior knowledge of the customs of the religion or its followers. The professional agent is therefore, in most cases, the only source of information on how the tourist should act or behave in the religious environment. In this sense the tourists become part of the religious observance (a private issue) in the public space (a tourist attraction). This is a good example of how RaE can be transferred into public space. The lecturer in tourism education, being also a manager in the tourism industry, reflected on experiences during visits to religious public spaces as tourist attractions. A pedagogical framework to incorporate religion and education (RaE) in the curriculum for tourism education will also be discussed.

Tourism Education Relating to Religious Public Spaces and RaE

In tourism education and tourism industry, educational excursions are conducted in order to have the travel agent experience the product (Roux, Christelle, 2009, p. iv). These tours include most cultural and religious sites in the tourism industry. In the non-structural interview with the lecturer (2010), she stated that during these educational excursions with new travel agents/students in tourism, one has an assumption that a uniform understanding exists by the various stakeholders (agents and tourists) on the religious sites being visited. In analyzing the processes and understanding the industry and the purpose of educational tours the following issues were mentioned: (i) the tour leader, normally from the sector of the tourism industry, conducting the educational excursion, whether a native to the country or not, does not have the necessary means or education to give the travel agents the needed information relating to religious areas being visited; (ii) tourist agents are not culturally or religiously aware of customs and/or have no understanding of religious practices or customs other than their own preconceived ideas (Roux, Christelle, 2009). Three examples during the interview were given to illustrate the above[2] (*verbatim*):

- "A travel agent named her donkey Mohammed, while on route to the Valley of the Kings in Cairo, Egypt. This was seen as utterly disrespectful, not only to the culture, but more seriously to the locals operating the tourism establishment who were accompanying us to the attraction."

- "Another agent's lack of understanding and religious 'finesse' was further demonstrated by not covering up her shoulders, chest and hips while entering a Mosque that was visited. The retail travel agent in question was isolated by the 'Tourism Police' in Egypt and told to be more respectful when entering places of worship and given a cloth to conceal the necessary areas. This problem is not confined to the tourism industry stakeholders only. Through my observations, many tourists have expressed this type of ignorant behavior when entering religious spaces or places of worship."

- "Istanbul's Blue Mosque still operates as a place of worship for the local community. Certain sections within the mosque have been cordoned off to allow visitors to enter, view and admire the interior of this world-renowned attraction. While visiting the Blue Mosque there were numerous individuals practicing their religion while being watched from behind the cordoned off areas. Overall the atmosphere was respectful. However, three tourists decided to get a better view and walked past the cordoned off area straight into the space where the devotees were praying, talking loudly and taking photos. Strangely the atmosphere did not change and no other tourist or tour leader informed them, but I see this as disrespectful, ignorant and offensive."

Having experienced these incidents it became apparent that there is a lack of a knowledge construct with regards to behavioral respect towards religious beliefs and/or the places of worship being visited. The lecturer further elaborated on her experiences as a Regional Sales Manager for a tourism wholesale company (2007-2009) conducting educational excursions also to various European countries for retail tourism agents. In her reflections she observed a considerable difference when entering cathedrals and/or churches. The retail travel agents could more closely identify with either the churches and/or cathedrals and showed more respect and keeping behind the cordoned off areas (where applicable) and showed their respect by being silent, as expected in a place of worship. This attitude indicated to her that "even though not all the temporary spectators were religious, their understanding of acceptable behavior within the religious space was much clearer. It can be argued that this is due to familiarity or personal religious beliefs". One can conclude with Margaret Werry's (2008, p. 17) statement that "tourism is arguably one of the only contemporary sites outside of the education industry where explicitly designated, non-vocational learning about other times, places and people takes place". The interview and reflections on this case study open an avenue for RaE, as an infusion into the discipline, and may contribute to foster respect towards religion in public spaces.

A Pedagogical Framework for RaE, Tourism Education and Religious Public Spaces

From the reflections above the following question was posed: Where does one draw the line when students or tourists and visitors, as outsiders, become part of this religious public and/or private space, and how does one interact with RaE and tourism education on these issues?

Firstly, one would prefer that religion in public space be seen as a private and/or public space for the devotees. Secondly, if this religious space is open to visitors (academics or tourists) who are not part of the religious community, it should be defined also as a spiritual and an educational center. This, we argue is where both values are imbedded in the notion to promote respect and understanding. The aim should include fostering the value of understanding the other, especially through observing the religious space, but also respecting the devotees' spiritual ambiance. When religious spaces are open as tourist attractions that generate an income for the religious places of worship, non-members of the religion cannot be excluded. Academic visits to religious public/private spaces add value to the principles and values of interreligious understanding, teaching-learning and contextualizing religious content to enhance respect and tolerance for the other (Roux, 2010).

The challenge for me and the lecturer in tourism education was to develop a pedagogical framework that contextualize a teaching-learning approach; foster respect and develop a knowledge construct for diverse world-views and to act accordingly. The practical component where knowledge can be constructed should be through developing critical thinking skills, discussing the social contexts and cultivating an appreciation and deep understanding of and for religious spaces. It brings two dimensions to the fore, namely appreciation and respect. It is in this realm that RaE brings a perspective to the content of the discipline.

One of the main developmental processes explored in tourism education and where RaE has an important role to play, was to examine content given to students/agents and to promote an understanding of issues aiming at improvement (Rothman & Thomas, 1994, p. 25; Roux, Christelle, 2009, p. 213). Rothman and Thomas (1994) also identified three main facets, namely knowledge development, knowledge utilization, and design and development. The aim of intervention knowledge in this specific case was to contribute to basic knowledge of human conduct (Rothman & Thomas, 1994, pp. 14-18; Du Preez, 2008; Roux, Christelle, 2009, pp. 214-216). Du Preez (2008, pp. 11-12) further argues that "applying knowledge of human behavior and conduct is a transformation of available knowledge" (in this case study, knowledge, perceptions and attitudes of students in tourism) into the application of concepts relevant to the students' knowledge construct and agents' practices. The aim was to create new strategies, content, programs, service systems "by means of a process of problem analysis, intervention design, early development, advanced development and dissemination" (Rothman & Thomas, 1994, pp. 8-14; cf. also Du Preez, 2008, p. 12; Roux, Christelle, 2009, pp. 216-217). The lecturer's facilitation strategies, methodological approaches, curriculum development for transformation and teaching-learning praxis were re-evaluated. A prominent aspect was the lack of critical thinking skills on diversity that might hamper a reflective approach and interactions towards new perspectives of religion in public space.

In order to illustrate the proposed pedagogical framework for tourism education and Religion and Education, where critical pedagogy and critical thinking will be part of curriculum development. One can define it as follows: Critical pedagogy and critical thinking form the basis of teaching-learning for the meaning of core notions of religious issues, morals, values and perceptions visible to society (i.e. the understanding of religious space). The knowledge imbedded in the learner comes either from her/his preconceived ideas or knowledge construct. These prior knowledges and ideas need to be deconstructed and re-interpreted into a newly reconstructed knowledge (in this instance religious knowledge applicable to tourism education). The new knowledge, with religion and education (RaE) content is infused into the discipline (commodity). In this process new knowledge is created, praxis is defined and infused in the social construct and the interaction between the disciplinary knowledge and religion, takes place.

CONCLUSION

Religion and Education (RaE) has the propensity to embrace many disciplines and to support different professional teaching-learning and professional training curricula. The experiences, internations and observations of the lecturer in tourism education brought us both to the conclusion that religion in public spaces is a complex education domain. When the notion of religion in public space is explored, RiE (religious education in schools and religion in education) as a subject only, it is just too limited to capture all the peripheral issues necessary to optimize the interaction between religious content, and the discipline where applications and meanings of core issues need to be incorporated. In this chapter I argued that we need to take a pragmatic stance towards RiE and its discourses. We need to explore new avenues for religion in pedagogy. RaE, as outlined in the proposed pedagogical framework, can contribute to the discourses on e.g. tourism education and can further also be explored in human rights education and religion. Tourism is a much larger commercial entity and vocational training programme than RiE in schools and tertiary institutions is. We need to enlarge the platform and input for RiE. This does not mean that RiE (in pedagogy) needs to be replaced and therefore RiE and RaE should not be in conflict with one another. My argument is that RaE provides new avenues and opportunities to stay relevant in education and contribute to religious understandings in public spaces.

ACKNOWLEDGEMENT

I wish to acknowledge the contribution of Ms Christelle Roux for her interviews, participation in the case study on RaE and Tourism education and her collaboration in developing the pedagogical framework.

NOTES

[1] Religion education is the new term used in the curriculum documents of the Department of Education, because of the legacy of apartheid imbedded in the terms religious education, bible education and right living needed to change.

[2] Direct words of the participant to explain the need for RaE in tourism education.

REFERENCES

Bowen, J. R. (2007). *Why the French don't like head scarves: Islam, the state and public space.* Princeton University Press.

Chidester, D. (2004). *Mapping the sacred in the mother city: Religion and urban space in Cape Town, South Africa* (www.mmiweb.org.uk/eftre/conferences_pages/).

Chidester, D., & Linenthal, E. T. (eds.). (1996). *American sacred space.* Bloomington: Indiana University Press.

Cornbleth, C. (1990). *Curriculum in context.* London: Falmer Press.

Du Preez, P. (2008). *Dialogue as facilitation strategy: Infusing the classroom with a culture of human rights.* Unpublished PhD dissertation, Stellenbosch University, South Africa.

Gergen, M., & Gergen, K. J. (2003). *Social construction: A reader.* London: Sage Publications.

Khondker, H. H. (2009). Dhaka and the contestation over the public space. *CITY, 13*(1), March.

Le Roux, M. (2003) *The Lemba: A lost tribe of Israel in Africa?* Pretoria, University of South Africa.

Martikainen, T. (2006). Consuming a cathedral: Commodification of religious places in Late Modernity. *Fieldwork in Religion, 2*(2), 127-145.

Potgieter, F. J. (2011). Morality as the substructure of social justice: Religion in education as a case in point. *South African Journal of Education, 31*, 394-406.

Rothman, J., & Thomas, E. J. (eds.). (1994). *Intervention research: Design and development for human service.* New York: The Haworth Press.

Roux, C. D. (2006). Innovative facilitation strategies for religion education. In M. De Souza, R. Durka, K. Engebretson, R. Jackson, & A. McGrady (eds.), *International handbook of the religious, moral and spiritual dimensions in education.* Dordrecht: Springer.

Roux, C. D. (2007). Hermeneutics and religion teaching and learning in the context social constructivism. *Scriptura (International Journal for Bible, Religion and Theology in Southern Africa), 96*(3), 469-485.

Roux, C. D. (2009). Religion in education: Who is responsible? *Alternation, 3*, 3-30.

Roux, C. D. (2010). Religious literacy and Human Rights Literacy as prerequisite for human rights education. In G. Durka, L. Gearon, M. de Souza, & K. Engebretson (eds.), *International handbook for inter-religious education* (Volume 4, pp. 991/1015). Dordrecht: Springer.

Roux, C. D. (ed.). (2012). *Safe spaces: Human rights education in diverse contexts.* Rotterdam: Sense Publication.

Roux, C. D. & Du Preez, P. (2006). Clarifying students' perceptions of different belief systems and values: Prerequisite for effective educational praxis. *South African Journal for Higher Education, 30*(2), 514-531.

Roux, C. D., & Walt, J. H. van der (2011). Paradigms, beliefs and values in scholarship: A conversation between two educationists. *Koers, 76*(2), 221-242.

Roux, Christelle (2009). *Developing an instructional training design for Trafalgar Tours sales managers.* Unpublished M.Tech Thesis. Faculty of Commerce, Cape Peninsula University of Technology, Cape Town.

Slattery, P. (2006). *Curriculum development in the post-modern era.* London: Routledge.

Werry, M. (2008). Pedagogy of/as/and tourism: Or, shameful lessons. *The Review of Education, Pedagogy and Cultural Studies, 30*, 14-42.

DOCUMENTS

2003. National Policy on Religion and Education. Department of Education, Pretoria: Government Printers.

2011. Curriculum Assessment Policy (CAPS): Life Orientation for Further Education and training. Department of Education, Pretoria: Government Printers.

AFFILIATIONS

Cornelia Roux
Faculty of Education Sciences
North-West University
Potchefstroom Campus
South Africa

DORET DE RUYTER

THE BEST AND THE WORST THAT HAS BEEN SAID AND DONE

Teaching Religious Ideals in Religious Education

THE BEGINNING

The highest flights of charity, devotion, trust, patience, bravery
to which the wings of human nature have spread themselves
have been flown for religious ideals.
(William James, 1902)

I was raised in a Protestant family from the middle of the sixties until the early eighties of the last century in a small village close to Amsterdam. Although my parents had different religious backgrounds, my mother's relatively liberal Protestant views were dominated by my father's orthodox Calvinist faith. His views became more liberal over the years, but being the eldest, the influence of the Calvinistic tradition was not only the strongest, but also lasted the longest. The Protestant religious beliefs of my parents influenced our family life in religious practices, like compulsory church attendance and confirmation classes, religious rituals like prayer and bible reading and it was quite clear that they hoped that I and my two other sisters would follow their religious path in life. Their Protestant faith also influenced their socio-moral values and ideals, which was visible in their donations to charity, their hospitality, and their insistence on moral obligations for instance to be honest, moral virtues like being fair and caring, and their views of an ideal world. They hoped and stimulated us to develop these moral qualities to the full. Finally, I remember my parents' expectations to make the most of our given talents, for example our intellectual capacities. We were aware of such expectations, because they would be disappointed with a grade if they knew we could do better or we would be reproached for lack of study. Fortunately, my parents were not overly demanding but (relatively) realistic in their expectations and did not expect perfection that one can aspire towards but will never achieve.

I. ter Avest (ed.), On the Edge: (Auto)biography and Pedagogical Theories on Religious Education, 151–161.

Ideals

Interestingly, when I look back, I remember that when I was a young adolescent I sometimes despised the expectations of my parents with regard to my intellectual abilities, being more interested in venturing out with friends than in learning Latin or Greek, more than their moral expectations. This might be due to the fact that I was interested in and committed to the big moral issues of that time, i.e. the cold war, apartheid in South Africa, global justice, and equality of persons irrespective or their gender-identity, religion, etc. My ideals resembled theirs; we marched for instance happily as a family in the anti nuclear bomb demonstrations in 1981 and 1983. In hindsight, it might be their upbringing that is one of the seeds from which my interest in ideals and human flourishing has grown.

Another seed was sown when I moved to Glasgow in 2000. Glasgow at that time was one of the cities with the most deprived areas in Europe. Coming from a country with a strong socio-welfare system and concomitant income tax policy, I was shocked by the enormous differences in wealth. I was more upset, however, by the related differences in the hopes of parents for the future of their children. I heard a story of one of my colleagues who had visited a student on placement that was typical for parents in deprived areas. It was a relatively innocent example, but nevertheless stuck in my memory. A boy in one of the extremely deprived areas in which the school was located had quite a talent for basketball. When the teachers tried to enthuse the parents to have him join a team and take lessons (which would be free), the parents declined with the remark that that was not something for them; they would never rise beyond the minimum. The fact that even being better than average in basketball was not to be expected from their son, became for me a telling example of a general loss of parental expectations in the possibilities and a better future of their children. I believed that ideals might be a key to ignite a flame of hope and I have been working on the subject of ideals in education since then.

THE ISSUE FURTHER EXPLORED

With regard to religious ideals, that form the subject of this contribution, I have defended the view that all schools, whether they are religious or state schools, should pay attention to religious ideals in addition to aspects like knowledge about holy books, beliefs, rituals, religious feasts, etc. (see De Ruyter, 2006; De Ruyter & Merry, 2009). I have provided two reasons for this claim. In this *liber amicorum* for Siebren Miedema, I primarily focus on the reason that teaching about[1] religious ideals in Religious Education (RE) furthers the development of pupils into citizens of liberal democracies, because this ties in well with Miedema's views on what he calls maximal interreligious citizenship education (2011). However, presenting religious ideals also has another purpose, which I will briefly address. These ideals can be an alternative source of values to the ones pupils encounter in mainstream society (see for a similar type of argument Brighouse, 2005) with which they can develop their identity and meaning in life. This ties in with another claim of

Miedema (2001, 2011), i.e. that learning about and from religions has import to the identity development of pupils.[2]

I should stress that I do not suggest that teaching about religious ideals is the most important part of RE, but do claim that it should be an aspect of RE. Nor do I mean to suggest that this will lead to a profound change in RE in Dutch schools, because it fits in well within the legal requirements in the Netherlands, which are defined in a general and minimal way – but it obviously depends how RE is currently put into practice in schools. The Dutch state prescribes various aims for primary and secondary schools. In one of these religions are explicitly mentioned, namely in primarily schools "pupils [should, DJR] learn essentials of religious movements that play an important part in the Dutch pluralistic society, and they learn to respect people's differences of opinion". For secondary education this aim is reiterated, although at a slightly more abstract level. All schools, of whichever signature, have to work towards this aim. I propose that the essentials of religious movements that are being taught should not be confined to central tenets and characteristic rituals or particularities of religious social codes, but in my view RE should also teach the ideals that religions profess.

I suggest that teaching about religious ideals within RE and citizenship education has two aspects. Firstly, religious ideals are to be taught. This can further pupils' understanding of some of the profound motivations of fellow citizens. Moreover, teaching about religious conceptions of ideals outside the religious domain like economic or moral ideals, which I call religious ideals in the broad sense, assists pupils to develop an understanding of similarities and differences between interpretations of ideals. As will become clear in the remainder of this text, teaching about religious ideals should not only involve an increase in knowledge and understanding, i.e. knowing which religious ideals believers may have, but also the ability to evaluate the ideals of other citizens. Secondly, the pursuit of religious ideals should be addressed. It is important that pupils learn to make a difference between religious ideals and the way in which these are pursued. While religious ideals have inspired people to moral excellence, think for instance of Martin Luther King, Ghandi or the Dalai Lama, or to religious exemplarity, for instance Theresa of Avila, or Siddhartha Buddha, it is also clear that religious ideals can bring people to the most abhorrent acts. History is marred with evil acts inspired by religious ideals. Precisely because persons attach high value to their religious ideals, there is the possibility that they will not refrain from trying to achieve their ideals in every possible way. Ideals can then become more valuable than other human beings: a person might not hesitate to sacrifice a few people for the sake of achieving her religious ideals.[3]

I will begin with a concise explanation of the concept 'religious ideals' and also clarify the distinction between (an evaluation of) religious ideals and the ways in which they are pursued. The fourth section describes what teaching about religious ideals may involve in relation to citizenship education. I will not describe in detail which religious ideals or which religious traditions have to be presented to the pupils. I would suggest that the main world religions should be represented, but local circumstances and the discretionary freedom of schools with regard to the specific content of curricular subjects may lead to a diversity in practices. Schools may opt to include religious views that are prevalent in their area or decide to pay more attention to the one religion than the other.

Finally, I should note that the focus of this contribution is on ideals of religions, but this should not be understood as the suggestion that non-religious worldviews are to be excluded from RE. On the contrary, with Van der Kooij and Miedema (2013) I defend the view that it is more appropriate to use the term Worldview Education instead of Religious Education, precisely because this underlines the (importance of the) inclusion of non-religious views on life. However, I have to confine myself and therefore focus on religious ideals. But what do we mean with 'religious ideals'?

RELIGIOUS IDEALS

Ideals refer to (a configuration of) characteristics of a person and situations or states that are believed to be excellent or perfect and that are not yet realised. They are ideas, dreams or visions, which makes it possible for people to dream of or envision the most superbly imaginable characteristics of persons or states. I define religious ideals as ideals that acquire meaning due to a belief in something transcendent or a divine being (De Ruyter, 2006). The term religious ideals can only be applied for those ideals that are related to such a belief. Thus, religious ideals are exclusive to those who have a religious conception of the good life.[4]

This definition of ' religious ideals' gives rise to two kinds of religious ideals. The first type may be called religious ideals in the *strict sense* and consists of ideals that are *constituted* by a belief in a transcendent being. These ideals are oriented towards the divine or are characteristic of one's relation to the divine. Such ideals are only pursued by people who believe in something transcendent or a transcendent being; the ideals have no meaning for people who do not share this belief. For instance, the ideal of devout believers may be to unquestioningly and completely follow the will of their god (see for instance Emmet, 1994), which can be incomprehensible to those who do not believe that this god exists. Abraham may serve as an example here. Not only did he leave his home to travel to an unknown destination because God had ordered him to do so, he was willing to sacrifice his son on the commandment of God. The second type of religious ideals refers to religious ideals in the *broad sense*. These ideals belong to other domains of life, but they are *influenced* by the belief in a divine being. Think for instance of moral, social, economic ideals. Although these ideals are held by many, they become religious ideals if they are influenced by a particular faith. For instance, it is possible to talk about Christian, Muslim or Hindu conceptions of the moral ideal of justice. The difference between the conceptions is due to the different interpretation of the ideals based on for instance a holy book, the tradition of a particular faith or the central creeds.

People who have religious ideals will also pursue these ideals. This can be explained as follows. People who have an ideal attach great importance to the characteristics of a person or a state to which the ideal refers. As these ideals are not yet realised, they are committed to the realisation of the ideal and therefore act in ways that they believe will be conducive to this end. However, although having an ideal influences a person's will and action, ideals do not specify the way in which they are pursued. For example, young pious men who firmly believe in a just world and hope that heaven will be established on earth before too long, may both pursue the ideal by praying because they believe that the new world can only be realised by God as well as by imposing their ideals upon the world by terrorist attacks.[5]

TEACHING RELIGIOUS IDEALS

The notion teaching religious ideals is quite vague and deserves further explanation, for which I will use a threefold distinction in the relation one can have to (religious) ideals. Firstly, it is possible that one knows about ideals of other people, but does not agree with them that the characteristics of persons or situations are perfect or excellent. For instance, I do not see anything excellent or perfect in pursuing fame or the acquisition of wealth and therefore do not believe these to be ideals. Secondly, one can recognise the ideals of others, but not have the ideals oneself. In this case one agrees with others that the characteristics of persons or situations are perfect or excellent, but one does not have or pursue these ideals oneself. For instance, I know that being a mother is an ideal for many women and recognise that it is an excellence indeed, but I do not have the ideal myself. Thirdly, people have and pursue certain ideals, of which I have already given several examples.

The second possibility, i.e. (teaching the) recognition of religious ideals, is complex in case of religious ideals in the broad sense. The way in which I defined religious ideals in the narrow sense implies that these can only be recognised within a (particular) religion. However, religious ideals in the broad sense may not only be recognised by adherents of a particular religion – who may also have and pursue the broad religious ideals of their religious tradition and community – others can agree that religious ideals in the broad sense indeed refer to excellences or perfections. However, although 'outsiders' can recognise the moral, economic, aesthetic or other ideal, they will not recognise the religious interpretation of it if they do not adhere to the religion(s). As I have said before, ideals tend to be abstract or relatively vague, for instance the ideal of justice or being just or the ideal of wisdom or beauty. Therefore, people of different convictions can agree on excellences or perfection *in abstracto*. If one recognises the ideal for non-religious reasons, it is possible to say that one shares the view that a characteristic of a person or situation is an ideal but one cannot call it a religious ideal. For instance, people will recognise that being a caring person is an ideal and many pursue this ideal. However, one may do so for humanistic reasons, for moral reasons or for religious reasons. But it is also possible that within a particular religious tradition people have different interpretations of the ideal and that they recognise the religious ideals of the other believers, but have and pursue their own interpretation.

155

For instance, within Christianity the ideals of humanity and justice have a particular conception, but charitable love and forgiving the offender to which Christians are called by Jesus in his Sermon on the Mount is interpreted in radically different ways by Christians.[6] Note that the abstract character of ideals helps pupils to discover that there may be more similarities between their own point of view and those of citizens they thought to be completely different and that there are more differences between their views and those from people within their own communities than they had expected. This allows them to develop more nuanced views against others and their own in-group.

In relation to the three types of relation of persons to ideals, it is possible to make a distinction between three types of intentions of teachers. Firstly, the aim may be that pupils know about religious ideals and understand why adherents to the religious tradition believe that these are ideals. This is clearly a form of teaching about religious ideals. Secondly, teachers may have the intention that pupils come to recognise religious ideals. They may believe there are good reasons for claiming that certain characteristics of persons or situations are excellent or perfect and that the pupils should understand and agree with these reasons too. Note that this intention of the teacher does not mean that the teacher indoctrinates her pupils. If she provides reasons, aims to convince pupils with her arguments, but does not force them, she educates and does not indoctrinate. This intention can be called teaching religious ideals. Thirdly, teachers may aspire that pupils will have and pursue the religious ideals too, which can be perceived of as an aspect of teaching into a religion. The last possibility does not fall within the two general of RE in the Netherlands that I mentioned in the introduction. It is not only not legally justified at public schools but also rejected on moral grounds, because as an institution of a liberal democratic state these schools are expected not to promote a particular conception of the good life, which teachers do in promoting the pursuit of religious ideals. Denominational schools may promote that pupils come to have and pursue particular religious ideals, but they do not have to and some do not do so.

Teaching about Religious Ideals and Citizenship Education

As I wrote in the introduction, the Dutch state prescribes that pupils learn that there is diversity of religious views (in other words, that they acquire knowledge) and learn to respect people's rights to have their own views on religious matters (in other words, that they develop a certain disposition). Note that the Dutch state does not demand that pupils learn to respect the views of fellow citizens, but to respect their freedom to have and live according to their own views. This is an important distinction, because some views do not deserve respect from a moral or liberal democratic point of view, for instance those that imply discrimination or suppression of particular groups. But it is also possible that one cannot respect the view of another because this is sharp contrast with one's own beliefs even though it does not fall below a moral standard or liberal political standard. When pupils do not learn to make this distinction, they may not learn what it means to be a tolerant citizen, for they may believe that only those who agree with them deserve their respect. Of course, they may acquire a tolerant attitude outside the school, but the state cannot be certain that they do. Pupils who are raised within an intolerant family or by parents with very strict religious views, possibly do not learn that others also have the right to have their beliefs.[7] However, precisely the fact that not all beliefs or the way in which ideals are pursued deserve respect shows the importance of an evaluation of ideals and their pursuit to which I will return in a moment.

Teaching about religious ideals is in my view instrumental, but importantly so, to citizenship education. The aim that pupils learn to respect diversity can in principle be combined with religious absolutism and religious pluralism, because respect for diversity can be conceived of as a strictly civic disposition that can be separated from one's personal views. Respecting that others have different views does not mean that one has to accept the view that there is a possibility that they may be right or that pupils need to learn to critically review their own conceptions of the good life (see for instance Steutel & Spiecker, 2011). However, I side with Miedema and Ter Avest (2011) in endorsing McLaughlin's maximal conception of citizenship education, which requires "a considerable degree of explicit understanding of democratic principles, values and procedures on the part of the citizen, together with the dispositions and capacities required for participation in democratic citizenship generously conceived" (1992, p. 237).

While teaching about a plurality of religious ideals does not necessarily have the intention that pupils will come to underwrite religious pluralism or fallibilism, these epistemological positions obviously will be discussed. When I look back at my own schooling, this is what I sometimes missed in teachers, and may be a personal reason for defending this position. For instance, while we read Lessing's *Nathan der Weise* with the parable of the three rings during our German lessons, raising critical questions with regard to the absolutist religious conviction of our German teacher was not appreciated. We analysed the parable in class and the teacher did explain that the rings stood for the three major religions, but he stopped a discussion about whether or not Lessing was right to suggest that we cannot know which of the three religions is the true.

Teaching the Pursuit of Religious Ideals

As I have mentioned, teaching pupils about religious ideals encloses teaching about the ways in which these ideals are pursued. In addition to teaching this content, citizenship education in a liberal democracy also requires that pupils are presented with criteria for evaluating these ideals and their pursuit. They should not only learn that citizens have various ideals and that people who exemplify these ideals are admired, but also whether or not admiration is appropriate. These criteria are also helpful to explain to pupils the difference between evaluating the religious ideals and the pursuit thereof.

In a previous article I wrote with Stijn Sieckelinck (2009), we introduced three sets of criteria to evaluate a person's commitment to and pursuit of her ideals. We suggested that the commitment and pursuit of ideals have to be rational, moral and prudent. The criteria of rationality and morality are particularly relevant in the context of this article. The criterion of prudence is related to the interests of the person who has the ideal. For instance, the pursuit of an ideal is not prudent if one thereby undermines one's own well-being. In citizenship education this criterion is less important than rationality and morality, because the central aim of citizenship education is not to enhance personal well-being, but the well-being of society and other citizens.

Sieckelinck and I described the criterion of rationality among others in terms of practical rationality, i.e. the way in which a person pursues her ideals should be intelligible in terms of means and ends. This criterion is also helpful in evaluating the pursuit of religious ideals where the consistency between means and ends can be called the logical-religious criterion. Take for instance the ideal that one love one's neighbour as oneself. Understood as an ideal, this imperative could be taken to mean that one loves all other human beings as oneself. It seems quite implausible that this ideal can be pursued by killing those who do not belong to one's religious in-group. However, loving one's neighbour can be pursued in various ways. A critical rational evaluation of religious ideals may not seem to be an intelligible exercise. While there may be reasons to believe this is the case for religious ideals in the strict sense, it is certainly possible to stimulate pupils to think critically about religious ideals in the broad sense and to ask them to investigate the sources for the religious conceptions of for instance economic ideals, moral ideals or social ideals, to compare them and to critically evaluate these conceptions.

The moral criterion is particularly important in evaluating the pursuit of religious ideals, be they moral ideals or not, but also in the evaluation of the religious ideals. Many religious exemplars are particularly seen as exemplary because of the moral quality of the ideals they pursue as well as the way in which they pursue them. In contrast, the intolerance of some believers, terrorist attacks and religious wars illustrate the immoral quality of the way in which they are pursued. Pupils and students need to learn that Martin Luther King, Ghandi and Shirin Ebadi are exemplary not only for their ideals, but also because of the way in which they pursue(d) their ideals. Equally, they should also learn that religious wars or terrorist attacks do not necessarily mean that the ideals of these persons are immoral. This assists students to make a nuanced judgement. With this I do not only mean that they should be taught not to simplistically generalise, for instance that all Muslims are violent, but also that they do not simply equate the pursuit of the ideals with the ideals themselves, for instance that Islam is an inherently violent religion. Learning to make these distinctions may be conducive to diminish intolerance against Muslims that is currently prevalent in the Netherlands and may also help to reduce feelings of perceived injustice of Muslims. These outcomes are important in civic education and are beneficial to building a tolerant liberal democratic society.

Thus far I have explored the idea that teaching pupils about religious ideals and assisting them to become good evaluators of religious ideals and their pursuit are important aspects of RE and citizenship education. Pupils learn about the important values of believers, why religious ideals and persons who pursue religious ideals are admired and that these ideals can be a source of great deeds as well as grave misdeeds. However, teaching about religious ideals may have another influence, namely that students learn from ideals. I will briefly address this issue.

Teaching about Religious Ideals and Learning from Religious Ideals

In a recent article, Miedema and Ter Avest argue that religious citizenship education, which in their view should be a combination of religious education and a maximal conception of citizenship education, is "fully combinable with what has been claimed elsewhere to be the aim of education in schools, that is that every child and youngster in every school should be able to develop her or his personal identity or personhood" (2011, p. 414). They suggest that religious citizenship education and identity development go hand in hand.

I agree with them, but I hesitate to use the notion 'self-responsible religious self-determination'. Even though they maintain that religious self-determination means that a person is able to shape the identity in relation to religion, not that s/he is a religious adherent and although they have a broad conception of 'religion', I think the terminology is confusing. But more importantly, I do not want to defend the position that all schools have a role in the religious development of their pupils, as I think they do suggest. However, I do believe it is valuable that pupils are presented with values that are not central to mainstream culture. An encounter with religious ideals provides pupils with alternative to develop their own identity, be it religious or not. It is possible that pupils come to recognise certain religious ideals or even see these ideals as a source of inspiration and motivation in their lives, even though this is not the intention of the school.[8]

As already mentioned, this could be true for broad religious ideals in particular. Moreover, it is not only possible that students will want to pursue these ideals *in abstracto*, but also recognise and have a particular religious conception of these ideals. For instance, there may be pupils who come to recognise religious conceptions of ideals like charity (or being 'materialistically' generous), chastity (or being sexually loyal to one person), or the view that the ideal person is someone who has certain traits of character rather than someone who has certain means. It should be noted, however, as I have said before, that these ideals are only called religious ideals if pupils not only have or recognise these ideals, but also a religious conception of them.

IN CONCLUSION

I have given several examples of the influence of my upbringing and education that I think have influenced (the development of) my academic views. I want to end with a teacher from my primary school, who also seems to have played a formative role in this respect (see also De Ruyter, 2006). When I was a fourth grade pupil, the Allende government was overthrown in Chile. My teacher invited the pupils to write a letter to Nelson Rockefeller asking him to explain the reason for the CIA's interference in Chile. The same teacher tried to convince us, following an idealistic national campaign, not to eat Outspan oranges, because they were grown in South Africa, explaining the situation in that county and why racism and discrimination are (religiously-) morally wrong. Even though both countries were on the other side of the earth, we were (at least in my recollection) very serious in our efforts to try to make the world a better place. One might argue that we were invited to think about ideals in a global setting at too young an age and that we were given a rather simplistic view of politics and the way in which they can be influenced. However, we did learn that it is important to think about a better world in which moral ideals, in our case also inspired by Protestant convictions, prevail. This example brings me to my final remark.

Presenting religious ideals that have inspired people and assisting pupils to develop the capacities to reflect upon these ideals is not only valuable for children as future citizens of a liberal democracy, but also for the pupils and teachers in schools. In thinking about religious ideals, pupils are invited to (literally) picture their own dreams, discuss with fellow pupils what their (religious) ideals are, why they have them and to discover the similarities and differences between their ideals. In doing so they not only practice and develop their moral abilities that they need as adults, but also contribute to the realisation of a moral democratic school in which pupils with a diversity of convictions are able to live and learn together. Having begun with a quote of an eminent pragmatist thinker, I believe there is no better way than ending a contribution to a liber amicorum for Siebren Miedema than with this Deweyan justification for teaching religious ideals.

NOTES

[1] In the next section I will further elucidate the idea teaching religious ideals. However, at this point it is important to clarify that I use 'teaching' (about/from/into) for the intention of teachers and 'learning' (about and from) for the effect on pupils. This effect can be intentionally pursued by the teacher (teaching into or teaching with the intention that pupils learn from), but it can also be the unintentional effect from teaching about.

[2] By referring to two of the central themes of Miedema, I also want to illustrate that while our research paths have separated since our intensive cooperation between 1993 and 1999, there are still clearly common themes in our current work.

[3] I agree with White who claims that RE should also include negative aspects of religions. In the context of this article, these would be the ways in which religious ideals are pursued, but can also be religious ideals that are considered to be morally heinous by those who do not recognise these ideals.

[4] 'Religious ideals' is the generic name of a category consisting of a wide range of ideals of specific religions, for instance Christian, Islamic, Buddhist, Hindu or Jewish ideals. These labels are quite general and can be specified into more specific denominational ideals, like Roman Catholic, Protestant, Eastern Orthodox ideals, etc.

[5] See, for example, Buijs, Demand, and Hamdy (2006).

[6] The abstract character of (religious) ideals, which makes possible personal interpretations of ideals draws our attention to another point that Van der Kooij, Miedema and I (2013) defend, namely that it is important to make a distinction between organised and personal worldviews.

[7] Actually, empirical research among adolescents and their parents points to a significant concordance with regard to Right-Wing Authoritarianism and Social Dominance Orientation in parents and adolescents (see for instance Duriez & Soenens, 2009).

[8] Obviously, if reflection can lead to recognition it is also possible that pupils adopt religious ideals in the strict sense (option c), which might for some be a reason to argue against teaching religious ideals in common schools.

REFERENCES

Brighouse, H. (2005). Channel one, the anti-commercial principle and the discontinuous ethos. *Educational Policy, 19*(3), 528-549.

Buijs, F. J. Demant, F., & Hamdy, A. (2006). *Strijders van eigen bodem. Radicale en democratische moslims in Nederland.* Amsterdam: Amsterdam University Press.

De Ruyter, D. J. (2006). Be ye perfect? Religious ideals in education. *Journal of Beliefs and Values, 27*(3), 269-280.

De Ruyter, D. J. (2006). Whose utopia/which ideals? About the importance of societal and personal ideals in education. In M. A. Peters & J. Freeman-Moir (eds.), *Edutopias: New utopian thinking in education.* Rotterdam/Taipei: Sense Publishers.

De Ruyter, D. J., & Merry, M. S. (2009). Why education in public schools should include religious ideals. *Studies in Philosophy and Education, 28*(4), 295-311.

Duriez, B., & Soenens, B. (2009). The intergenerational transmission of racism: The role of right-wing authoritarianism and social dominance orientation. *Journal of Research in Personality, 43*(5), 906-909.

James, W. (1902). *The varieties of religious experience. A study in human nature.* Available via: http://selfdefinition.org/christian/William James -- Varieties of Religious Experience.pdf. Downloaded 4 February 2012.

McLaughlin, T. H. (1992). Citizenship, diversity and education. A philosophical perspective. *Journal of Moral Education, 21,* 235-250.

Miedema, S., & Ter Avest, I. (2011). In the flow to maximal interreligious citizenship education. *Religious Education, 106*(4), 410-424.

Sieckelinck,S. M. A.,& De Ruyter, D. J. (2009). Mad about ideals? Educating children to become reasonably passionate. *Educational Theory, 59*(2), 181-196.

Steutel, J., & Spiecker, B. (2011). Civic education in a liberal-democratic society. In D. J. de Ruyter & S. Miedema (eds.), *Moral education and development: A lifetime commitment* (pp. 193-208). Rotterdam/Boston/Taipei: Sense Publishers.

Van der Kooij, J. C., De Ruyter, D. J., & Miedema, S. (2013). 'Worldview': The meaning of the concept and the impact on Religious Education. *Religious Education, 108*(2).

AFFILIATIONS

Doret de Ruyter
Department of Research and Theory in Education
VU University Amsterdam
The Netherlands

FRIEDRICH SCHWEITZER

RELIGIOUS EDUCATION, IDENTITY AND FAITH IN (POST-)MODERNITY: MORE THAN A BIOGRAPHICAL APPROACH?

A Personal Attempt at Finding the Red Thread in My Academic Work on Religious Education

INTRODUCTION

When I was a young boy, maybe of seven years,
I envied an older boy who told me that he now had time
to do something with me, exactly one hour.
Little did I realize that me not having time, "exactly one hour",
really meant that I had all the time in the world.
Today, I sometimes envy those colleagues who have their clear-cut approaches to
religious education, "exactly defined".
Do I not realize that I, also, may have one?

I rarely think about 'my approach' to religious education. Yet sometimes others tell me that my name stands for a biographical approach. Are they right?

My more than 30 years of work in this academic area after graduation should have produced enough evidence for whatever model I might actually have followed. This is why I start this essay with biographical reflections on my work, trying, as it were, to look over my own shoulder. My biographical reflections will, however, not be personal in the sense of a psychological narrative. The space available in a necessarily short chapter would hardly allow for developing such a narrative in any depth, and without at least striving for such depth it would be deemed to turn into a contradiction in itself.

MY APPROACH TO RELIGIOUS EDUCATION: A BIOGRAPHICAL SKETCH

In this section, I will try to give readers a brief overview on my work in the field of religious education. In doing so, I will roughly follow the chronological order.[1]

Bringing Together Theology, Education, and the Social Sciences

I come from a family that has a long history with the pastoral profession. For several centuries, the male ancestors on my father's side were all ministers. Yet this tradition came to an end when my grandfather decided that he wanted to

I. ter Avest (ed.), On the Edge: (Auto)biography and Pedagogical Theories on Religious Education, 163–174.

become a medical doctor. He became the founder of a new tradition for the family. Until today, there are a number of medical doctors in my family, including my brother and my daughter.

Quite independently of the choice of a subject there was no doubt with my parents or myself that I should go to university. I had always been a very good student and finished the German Gymnasium as prospective recipient of an elite-type scholarship.

When I actually entered the university in 1974, I was rather unclear what course of study I should pursue. I had a strong interest in education but even more in understanding human life. This vaguely defined interest – at that time, it did not appear vague to me at all but very much to those I talked to about my plans – finally brought me to theology and, a little later, to education which means that I actually pursued two degrees, one in theology and one in education. What made both fields so exciting for me at that time was the (re-)discovery of the social sciences that was going on in parts of both fields – sociology and psychology most of all but also a number of related disciplines like cultural studies.

Prime examples were the writings of Erik H. Erikson, Lawrence Kohlberg, and George Herbert Mead as well as of Jürgen Habermas who drew on their theories for his social philosophy. Their work strongly influenced my thinking at that time. It was no surprise then that the formation and development of personal identity became the topic of my dissertation (Schweitzer, 1985), partly written at Harvard University in the early 1980s where, again, I followed my dual interest in theology and education, and partly at Tübingen University where I eventually earned my doctoral degree (in social sciences). It was during my time as a postgraduate student in the United States when it first dawned on me that my teachers back in Germany as well as the famous libraries there might in fact not know or hold everything that could be important for me. Ever since, trying to internationalize my own work and consequently the understanding of religious education has remained a strong motive for me. A few years later, ISREV (*International Seminar on Religious Education and Values*) became a true haven for me in this respect.

Beyond my dissertation, I wrote a number of books strongly influenced by Piagetian developmental psychology – including its religious varieties set forth in the theories of James W. Fowler and Fritz Oser who also had become personal friends of mine – as well as by psychoanalytic approaches and sociological perspectives. These books of mine covered topics like 'Life History and Religion' (Schweitzer, 1987), 'Religious Education in Adolescence' (Schweitzer, 1996), or 'Developmental Psychology and Teaching Religion' (Schweitzer et al., 1995). Another major study, my theological habilitation (Schweitzer, 1992), addressed a similar topic, 'The Religion of the Child'. Yet for the most part, this book was based on historical research (inspired among others by the seminal work of Philippe Ariès), tracing Protestant views of the child and of childhood religion since the time of the Reformation and especially after the onset of modernity. For my own approach, this piece of research opened up a whole new domain that I had not been introduced to when I was trained. Due to the emphasis on social scientific approaches, the value of historical understandings had all but disappeared from the academic curriculum in our field. I never became a real history scholar but I have remained interested in what sometimes is called the historical-systematic approach, i.e., the attempt of understanding key concepts in the field of education by studying their vicissitudes in history. In my case, this mostly refers to understanding how the meaning of religious education has changed under the impact of social and cultural modernization. Until today, the clearest and most impressive example of the new ways of thinking about religious education can be found in the work of Jean-Jacques Rousseau.

In many ways, especially through working on Rousseau's *Emile*, published in 1762, and through encountering his plea against religious education in childhood it became clear to me that there was a true watershed between what people took for granted in catechetics before and in religious education after the eighteenth century. What was new – and still continues to play a major role until today – is the conviction that even the most important beliefs or dogmas cannot legitimately override the needs and limits of the human being that, in the philosophy of education, is referred to as *educandus*, i.e., the young person. The same is true for the claims of reason. Religious education has to be clear on how the religious traditions and convictions relate to the insights of modern science and how the young person can come to terms with conflicting interpretations of reality.

The longer I worked on the history of religious education, the clearer it became to me that this kind of attitude was not only due to personal choice of to a certain philosophical stance. Instead it was itself the expression of a society and culture that had deeply changed, among others under the impact of forces like industrialization and urbanization.

The Need to Broaden My Views: The Meaning and Scope of Academic Disciplines

Broadening my approach in order to include historical research coincided with another new interest that refers to theoretical questions concerning the meaning and scope of academic disciplines. Since the early 1990s, I have been interested in practical theology which, to some degree at least in the German speaking world and as far as it concerns theology, is considered the umbrella or 'mother' discipline to which religious education belongs as one of its sub-disciplines (cf. Schweitzer & Van der Ven, 1999). At that time, Friedrich Schleiermacher's work in theology as well as in education started to fascinate me. Just like myself, Schleiermacher was deeply interested in both, in theology as well as in education. Moreover, his famous writings on the philosophy of education but also his speeches on religion after the Enlightenment allowed me to develop a new understanding of my own work as premised on the ideas of modernity. I consider Schleiermacher the true father of the modern discipline of religious education that took over from the earlier period of traditional catechetics.

Especially during the first decade of the new century I was able, together with Richard R. Osmer of Princeton, to conduct an international comparative study on the development of religious education in Germany and in the United States during the twentieth century (Osmer & Schweitzer, 2003) – a study that, at least for us as

165

authors, made it clear how the unfolding landscape of religious education in two different locations can be interpreted meaningfully by understanding the respective changes as different but parallel responses to the challenges of social and cultural modernization. This study became the starting point for a major project on the same topic referring to Germany (Schweitzer & Simojoki, 2005; Schweitzer et al., 2010a, 2010b). This research used religious education journals as its material object in tracing the development of religious education as a modern discipline.

At the same time, I had the opportunity to expand my empirical work as well – with studies on religious education at school, on religion in German kindergartens, and also on confirmation work. Especially the study on confirmation work that was carried out in seven European countries, allowed me to come back to my international interests and to cooperate with many colleagues from other countries (Schweitzer, Ilg, & Simojoki, 2010).

PLURALISM: A KEY CONCEPT FOR RELIGIOUS EDUCATION

I do not remember when the concept of pluralism first became important to me and my work. In my articles it starts to show up in the 1990s. I assume that there was an influence from a number of directions – from the first debates on multiculturalism in the 1980s, from my increasing international exposure but also from the philosophical discussions on postmodernity. In any case, this concept has deeply influenced my work ever since.

In the year 2000, I was invited to be the Stone Lecturer at Princeton Theological Seminary. This lecture series gave me the chance to review some of my work within an international context. I chose to do the Stone Lectures on "The Postmodern Life Cycle" which also became the title of the book I later developed from these lectures (Schweitzer, 2004). In terms of my understanding of religious education, it added at least two new insights for me:

- The traditional understanding of the life cycle (Erik H. Erikson) as well as of human development (Kohlberg, Fowler, Oser) is in need of a new framework. The new framework must also include our understanding of personal identity because the traditional guiding images of identity formation do not remain the same in postmodernity.
- Given the increasingly plural situation in western societies—culturally but also religiously – the concept of pluralism must play a key role for our understanding of religious education. Plurality is the situation we have to face. Principled pluralism that equally avoids fundamentalism as well as relativism in the response to plurality, should be the aim of religious education.

The Ecumenical and Interreligious Dimension

More and more, plurality includes the presence of different religions and of different religious traditions that are also pluralistic in themselves. Given the presence of Islam in Germany, it is no surprise then that my work has come to include more and more questions of interreligious education, especially during the last ten years. Confining my interests to just one tradition without being aware of other traditions could hardly make sense anymore. In addition to this, it became clear to me that religious education can only make a contribution to society if it is open to the pluriform religious situations characteristic of the present time.

A first step in opening up for other traditions beyond Protestantism has been the intensive cooperation with my Catholic colleague Albert Biesinger here at Tübingen. In a cooperative manner that is still rare in Germany, despite the characteristic situation with the two denominations as the major religious bodies in this country, together we conducted several research projects on ecumenical cooperation in religious education, lectured together, taught together and supported each other in our research interests and in organizing conferences and public events in relationship to religious education (Schweitzer & Biesinger, 2002).

With more than four million Muslims living in Germany, especially cooperation with Muslim religious educators has become an important and enriching experience for me as well. Looking at processes of teaching from a Christian as well as from a Muslim perspective made me aware how far our views are impregnated by deeply rooted religious presuppositions, not only concerning content (which is to be expected) but also concerning the understanding of the child or the meaning of learning itself. At this point, this cooperation still is in its early phases for me. I clearly hope to do more work in this direction in the coming years, for example, by conducting a study on how young people deal with religious differences and how they can be supported in finding peaceful and tolerant ways of living together with others who are different from them.

So far in this interreligious cooperation, an experience from interdenominational – Christian ecumenical – cooperation with Catholic colleagues repeated itself. The more I have worked with colleagues with religious backgrounds different from my own, the more I have become aware of my own theological convictions as a Protestant. For me, the bible remains a decisive basis for my personal faith as well as for my understanding of theology or my understanding of what the church should be. Moreover, the justification never through my achievements but by "faith alone", obviously is one of my deepest convictions.

DOES IT FIT TOGETHER? CONTOURS OF MY APPROACH TO RELIGIOUS EDUCATION

In this section, I leave behind the biographical mode in order to describe my understanding of religious education (as a summary cf. Schweitzer, 2006). This understanding is related to praxis but the focus is on my academic approach.

Religious Education as a Modern Discipline: Interdisciplinary and Dialogical

From my perspective, there can be no doubt that religious education is a modern discipline. In Germany as well as in many other western countries, this discipline has come to replace traditional forms of catechetics, not because of a free choice of modern-minded educators or theologians but due to the pressures of social and cultural modernization described above.

In my view, however, it is not enough to understand religious education as a modern discipline in the sense of history. It is certainly true that this discipline – and even the term itself – has come into existence not before the nineteenth century or, concerning the new term, not before the twentieth century. When I call religious education a modern discipline, I also refer to the normative implications of this historical development. Religious education *must* be modern—it has to face up to modernity with its specific truth claims – because otherwise it will not be able to do justice to the needs of today's inhabitants of the western world.

The pressures of modernity make themselves felt simultaneously in different ways. One important example is the impact of competing truth claims that religious convictions now encounter in society – truth claims of non-religious worldviews or, in a more general sense, the truth claims of science. The tension between faith in God as the creator on the one hand and evolutionary theory on the other may be taken as a corollary of this competition. Parallel to this article, I am working on a small book addressing the conflicting views of creation, evolutionary theory, creationism, and intelligent design (Schweitzer, 2012). In this book, I argue for a complementary understanding of science and religion by pointing out that they are different ways of looking at the world and that both are needed and can be maintained at the same time, although they cannot be unified by a single overarching theory or explanation.

Moreover, ever since the Enlightenment, religious education has been criticized for not meeting the standards of what should be accepted as educational. From Jean-Jacques Rousseau to Paul Hirst, philosophers of education have suggested that "Christian education" is a contradiction in terms. All education must be open-minded and therefore open-ended. According to this view, education can never be Christian because this would exclude the very openness on which true education is premised.

This kind of critical argument implies, at a more practical level, that philosophers of education have assumed the right to evaluate the educational quality of religious education. The most famous example for this is again Rousseau. From his perspective, even the best theological arguments can never be enough to justify pedagogical practices. The only grounds on which such practices can be justified must be educational. Rousseau's plea against religious education in childhood means just this. It was hardly meant to introduce a new kind of education without religion – something no one could realistically expect in the eighteenth century – but to demonstrate the new power of educational principles that, for Rousseau, must have precedence over any religious dogma.

It is easy to see that, at least in recent decades, what used to be academic debates between professors or philosophers, has turned into popular issues. Due to the process of individualization as described by many sociologists, the former authority of institutions like the church is on the wane. The fact that a church maintains certain views or that a certain pedagogical program is offered by a church no longer is considered a reason for agreeing to it or to assume a high quality of such a program.

In my understanding, a first consequence for religious education must be to develop an approach that is capable of facing up to such challenges. For me, the new designation – religious education – means just this: a modern discipline, a discipline in line with the requirements of modern life and most of all with the actual experiences of growing up in a pluralistic society.

It is no coincidence that this discipline also implies interdisciplinary cooperation. Theology cannot be the only source on which religious education can draw. Other disciplines like education and the social sciences must be partners in constant dialogue for religious education – even if, as experience seems to show, these disciplines often are not very likely to be responsive to questions relating to religion (Schweitzer, 2003). In my own work, for example, developmental psychology has played an enriching role in helping us understand the ways in which children make sense of the world. Most of today's academic psychology, however, does not show much interest in religion anymore.

The more pluralistic society becomes, the more there is a need for additional partners in dialogue. Religious and cultural studies must inform religious education about the religious situation of our present. Recently, the attempt of establishing not only Islamic Studies but full-blown Islamic Theological Faculties in Europe points to another necessary partnership. To teach about Islam within Christian education necessarily includes not only expertise concerning Islam but also requires listening to the self-understanding of Muslims. It is fascinating for me to read the Quran and to compare it to the Bible. Comparing the stories of the birth of Jesus in the Gospel of Luke and in Sura 19 is an example that is becoming popular in religious education. Yet how can I understand the meaning of what is said about Jesus in the Quran without the cooperation and help of Muslim scholars? In this respect, not only cooperation with Muslim colleagues has been of help for me but also the Muslim students attending my classes have become important partners in dialogue. I find it quite enriching to work with classes that are religiously diverse, and I am also convinced that students of Christian theology can greatly profit from the interreligious encounters that such classes can entail.

Finally, we also have to be aware of the disciplinary presuppositions for modern religious education. Traditional catechetics simply was part of theology. Catechetics often was understood to be an immediate outcome of dogmatics. With the new discipline of practical theology, religious education could assume a new position within the theological course of study, thus gaining more independence from doctrinal issues and more openness for educational aims. At the same time, religious education became an object of study within general education and other disciplines that claim independence from theology altogether. The disciplinary constitution of religious education must be in line with this situation, allowing for multiple disciplinary relationships within the academic world.

FRIEDRICH SCHWEITZER

PRINCIPLED PLURALISM AS THE AIM OF RELIGIOUS EDUCATION

The context in which religious education is taking place, is increasingly plural. Most often, two dangers are identified as characteristic of such a context. The one is fundamentalism which is then interpreted as the attempt of withdrawing from the ambiguities of the cultural and religious situation by fully identifying with one and only one position and truth. The other danger is relativism. In this case, the ambiguities are redefined, so that they no longer will threaten the individual but can be experienced as enriching choices.

Contrary to both of these attitudes, principled pluralism is not opposed to the plural situation and it is not premised on not accepting permanent tensions between different truth claims. Yet not all options are considered of equal value either. Instead, education should afford the individual person with the ability to make critical choices, on the basis of considered judgment.

Principled pluralism should not be viewed as an abstract ability. With religion, there is little space for the disinterested bystander. Moreover, while religious identities cannot be the aim of religious education for a whole number of reasons, religious education should still support young people in the process of developing such an identity in the sense of finding possibilities for at least partial identifications with a religious tradition or – as seems the case more often today – for combining elements from different traditions in a responsible manner. From this perspective, principled pluralism as the aim of religious education can also be seen as simultaneous support for both, religious identity and dialogical abilities.

Biographical and Child-oriented

Within the framework of religious education as a modern discipline, the biographical approach takes on additional meaning. This approach can be appreciated for its effectiveness. Taking people seriously in their biographically determined situations is the only way for religious education to effectively reach today's children, adolescents, or adults.

Yet the biographical approach implies much more than a certain didactic technique. It means that the specifically modern situation of individual subjectivity that is claiming indispensable rights vis-à-vis all traditions and institutions, must be taken seriously from the beginning. In this situation, these rights can not be overruled by the objectivity of the content to be learned or by social institutions invested with an authority prior to the rights of the individual.

Moreover, the biographical approach is premised on the valuation of experience. Ever since the Enlightenment, there has been the demand that religious faith should be in line with personal experience. Modern people tend to believe only that which they can verify from their own experience. The decisive question for them is what makes sense to them, in accordance with their personal experiences.

From a somewhat different perspective, the tendency of child-orientation is another variation of the new valuation of the individual person. Modern religious education then must be child-oriented from the beginning. And again, the question

170

of what can count as appropriate for children cannot be determined by religious education without reference to general education and the social sciences.

In my own work, I have tried to extend the principle of child-orientation in order to connect it to a children's rights approach (Schweitzer, 2000). The children's rights movement is a typical twentieth century phenomenon, exemplifying the modern turn in general education. For religious education this implies that it should be based on children's right to religion, in the sense of having access to educational or nurturing resources that will support the child religiously.

METHODOLOGY

The understanding of religious education described so far, also presupposes a certain methodology. In this respect, the threefold approach of historical, systematic, and empirical methods offers a first orientation that I still consider helpful. Historical and hermeneutic methods are indispensable for appropriating the religious and cultural traditions on which religious education has to draw. These methods are also needed in respect to the traditions of religious education itself. Yet as helpful historical insights may be, there also is the need for a comprehensive theory of religious education that is based on systematic and analytic methods. Moreover, empirical approaches play an important role in religious education in different respects. Interdisciplinary relationships to the social sciences and to general education often refer to empirical research. Within religious education itself, there is an increasing need for empirical research as a basis for testing and evaluating its own effects.

Sometimes methods of evaluation are considered another methodological approach in religious education. While this may make sense in terms of the aims of such research, the methods used by it inevitably tend to be the ones mentioned above. The same holds true for international comparative research in religious education that, in my understanding, should play a much stronger role in the future.

Faith and the Need for Theology

Some religious educators have used the argument of modernity for severing the traditional ties between religious education and theology. The best example probably is religious education in the UK where at least main representatives of the discipline claim that religious education is much better off without theology.

In my own understanding, the relationship between religious education and theology can only be given up at a high price. Religious education is in need of theology in order to authentically include the self-interpretations of religious traditions. Theology is also needed for interreligious dialogue. A religious studies approach tends to bypass the different theological positions in favor of more abstract interpretations. Yet true dialogue presupposes difference.

Finally, religious education is in need of theology for having a disciplinary background, especially in the field of didactics and the school where the different subjects typically presuppose such a discipline. This is not the place for an

171

extensive discussion of the question why I do not consider religious studies as a suitable candidate to replace theology ion this respect. Suffice it to say that it is the normative and critical dimensions of theology that make it indispensable for religious education.

A MODEL FOR THE PEDAGOGY OF RELIGION: DIALOGICAL DIDACTICS WITH CHILDREN AND ADOLESCENTS AS THEOLOGIANS

Dialogical Didactics

In the context of German religious education, I have used a designation for my preferred didactical model that does not seem to lend itself to easy translation into English (Schweitzer et al., 2003). The designation is *Elementarisierung*, a concept that goes back to Pestalozzi in the late eighteenth century and to Wolfgang Klafki, the major twentieth century German representative in the field of general didactics. In the present context, I call it *dialogical didactics* because the different meanings of the term dialogue play a crucial role for this model.

In its first meaning, didactics is dialogical when it allows for a dialogical relationship between the learner as active subject and the content of teaching and learning. This understanding excludes all approaches to teaching and learning that are exclusively focused on the objective side of the relationship between learner and content (objectivist didactics). Instead it provides space for creative dialogue at different levels – the level of the learners' life worlds that must be addressed but also of their ways of making sense of things, for example, in terms of personal structures of cognition and interpretation. Moreover, the model also includes reference to truth claims and foresees critically examining different truth claims as part of the process of learning and teaching – an aspect that, in my understanding, must be part of religious education.

At another level, didactics is dialogical when it includes not only one religious tradition as it was the case with catechetics. It then refers to different denominations within Christianity but also to different religions like Judaism and Islam or other religions, depending on the context. Increasingly, it must also go beyond the religious sphere in order to include non-religious worldviews as well.

In my own work that, especially in this respect, builds upon the prior work of my academic teacher Karl Ernst Nipkow, I am using a model with five different dimensions specifying different aspects of didactics: content structures; experience; ways of constructing reality (especially in terms of cognitive structures); methods of teaching and learning; dealing with truth claims.

Children and adolescents as Theologians

Especially in the German speaking countries, child theology has become something like a movement within religious education (Schweitzer, 2011). In my understanding, this approach must include the theology produced by children (*theology of children*), theological conversations with children (*theology with children*), as well as theological impulses that children can work with (*theology for children*). More recently, this approach has been extended in order to also include adolescents (Schlag & Schweitzer, 2011).

In my understanding, viewing children and adolescents as theologians can become an important addition to the didactics of religious education. The understanding of a dialogical pedagogy of religious education already includes a strong emphasis on children and adolescents as active subjects. Suggesting to consider them as theologians takes this emphasis even further. It does not mean, however, that the difference between academic theology on the one hand and the theology produced by children or adolescents on the other should be overlooked. Yet it does mean to take seriously that not only adults in theology are reflecting about their faith but that this reflective activity can also be found with children and adolescents.

Yet at the same time, framing the understanding of children and adolescents as theologians didactically and insisting on the need for (religious) education is what distinguishes my approach from the well-known naïve attempts of expecting everything from the children themselves, i.e., from children that, beforehand, had to be idealized.

MORE THAN A BIOGRAPHICAL APPROACH?

In the beginning of this essay I made reference to those who tell me that I stand for a biographical approach to religious education. Are they right? I think, only to a degree.

They are right in terms of my many efforts and publications that are meant to do justice to children, adolescents, and adults as individual persons with a certain background, from certain life worlds and with their biographies. They are wrong to the degree that my focus on biographies hinges upon a much broader social, societal, and religious framework.

NOTES

[1]   Since this is an essay on my approach to religious education I limit the references to my own publications. Moreover, I will only reference books.

REFERENCES

(Books by Friedrich Schweitzer, some of them have been translated in other languages, Danish, Dutch, Hungarian, Japanese, and Korean; the English titles are original publications)

Schweitzer, F. (1985). *Identität und Erziehung. Was kann der Identitätsbegriff für die Pädagogik leisten?* Weinheim/Basel.
Schweitzer, F. (1987). *Lebensgeschichte und Religion. Religiöse Entwicklung und Erziehung im Kindes- und Jugendalter.* München.
Schweitzer, F. (1992). *Die Religion des Kindes. Zur Problemgeschichte einer religionspädagogischen Grundfrage.* Gütersloh.

FRIEDRICH SCHWEITZER

Schweitzer, F. (1996). *Die Suche nach eigenem Glauben. Einführung in die Religionspädagogik des Jugendalters.* Gütersloh.
Schweitzer, F. (2000). *Das Recht des Kindes auf Religion. Ermutigungen für Eltern und Erzieher.* Gütersloh.
Schweitzer, F. (2003). *Pädagogik und Religion. Eine Einführung* (Grundriss der Pädagogik/ Erziehungswissenschaft Bd. 19). Stuttgart.
Schweitzer, F. (2004). *The Postmodern Life Cycle: Challenges for Church and Theology.* St. Louis.
Schweitzer, F. (2006). *Religionspädagogik* (Lehrbuch Praktische Theologie 1). Gütersloh.
Schweitzer, F. (2011a). *Kindertheologie und Elementarisierung. Wie religiöses Lernen mit Kindern gelingen kann.* Gütersloh.
Schweitzer, F. (2011b). *Menschenwürde und Bildung. Religiöse Voraussetzungen der Pädagogik in evangelischer Perspektive* (Theologische Studien NF 2). Zürich.
Schweitzer, F. (2012). *Schöpfungsglaube – nur für Kinder? Zum Streit zwischen Schöpfungsglaube, Evolutionstheorie und Kreationismus.* Neukirchen-Vluyn.
Schweitzer, F., & Osmer, R. R. (2003). *Religious education between modernization and globalization. New perspectives on the United States and Germany* (Studies in Practical Theology). Grand Rapids.
Schweitzer, F., & Schlag, T. (2011). *Brauchen Jugendliche Theologie? Jugendtheologie als Herausforderung und didaktische Perspektive.* Neukirchen-Vluyn.
Schweitzer, F., & Simojoki, H. (2005). *Moderne Religionspädagogik. Ihre Entwicklung und Identität* (Religionspädagogik in Pluraler Gesellschaft 5). Freiburg/Gütersloh.
Schweitzer, F., & Ven, J. A. van der (1999). *Practical theology – International perspectives* (Erfahrung und Theologie 34). Frankfurt/M.
Schweitzer, F., Nipkow, K. E. et al. (1995). *Religionsunterricht und Entwicklungspsychologie. Elementarisierung in der Praxis.* Gütersloh.
Schweitzer, F., Biesinger, A. et al. (2002). *Gemeinsamkeiten stärken – Unterschieden gerecht werden. Erfahrungen und Perspektiven zum konfessionell-kooperativen Religionsunterricht.* Freiburg/ Gütersloh.
Schweitzer, F., Nipkow, K. E. et al. (2003). *Elementarisierung im Religionsunterricht. Erfahrungen, Perspektiven, Beispiele.* Neukirchen-Vluyn.
Schweitzer, F., Ilg, W., & Simojoki, H. (2010a). *Confirmation work in Europe: Empirical results, experiences and challenges. A comparative study in seven countries.* Gütersloh.
Schweitzer, F., Simojoki, H. et al. (2010b). *Religionspädagogik als Wissenschaft. Transformationen der Disziplin im Spiegel ihrer Zeitschriften* (Religionspädagogik in Pluraler Gesellschaft 15). Freiburg.

AFFILIATION

Friedrich Schweitzer
Evangelisch-Theologisch Fakultät
Universität Tübingen

JACK SEYMOUR

RELIGIOUS EDUCATION AMONG FRIENDS AND STRANGERS

Contributions of Revisionist Educational History to Public Living

INTRODUCTION

*We engage in rituals
reinforcing identity and values,
playing and celebrating together;
and we are given artifacts,
like my knife and watch,
that carry meaning.*

Growing up surrounded by an extended family focused my identity and vocation. I was named after my grandfather, Jack. Many a day, I would sit with my grandmother as she told family stories, intentionally focusing on what it meant to be a 'Seymour'. My grandfather had died when I was five. As a result, my grandmother wanted me to know him and the obstacles he had overcome. She was amazingly truthful about strengths and weaknesses. With a limited public education, my grandfather trained himself, completing a high school equivalency and even some college. From working as a field hand, he moved to manage a factory that helped to build the automobile industry. My grandmother wanted me to know the values that Seymours' embodied: hard work, faithfulness, availability for others, and commitment to public life. Her stories reinforced my 'identity'.

After my grandfather's death, I was given artifacts that were his – a knife and a watch. I still have them in my desk drawer. They remind me of the virtues my grandmother inculcated. In fact, only recently did I realize that on the desk where I write are pictures of my grandparents, my parents, and my brother. They all look at me as I work; family expectations are still being communicated.

Furthermore, on Sunday afternoons, extended family members would often gather at my grandmother's home, some coming as far as 40 miles. As we played and dined together, values of our family heritage were further imprinted. Together we learned as we watched the family confront new circumstances.

In many ways, my family story parallels how faith is learned. Together those of us who share a faith are told stories that focus our identities and commitments, similar to my grandmother's stories forming lived virtues; we are surrounded by trusted communities that live our values, similar to the family gatherings that embody meanings and expectations; we engage in rituals reinforcing identity and

I. ter Avest (ed.), On the Edge: (Auto)biography and Pedagogical Theories on Religious Education, 175–185.

values, playing and celebrating together; and we are given artifacts, like my knife and watch, that carry meaning.

LEARNING RELIGIOUS FAITH

A religious faith is learned as stories and concepts are taught, as trusted communities nurture, as rituals of identity are engaged, and as sacred artifacts are shared. Faith also develops through the ways new circumstances are encountered – meanings are confirmed, are expressed in new ways, or even reshaped.

Therefore, learning a faith is a dynamic cultural project. A *cultural project* because it occurs explicitly and implicitly in the midst of a community of meaning – a community that shares stories, concepts, expectations, and hopes; *dynamic*, because deep meanings and values are always encountering new experiences and challenges. Most often new knowledge and new perspectives are mediated into those cultural patterns – *formation* continues as faith is re-enforced. Yet sometimes, contextual realities or new knowledge so challenge that those deepest meanings are shifted – *transformation* occurs (Seymour, Crain, & Crockett, 1993, pp. 31-39).

An example of this learning process is the development of the early Jesus movement into the Christian church. By the end of the first century, a Galilean movement rooted in Jewish culture had taken on characteristics of Roman civic administration. A localized Jesus movement consisting of disciples and followers became institutionalized into a growing church including persons very different from the originating twelve. In fact, that new 'church' even had to define who was in and who was not (thus concerns for heresy). Of course, none of these shifts occurred without disagreement. The process of 'cultural learning' is filled with contest. Groups affirm new meanings and others challenge their legitimacy.[1] For example, the connections with Rome further separated Christianity from its Jewish heritage. Or, doctrines defined by the early ecumenical councils united parts of the Christian movement, yet intentionally separated others.

Religious education is taught through a dynamic cultural process. *Friends* (here I mean those within a religious tradition) are taught to share and live out of common convictions, even with disagreements (also true for families). By sharing a common story, recognizing common artifacts, and engaging in common social practices, persons are taught a faith.

Religious Diversity

Yet, we live in a world made up of multiple communities. Religious diversity affects public life. Most Western democracies consist of diverse groups of people who hold diverse understandings of values and commitments. Even though one tradition may be more dominant, public life cannot be controlled by it. For those outside a dominant tradition (*strangers*), stories seem peculiar, artifacts are quaint, and social patterns are confusing or offensive – for example, a greeting with a hug may be much too intimate. Nevertheless, in our world of instant and global communication, we must find ways to share life on our planet. We must find ways to live our passionate faith commitments with 'strangers' in the public arena.[2]

Therefore, while religious education attends to how a particular community of 'friends' define or reinforce cultural patterns, to live in a diverse world requires contributions of both friends and strangers. We must engage religious commitments and values across traditions. If we do not shape public life in ways so we can thrive together, we will retreat to separate territories or continually fight.

These two questions of how a particular faith is dynamically passed on though time (with 'friends') and how that faith engages strangers have been central to my scholarship. Both are complementary and essential questions for religious education today.

Friends and Strangers

The methods I have found fruitful to address these questions include historical and ethnographic analysis. Gravitating to these methods was natural. I became interested in history as I mined my grandmother's stories of family responses to cultural changes. Also the conflicts I experienced between my family's faith, which included openness to people who were different, with my church's rigid definitions of truth drove me to ask religious questions. Luckily, at about the same time, during the social conflicts over race, war, and gender in the 1960s, I encountered public religious leaders working for the common good. Furthermore, studying religious and educational history has brought light on the processes of cultural change – on how religion contributes to public learning and living.

In this essay, I will develop a definition of education grounded in historical scholarship and define a method of 'critical, revisionist' educational history. Furthermore, I will offer implications for both religious education for friends and strangers. I hope these suggestions will inspire us to ask: *how do we teach faith traditions and how do we cross religious boundaries to build a world where we can live together?*

ON DEFINING EDUCATION AND RELIGIOUS EDUCATION

How does a tradition become the defining worldview for a people? How does a tradition develop and change, yet remain in continuity with its past? These are fundamental questions which historians of education have been asking in the U.S. since the beginning of the last century. An example is reflected in a book title published at the turn of the 20th century: *The Transit of Civilization from England to America in the Seventeenth Century* (1901). Edward Eggleston, at the end of a rich career, consisting of congregational ministry, editing, and writing, sought to define how the culture of the U.S. had become 'English'. Because of colonization, the identity of the nation could have become French, Dutch, or Spanish. Being enemies with England through bloody wars (of 1776 and of 1812) could have divided the U.S. from 'English' culture. Eggleston concluded that the cause for the 'transit' of English civilization to the U.S. was a *dynamic cultural education*

177

process, rooted in the social processes of trade, commerce, language and communication, as well as schooling.

Eggleston's work was taken up by educational historians. His insights helped to expand the understanding of education, seeing it as a complex practice of socialization where the values and convictions of a people were transferred and transformed through social participation.[3] For scholars of education, the conclusion became clear – any definition of education must be expansive. While schools teach, education also involves cultural practices – dynamic processes of formation and transformation.

Lawrence Cremin, professor and president of Teachers College in New York City, filled out this idea in his monumental, Pulitzer-winning, three-volume *American Education (The Colonial Experience 1607-1783; The National Experience 1783-1876;* and *The Metropolitan Experience, 1876-1980)* published from 1970-1988. He defined education as "the deliberate, systematic and sustained effort to transmit or evoke knowledge, attitudes, values, skills, and sensibilities" (Cremin, 1970, p. xiii). To reclaim Eggleston's word, education consists of *intentional efforts* to "transit" a culture through time. Just like families seek to pass on a heritage, cultures are passed on through explicit teaching and through storytelling, artifacts, and rituals.

Cremin's history profoundly demonstrated how the 'culture' of the U.S. was drawn from many sources and how its identity and vocation were 'dynamically' transmitted and revised as it passed through the challenges of historical experience: urbanization, depression, wars, immigration, and profound economic changes. He argued that education must be considered "comprehensively, relationally, and publically" (Cremin, 1975, p. 57). In other words, we broaden our view of education realizing that it occurs through many social procedures (comprehensively), see the interconnections of these procedures with each other (relationally), and initiate conversations about their effects (publically).

At the heart of education is 'public dialogue' seeking to evaluate the impact of education on persons and communities. In the spirit of a biblical prophet, Cremin argued that the function of the educator is "prophesy, or the artistic linking of tradition and aspiration" (Cremin, 1975, p. 96). Educators examine the variety of social procedures that teach, their interrelationships, and their outcomes. The educator then 'problematizes' the findings so that people can question – exploring the deepest meanings in their traditions and the hopes that guide their living with the realities that they encounter. Education is thus an arena of controversy and public decision-making.

Such a prophetic task is no less true for a religious educator. For example, from an originating experience in the Jesus movement, groups expanded in multiple directions. Jesus' brother James continued a Jewish renewal movement in the heart of Jerusalem. Paul spread a reconstruction of the Jewish tradition into the urban centres of the Roman Empire inviting Gentile 'God-fearers' into the way of Christ. Then other disciples and enthusiastic spirit-led converts communicated their messages in new ways in new contexts. By the end of the first century, multiple 'trajectories' of early Christianity were present (see e.g. Ehrman, 2005). Engaging pluralism was part of the Christian movement from the beginning. Persons sought to teach their perspectives and to interact with others who had very different views – some within the Christian communities themselves and many outside who held perspectives of Roman society and of other religious traditions, like Judaism.

Very public questions about what was true and what was false were raised within these emerging Christian communities themselves, even as 'Christians' were oppressed in the wider Roman society. Strategies for teaching were developed that formed believers, challenged those outside the consensus, and, through 'apologetic writings', sought to make connections with the wider society.

Education/religious education is a process of negotiating meanings (see Seymour, 1987). Deep commitments and practices that conserve, transform, empower, or control are contested. Education makes friends and excludes former friends; education encounters and invites strangers. Understanding and engaging the dynamic cultural processes of passing on a faith and claiming new meanings in new times are at the heart of the work of the educator and religious educator.

REVISIONIST HISTORY AS AN APPROACH TO EDUCATION

History tells the story of a people – recognizing how a peoples' faith is transmitted and transformed across time as well as how it continues to be taught and learned. What is lost or gained in the transitions across time, how are groups included or excluded, what 'dangerous memories' are forced underground, and how is the faith dynamically transformed to address new realities without losing its integrity?

For example, in New England in the mid-1800s, public school systems were being formed. Populations included mainly Protestant Christians and some Catholic Christians. The content of the school curriculum was contested (influenced by demonstrations and violence). As school boards increasingly required the use of the 'Protestant' King James Version of the Bible in the curriculum, Catholics, in turn, to protect themselves founded parochial schools where their perspectives and values could be taught. In telling this story, the historian's task is complex weaving among events and interpretations. How the story is shaped and who are identified as founders is affected by the historian's motives and perspectives. Therefore, transparency is required – what is the frame of reference empowering the historian?

Different Frames of Reference

A similar example from today's news: conversations about school choice – about public schools and charter schools. Who determines the values that shape the public's education? Who funds public education? One story: an amazing charter school foundation, the Seton Education Partners, seeks to offer hope to students in disadvantaged neighbourhoods by providing both a 'public' education and Catholic values. Yet, the conflict is obvious: how are Catholic values and non-sectarian public schooling to be reconciled? Similar contests occur over religious perspectives in schools in many other places in the world, e.g. the wearing of

179

Muslim religious clothing in French schools. How will these stories be told? Whose perspectives will be highlighted and why? If the historian is to contribute to public dialogue, he or she must be truthful about the frame of reference affecting the narrative told and the conclusions reached.

History thus offers insights into the ways differences among groups are suppressed as well as how options for living together across differences are learned. The method I use is revisionist history (see Seymour, 1987; see also Seymour, O'Gorman, & Foster, 1984). *Revisionist*, because in shaping the narrative, the voices excluded and suppressed are re-engaged; *cultural*, because it looks at social processes of transmitting and transforming; *history*, because it seeks to reveal the cultural patterns that set trajectories into the present, defining how dialogue occurs and options are limited.

History then begins with questions about current realities and is combined with ethnographic research to examine how educational processes are experienced by real people (see Crain & Seymour, 1996). Furthermore, history becomes a form of *advocacy*, seeking to affect the practices and commitments of the present. The ways a tradition seeks to pass on its heritage are respected as well as the values and perspectives of those excluded are also honoured. The hope is that such a 'problematizing' of the story of education will provide occasions for public conversations about the kind of community a people wants to create and hopefully to *thrive in*.

An Example

Below is an example of the revisionist method:
1. Choose a problem – Define why it is important.
2. Clarify the question – Why are people interested in it? What difference might it make?
3. Explore the question.
   a. Be particularly sensitive to historical choice-points when certain patterns triumphed over others. Attend to the minority strands that have been forced underground in official histories.
   b. Consult a broad range of sources, going beyond 'official documents' to alternative sources e.g. individual diaries, oral stories, family traditions, minutes of meetings, and modes of social communication like popular magazines, curricula, and educational handbooks, as well as interviews, as is possible, with present persons affected by decisions.
4. Develop and argue a perspective.
   a. Draw the reader into the problem that initiated the study.
   b. Define the thesis clearly and openly.
   c. Make apparent the motivations and ideological perspectives within which the study is written.
   d. Develop an argument. Take a position.
5. 'Problematize' findings for public conversation.

    a.   Turn the study back on itself to examine the impact of the narrative on present educational policy-making.

    b.   Define the questions which need to be engaged in public conversation and decision-making about the world we inhabit and our hopes for building the future.

Cremin is therefore correct: education is about prophesy. The religious educational historian stands at the 'artistic linking of tradition and aspiration'. The educator examines social procedures that teach, their interrelationships, and their outcomes. The educator 'problematizes' findings so that the wider public can engage the deepest meanings in their traditions as well as the hopes that guide their living with the realities that they encounter – so they can contest about which meanings and convictions will be communicated, by whom, to whom, and with what force. In other words, religious education engages the social procedures by which the faith is communicated within a religious tradition. Are the traditions and aspirations of the faith respected? Furthermore, how do these traditions affect wider public cultural realities – including people who, in fact, share other religious views? Does religious education assist the human community and the natural world to thrive with life chances and hope? Both forms of religious education are addressed: religious education with *friends* who share a worldview – defining the patterns for dynamically teaching a faith perspective into the future; and religious education with *strangers* – partnerships with those who differ to build a world where we can live together.

AN ILLUSTRATION: REVISIONIST RELIGIOUS EDUCATION AMONG FRIENDS

In a recent essay, I used revisionist cultural history to explore an issue within the Christian religious tradition. I sought to link 'tradition and aspiration' and 'problematize' discussion within the 'mainline' Christian community (Seymour, 2003; see also Seymour, 2004). Let me illustrate: I examined the "deep theological differences [that] threaten to divide Protestant denominations" and "block mission".

Religious Education among Friends

Then through an exercise in historical retrieval, I described a previous divisive controversy in Christian education between the liberal religious education and neo-orthodox Christian education movements in the 1940s and 1950s. Both sides of this controversy so expressed their disagreements that name-calling resulted. Rather than simply narrating the divisiveness, I pointed to areas where they together had to address the realities in which they found themselves. I both affirmed the differences that divided the movements and focused the common questions they were addressing, thus raising questions (problematizing) for public conversation today.

    From the analysis, I advocated for two simultaneous tasks on the part of diverging groups within mainline Protestantism: (1) educate for a theology of

181

identity that builds up and clarifies the integrity of each separate group and (2) educate for a theology of coalition, recognizing that both are dealing with common social and religious issues. I asked if engaging in a common project to address common issues might provide an adjustment in the tone and divisiveness of the conflict (Seymour, 2003, 2004).

> Yet, in addition to this identity-building and identity-clarifying task, there is another task of theology – exploring and claiming the coalitions and options that contribute to the good of the human community? Today, various 'sides' of the theological debate seem to have reverted into a tribalism that stifles conversation. How are perspectives of differing communities shared, conversations engaged, and coalitions for healing built? (Seymour 2003, p. 361)

I pleaded for respect and conversation, affirming that differences needed to be expressed, but also pointing to places where common coalitions could be built. Thus, using revisionist history, I engaged a current problem.

> As Christian religious educators, we need to reclaim our theological nerve, because a gracious God is calling us to offer an identity and faithful practices in the midst of the incarnated realities of human living. … May we seek to assist in the formation of Christian identity at the same time we work in partnership with to build coalitions seeking to repair creation. Such is the task and vocation of practical theologians of education. (Seymour, 2004, pp. 283-284)

Religious Education among Strangers

In 2007, the Center for Jewish Education of the University of Haifa in conjunction with The Von-Hugel Institute of St. Edmund's College, England convened a conference about religious schooling in liberal democratic societies (see Alexander & Agbaria, 2012). In an interfaith atmosphere, we sought to communicate how religious education across traditions might build partnerships.

My task was to speak from a Christian perspective. We enter interfaith conversations with hospitality, yet we also offer a particular faith perspective – for me, 'following Jesus'. I respectfully sought to contribute to the conversation.

Of course, the group gathered in openness, yet the diversity of the group, both religiously and culturally, could have resulted in significant divisions. By publically addressing a common problem, religious schooling in democratic societies, we engaged in religious education for public living. We learned much about each others' commitments. In fact, we embodied a way into the future. The conference conveners assumed working on a common issue might build partnerships. It did.

Again, using historical analysis, I examined moments where persons sought in the public square to educate across differences, where persons of differing faiths gathered together. One such incident was the racial justice movement of the 1960s when persons of various religious communities drew from their traditions to call the U.S. back to its traditions and aspirations of freedom, equality, and responsibility.

From this historical analysis, I offered that building community is not a process of gaining agreement. Rather, building community is a *project*, differing voices work together from their own perspectives to address an important common public concern – again, in this case, racism.

> *Community is a project and a gift* building the future. As we work on projects together, we build community (our communities); we create the future. We also discover the depth of our differences and our common hopes. Building community is the project, often painfully realized, slowly and with much effort. Then, when in our combined effort, we find moments of connection, community is a gift. Connection renews our efforts for the hard work of community building. (Seymour, 2012, pp. 243-244)

From that experience, I concluded that religious education among strangers has three tasks:

First, each community must truthfully and critically teach its own faith perspectives. We need to be fulsome and honest. For example, Christians need to be honest that they are not of one mind. They also need to acknowledge that the name of Jesus has been used to oppress others.

Second, each community must find occasions to teach in partnership with those from other traditions. When we study together, examining texts we hold in common or common problems, honestly listening to each other, we hear each other's commitments. For example, such sharing with integrity is exactly what Jewish and Christian theological students reported after participating in an interfaith class.

> They bring their vulnerabilities. They are offered a new lens through which to view their sacred texts. They are challenged to articulate their beliefs and explain aspects of their tradition to their study partners, often helping them to clarify their relationship to their own tradition, to their sacred literature and to God. As a semester progresses and trust develops, ... What results is a broadening of their definitions of 'Jew' and 'Christian' to include nuance, narrative and diversity.

Third, as we address common problems together, we build coalitions. Suzanne Rosenblith and Scott Priestman, who wrestle with how state legislatures choose textbooks for public school courses on religion, have asked if some mutually acceptable criteria for public religious discourse can be identified (Rosenblith & Priestman, 2004). I agree with them. We need to seek such criteria. We must make the effort. Beginning with our individual traditions, we must extend dialogue exploring together criteria for public religious conversation (Seymour, 2012, pp. 236-242).

AGENDA FOR RELIGIOUS EDUCATION AMONG FRIENDS AND STRANGERS

In conclusion, from within my own tradition let me summarize some ways of understanding religious education among friends and strangers.

First, the religious educator passes on deep commitments and reminds believers of their traditions. Religious education among friends prophetically calls persons back to their traditions. That is what my grandmother was doing when she told me what 'Seymours' did and did not do. Or for Jesus, that was the content of his encounter with the rich young ruler (Luke 18). Jesus reminded the young man of what he already knew, that he was to love God and neighbour (the *shema* that guided and guides the Jewish community). Jesus reminded him of the heart of his tradition. Religious education for friends is reminding us of the commitments at the heart of our traditions.

Yet, second, again among friends, the religious educator focuses on connecting tradition and aspirations. For example, when Jesus taught for the first time in his home community (Luke 4), he was invited to read the *haphtarah* for the day. He read the words from the scroll of Isaiah about the promised time of God's activity in the world – when good news is given to the poor, release provided for captives, sight for the blind, and freedom for the oppressed (Isaiah 61). The community first 'marvelled' at his communication, yet became filled with fury when he challenged them to faithfulness by reminding them that God offered grace even to 'strangers'. Indeed, education is contested. He challenged their faithfulness with the aspirations of the tradition – clearly prophesy.

Finally, religious education among strangers is joining in common projects. As Jesus walked through Samaria, he encountered a woman at the well. He began to talk and witness to her; she argued with him. She could not understand why he would talk to her, a woman and a stranger. Through their conversation, she came to understand the gift he offered. They connected traditions. As a result she gathered everyone in the village and extended the conversation into her community. Common projects bring those separated into a common space considering how to inhabit it in ways that build each other up.

The prophetic act of the educator is to remind friends of their traditions and aspirations and to reveal the effects of our actions. The prophetic act of the educator is also to join with strangers working together on projects in the public space we share. Revisionist historical research is a tool calling us to engage the prophetic acts of religious education for friends and strangers.

NOTES

[1] Siebren Miedema's excellent work on the educational philosophy of John Dewey assists us to examine this process of contestation and of critical, political education. See e.g. Miedema (1995, 2012) and his essays with Biesta (Biesta & Miedema, 1996).

[2] I am using 'friends' here to refer to education within in one's own religious community; 'strangers', in turn, means seeking to learn from and to engage in religious education with persons who are outside one's religious community. While I know strangers often become friends, I am simply using the words to designate religious education within and outside of one's own religious community. One aspect of religious education is basically about inculcating people into a dynamic religious

tradition. Therefore Christian education is about inculcating persons into the dynamic Christian tradition using all aspects of critical analysis and critical pedagogy. Yet, religious education also has another dimension with 'strangers'. Here we engage with 'partners' from various religious traditions and some with no religious tradition to affect our common public life. I think this second aspect is so critical because we basically live in a world of strangers – a world with tremendous differences and a plurality of perspectives. We need to learn how to live together on the common globe we share. That is a task of partnership.

[3] Again social participation is seen in Siebren Miedema's use of and analysis of Dewey.

REFERENCES

Alexander, H. A., & Agbaria, A. K. (eds.). (2012). *Commitment, character, and citizenship: Religious education in liberal democracy.* New York/London: Routledge.

Bailyn, B. (1960). *Education in the forming of American society.* Chapel Hill, NC: University of North Carolina Press.

Biesta, G. J. J., & Miedema, S. (1996). Dewey in Europe: A case-study on the international dimensions of the turn-of-the-century educational reform. *American Journal of Education, 105*(1), 1-26.

Crain, M. A., & Seymour, J. (1996). The ethnographer as minister: Ethnographic research in ministry. *Religious Education, 91*(3), 299-315.

Cremin, L. A. (1970). *American education: The colonial experience, 1608-1783.* New York: Harper and Row.

Ehrman, B. D. (2005). *Lost Christianities: The battles for scripture and the faiths we never knew.* New York: Oxford University Press.

Miedema, S. (1995). The beyond in the midst. The relevance of Dewey's philosophy of religion for education. In J. Garrison (ed.), *New scholarship on Dewey* (pp. 61-73). Dordrecht/Boston/London: Kluwer Academic Publishers.

Miedema, S. (2012). Maximal citizenship education and interreligious education in public schools. In H. A. Alexander & A. K. Agbaria (eds.), *Commitment, character, and citizenship: Religious education in liberal democracy* (pp. 96-102). New York/London: Routledge.

Rosenblith, S., & Priestman, S. (2004). Problematizing religious truth: Implications for public education. *Educational Theory, 54*, 365-380.

Seymour, J. L. (1987). Power and history: History as 'critical' analysis. *Religious Education, 82*(3), 349-359.

Seymour, J. L. (2003). Holding onto hope: Addressing theological conflict through Christian religious education. *Religious Education, 98*(3), 348-364.

Seymour, J. L. (2004). The clue to Christian religious education: Uniting theology and education, 1950 to the present. *Religious Education, 99*(3), 272-286.

Seymour, J. L. (2012). Constructive, critical, and mutual interfaith religious education for public living: A Christian view. In H. A. Alexander & A. K. Agbaria (eds.), *Commitment, character, and citizenship: Religious education in liberal democracy* (pp. 226-244). New York/London: Routledge.

Seymour, J. L., O'Gorman, R. T., & Foster, C. R. (1984). *The church in the education of the public: Refocusing the task of religious education.* Nashville: Abingdon Press.

Seymour, J., Crain, M. A., & Crockett, J. (1993). *Educating Christians: The intersection of meaning, learning, and vocation.* Nashville: Abingdon Press.

AFFILIATIONS

Jack L. Seymour
Garrett-Evangelical Theological Seminary
Evanston, Illinois, U.S.A.

GEIR SKEIE

IN SEARCH OF A RELIGIOUS EDUCATION APPROACH

INTRODUCTION

We are certainly shaped by 'significant others',
but these people are also part of a larger context.

I started my career as a religious educator at first by something that seemed almost a coincidence, but it continued as a personal choice. Through these years of teaching and researching, I have not really developed my own proper 'approach' to religious education. Still, one could assume that if somebody read through my writings, they would find characteristics that may disclose some kind of approach. In this contribution, I have myself tried to capture some recurring themes and perspectives in a spirit of self-reflection by recapitulating some of my work in retrospect. Looking in the rear-mirror, as a researcher of religious education, I see myself as influenced by the historical context of my younger years as well as that of my active years as a researcher. Influence is not a linear process; it is interwoven with the ambition to articulate my own reactions to the same historical context. This dialectic between being influenced by context, and trying to influence context is not easy to unpack, but by presenting a narrative partly interrupted by reflection, I hope to achieve some more clarity in my own thinking, and also to offer some food for thought to the reader. Still, the following reflections are only bits and pieces of a story, many people and many experiences are left out and this of course raises questions about choice and interpretation that will remain unanswered here. Among the things I have included, however, are parts of a personal 'religious' biography that may be relevant to the overall picture. Both this element, as well as other parts, are included in order to account for different influences and to recognise that these are not only 'personal', but also historical.

SIGNIFICANT OTHERS IN EARLY YEARS

We are certainly shaped by 'significant others', but these people are also part of a larger context. This can be illustrated with the story of my parents who both grew up in families marked by low-church lay people's organisations, with a pietistic and puritan profile. Their parents, my grand-parents, were strong and self-conscious individuals, probably seeing themselves as part of a large movement of

I. ter Avest (ed.), On the Edge: (Auto)biography and Pedagogical Theories on Religious Education, 187–198.

committed Christians with working class and farmer background and with roots back to early 20th century revivalist movements. Their life was simple in material terms, but oscillated between workplace (mainly the men), home and different (also leading) activities in Christian mission organisations. My parents were young during the war and benefitted from the changes in society opening education to larger parts of the population after 1945. They took part in the modernisation process by entering into the town life as part of the educated middle class, distancing themselves from the conservative Christianity of their parents, but not leaving the church altogether. By doing this, they mirrored much of the development in post-war Norway where development, enterprise, welfare state and increasing wealth were influential elements.

In spite of their own distancing from a conservative Christian background, my parents sent me as a child to different religious children and youth organisations. I remember, being about nine years old going to such a children's group which consisted in reading aloud from a book called 'For my mother's sake', about children learning to be well behaved, mainly with the help of Chrsitian influene. While listening we made small handicraft products. Later I joined the Methodist Church scout groups, which was much more fun; roaming around in the woods, learning to survive there and to develop different scouting skills. During the years to come, I passed through a varied spectrum of Christian organisations, starting with rather fundamentalist ones and 'ending up' as a young student with Christian Socialists and the radical Student Christian Movement.

Influenced by some of the charismatic Jesus-revolution trends of the early 1970's as well as the anti-Vietnam war movement I started to study theology. It was a choice between that and social sciences, which I saw as being close to my school interests in upper secondary and also a way of following up my political activism. I thought of becoming a journalist afterwards. When the final choice was theology, this also became part of a political agenda in different ways, since I belonged to a group of of young people who thought that the main stream church was in need of a 'reformation', more in political and ethical terms than in theological terms. We were engaged in demands for global justice, equal rights and also for installing a more communicative liturgy. Not surprisingly, this turned out to be more difficult than imagined, and after a few years trying to get permanent work as a pastor, observing open and hidden power from the clerical hierarchy, I took the opportunity to apply for a post in teacher education. The local bishop even advised me not to become a minister since he thought I was much too concerned with politics, my family was not sufficiently active in parish life and my theological position seemed dubious to him. This did not make a clerical career easier.

I have later learned that a large part of my fellow student cohort at the theological faculty gradually left church related jobs for completely different careers. From time to time I have met some of them and they have told similar stories about push and pull factors. Many were involved in youth work in local parishes during student years and felt marginalised because their methods were not approved, others did not find a place to discuss seriously their thoughts about religion and church. I know theologians who have become journalists, musicians, researchers, consultants, managers and politicians. They are working in private and public sector and most are happy with their choices. Few regret the study of theology as such, they rather describe it as useful and enriching in many ways. Some do not have any church relations, while others are active as' lay' members in local church councils. In retrospect it is interesting to see that much of what caused inner-church confrontation in the 1970s and early 1980s has become less controversial later and to some extent been adopted as official church positions (support for global justice and 3rd World independence movements, criticism of Israeli occupation of Palestine, women's liberation, increasing gay liberation, environmental issues, etc.).

BECOMING A RELIGIOUS EDUCATOR

I started my career as a religious educator at first by something that seemed almost a coincidence, but continued as a personal choice. After ending my short career as part of the clergy, I still had an academic interests and even research drive. I got the opportunity to develop this when a possibility came along to work in the regional university college with teacher training. I continued to work there for several years, not only with teaching, but with administrative work of different sorts. Finding myself in teacher education, more precisely in religious education, I soon discovered that my background lacked important competences related to teacher's work. I needed to be re-socialised and re-educated, but I also felt more at home in this as a working context, than in the somewhat strict and hierarchical church setting. Gradually I discovered that hidden agendas, power play and personal vendettas, also can be part of academic life. Some times this happened between peers who saw their own field of research threatened by others' success, or conceived their department mainly to be at war with other departments over resources. At other times leaders had personal preferences in terms of subject areas or persons and played a manipulative game of divide and rule. But in spite of such disturbing experiences academia also proved to be full of generous and genuinely knowledge seeking colleagues as well as many committed students. This is still the case while new public management, enterprise ideology and 'the audit society' is continuing to change higher education globally.

Entering into the world of *teacher training* in the 1980s I discovered that the education of teachers in Norway was getting more research oriented, after having relied much on a mix of subject area knowledge, general educational theory and practice with supervision. This 'mix' was presented by teacher trainers who for the most part had been teachers themselves, but after further studies were qualified as academic staff. Historically, theologians, who for the most part were teaching religious education, had earlier been instrumental in establishing many of the local teacher training institutions hundred years earlier. For some generations, they also were the only staff with full academic background, and often among the few who actually did research. This research was often part of traditional academic theological research within their field of interest, and later in their careers several of them moved from teacher training to more prestigious positions in universities.

The close relationship between church and teacher training were also reflected in the ethos of primary school teachers, where the ideal of 'the Christian teacher' for a long time was prominent and even strong within teachers' unions. My own reflections on this history went in the opposite direction. Having my own negative experiences with conservative and hierarchical church power, I saw the declining, but still traceable influence in teacher training as illegitimate. It was part of an alliance between church and state as much as the remains of a cultural hegemony of the Lutheran Church of Norway. Gradually the role of Christianity was changing in a society that was becoming more diverse and people also started to acknowledge that the diversity had been more present also historically than earlier recognised.

Colleagues and Friends

In the collegial meetings with RE teachers nationally I developed many life –long relationships, one example is Sissel Østberg with whom I early got in touch. She was at the time one of the very few RE teacher trainers with a history of religions background. We became both colleagues and friends and both felt strongly that religious education in primary and secondary school as well as in teacher training should be changed into a broad, multi-faith subject, reflecting the global diversity, the increasing presence of world religions in Norway and the general diversity of spiritual and world view positions represented in the population. Sissel had a broad background in history of religion with earlier studies of ancient religion in the Middle East and a growing interest in present day Islam. She later developed this into a PhD under the supervision of Robert Jackson in Warwick. Through her I developed my insight into religious diversity and also the commitment to the values of tolerance, mutual recognition of religions and world-views and the attentiveness to the needs of children and young people from minority background. Sissel later became vice-chancellor of Oslo and Akershus University College of Applied Sciences and today she is a national figure in issues related to minorities and inclusion.

Sociocultural Diversity and 'Norwegianness'

During the 1970s and 1980s the cultural and religious composition of Norwegian local communities had changed a lot through family-immigration related to earlier work-migration as well as increasing numbers of refugees and asylum seekers. Not only the cities became more diverse, but also the less densely populated countryside. This made many small schools more diverse and debates about inter-cultural education became local. Myself, I became instrumental in starting up courses in inter-cultural education in Bodø, Northern Norway were I then lived and worked. Parallel to this also recognition of the rights of the Sami population became formalised and I was quite involved in developing a distinct teacher education for the local Lule-Sami community of the region of Bodø. From this I learned a lot about generations of oppression and minority life and what it means to be a minority within a minority.

These and other events told me that my role in teacher training had to be revised or negotiated in some way. I saw strength in this historical tradition of theologians in teacher training mainly in the willingness to accept and participate in the educational enterprise as a broad cognitive, affective and value-based practice (the Bildung perspective). The weakness was the tendency to identify or confuse general education with the formation of what may be called 'Christianness' and 'Norwegianness' and often a combination of the two. Here, borders between religion and nationality seemed to be more or less consciously blurred in an effort to make all belong to the same 'culture'. As a reaction to this, I started to research the foundations of religious education.

Research

In the early 1990s I was challenged to develop a PhD project in cooperation with the University in Trondheim, which at that time was the closest University where research into religion and education was done. Initially the cooperation with the university was more general in its setup, but I discovered that what they were mainly interested in, was to recruit individuals for research training. In my case this was helped by my PhD supervisor, Professor Ole Gunnar Winsnes. His research background was partly within empirical study of children's religious socialisation and partly in theoretical and methodological issues related to the empirical research of religion. He was considered to challenge the then dominating theological perspective on religion in education, but was trained as a theologian himself, initially. One of his main influences came from sociology of religion, particularly Thomas Luckmann, who regularly came for research seminars in Trondheim during these years.

INTERNATIONAL IMPULSES AND NATIONAL DELVELOPMENTS

Based on the critical reflection I had raised regarding the semi-confessional Norwegian public religious education, my PhD project sought to develop a theoretical basis for religious education as a 'culturally conscious' field of research and practice. I saw, and still see religious education research mainly as a field of investigation where different disciplines meet in order to challenge each other and to solve research questions. In the early 1990s I was glad to discover that the Norwegian situation resembled dilemmas and debates in other countries, and since my PhD work circled around concepts like 'pluralism' and 'identity' and 'culture', I could benefit from the current international debate in several disciplines. Early in the PhD work my supervisor introduced me to the International Seminar on Religious Education and Values (ISREV), and when I first participated in 1993, I discovered that my preoccupation with plurality and pluralism was received with great interest from international colleagues. This lead to my first publication in an international journal in 1995. Several of the people I met at my first ISREV have been close colleagues since then, like Hans Günter Heimbrock, Robert Jackson and Sven G. Hartman, others like Siebren Miedema, I met later. These are examples of the many colleagues who have generously shared their views, invited me for visits, introduced me to networks read drafts and supported my career in different ways.

Change of RE Curriculum

When the PhD thesis was finished in 1998, big changes already had happened to Norwegian RE. After the establishment of a general core curriculum in 1993, emphasising national heritage rather than Christianity as a personal faith, a process started with a white paper commissioned by the minister of education in 1995. This lead to a complete change of the RE curriculum from confessional to a multi-faith profile in 1997. It meant the full inclusion of world religions, secular world-views and also philosophy in the school subject grades 1-10, plus one year in upper secondary. The aim of RE was to learn about religions, learn about oneself and to learn to live together.

The result was certainly going in the direction of my own thoughts at the time, but I had no influence over the process. Actually, I was not entirely satisfied with the result and part of this criticism found its way into the PhD as well. I argued that the removal of a Christian confessional RE was not fully accomplished, since it was still very much dominated by the Christian religion. This dominance was both in terms of quantity of content and in the less explicit cultural hegemony of a Christian influenced majority culture. This proved to be a problem to many more than myself, and during the years from 1997 the RE subject curriculum has been changed several times. Today it presents itself as a more mature multi-faith subject, even if that does not mean that all debate is over. The quantitative dominance of Christianity has been adjusted, the lack of clarity about illegitimacy of confessional influence on students has been improved and the underlining of learning about religion as the main objective has been emphasised, resulting in less emphasis on the personal dimension. This last element was much influenced by the decisions of the UN Human Rights committee and the European Human Rights court and has been much discussed (Lied, 2009).

It is interesting to observe that through all these changes, the general core curriculum has been kept intact, with its emphasis on national heritage and portraying the Christian religion as something like a 'common culture'. This was seen as an example of the inconsequence sometimes built into curricula, and also as an example of how religion is used as a political instrument for social cohesion. By referring to Christianity and Humanism as the sources of 'common values', religion is included in the very foundation of public education through the school law and this I consider to be a political use of religion in order to secure social cohesion. It uses religion as a source of commonly shared meaning and the function of religion is sociologically speaking an ideological foundation of society. Even if The Church of Norway is not using this to justify aggressive proselytisation or to claim political influence, there is a public role offered partly explicitly and partly tacitly by the representatives of the state. The difference from the function of religion as a 'canopy' in earlier times is perhaps that religion is not so much treated as a personal faith, but rather as a shared tradition irrespective of faith. This comes close to what Bellah called 'civil religion'. It is interesting to observe that in a time when religion is usually thought to be expelled from the public sphere and 'privatised', it is coming back in the 'depersonalised' shape of 'common values'.

THE ROLE OF CHURCH AND RELIGION

The above observations and critical perspectives I find to be drawing on my early inspiration from and preoccupation with Marxist thought about religion, where one part of the analysis was that even if religion is not part of the 'base', it can play an important role in the 'superstructure' and that the relationship between the two is seen as dialectic. Not all Marxist thinking treated religion as something to be combatted; both Karl Marx himself and several others kept a focus on the social function of religion, not the claims about existential issues. Drawing on such impulses, I have myself considered the political dimensions of religious education to be important and interesting from a research perspective (Skeie, 2001, 2006a). In a secularised country like Norway, one could expect that religion was obsolete as a political instrument, but as I have tried to show, this is not the case. The present dismantling of the state church system is met with surprisingly strong opposition from parts of the population. In many ways The Church of Norway seem to be considered by parts of the population almost as a welfare state institution, offering collective rituals in certain life phases. Confirmation still has a strong position, with about 80% of the cohort taking part, and this is mirrored by the Humanist Association's use of the same term in their 'civic confirmation', which is the parallel secular Humanist ceremony for 14 year olds. In this ceremony the whole family is invited to a large hall in the local community where a collective ritual is concluding a period of some months with teaching and learning about issues like values, ethics, social responsibility, international solidarity and human rights.[1] In many ways this resembles the confirmation period in many parishes.

In addition to playing a significant collective role in 'rites de passage' like confirmation, the church has also played a central role in traumatic local or national events. The last example is *the massacre of 22 July 2011*, which was followed by services in the churches many places and with broad participation both from political leaders and general population. The political leaders tend to claim that this is not to be seen as an 'official religious service', but that they participate because of being invited. The prime minister's speech in the Cathedral of Oslo two days after the 22nd July event did not mention God, religion, church, but he mentioned 'evil', 'national tragedy' and expressed strong personal emotions, in particular 'loss' and 'grief', ending like this: "Now life is at its darkest for you. You shall know that we are there for you".[2]

The Church of Norway was quite careful not to exploit these rituals for its own purposes and tended to focus on the broad participation. There is no secular institution really rivalling with the church is situations of national trauma. It is interesting, though, that school sometimes may play a similar role in a smaller scale. This is often seen in cases when something tragic happens to children in the local community. Local, school-based rituals have been developed, sometimes in cooperation with the local church, but often not so. This practice is beginning to be researched by some colleagues. The ritual element is usually modest, but almost every time the lightening of candles is a central part (Haakedal, 2009).

Christian Religion in Curriculum

I see these examples as signs of the Christian religion playing a role similar to the one reflected in the general core curriculum of the school, and by this displaying a connection between the political and everyday life. We may see the Christian religion and the Church of Norway representing structures of meaning that are changing very slowly, and the concept of secularisation may not be ideal in order to capture the complexity of the process. New perspectives from theory of post-secularity and (re-) sacralisation are among the impulses here. What is somewhat puzzling, even disturbing, is that there is a tendency of homogenisation related to this, and this is not fitting with the general plurality of present day Norwegian society. Usually we want school and society to be inclusive, but inclusion becomes problematic when it does not reveal the differences that are supposed to be included. What then seems to happen is that a big 'we' is offering to include 'others' without asking questions how 'we' and 'others' are defined. A possible analysis of this, points in the direction of the preoccupation with 'sameness' that seems to run through Norwegian culture and society, according to several sociologists and ethnographers (Gullestad, 1992). If they are right, it may be that religion is working as a tool for constructing social cohesion because it still can invoke some kind of 'sameness' and at the same time 'Norwegianness'.

Religion in the Public Domain

Why is not religion replaced with something else, that could create 'sameness' without excluding minorities and that would fit better with a highly secularised society? One possible explanation could be that the public or collective role of religion has been underestimated, following the emphasis on the individualisation and privatisation of religion in modern societies. It may be that the historical role of religion is more difficult to replace than some expect. This line of thought even challenge the way religion is conceptualised. In Scandinavia, at least, there is a tendency to focus either on the existential dimension (big questions about life) or on truth claims related to ontology. When the focus is on the first, a common position is that personal views on life may conflict a lot, but should be tolerated and respected as should the right to organise according to faith and to take part in collective rituals based on these individual beliefs. In the second case, the discourse tends to follow a more than hundred years pattern of world-view debate where the agenda is picture faith and science as complete opposites and where there are ready made positions. This can be exemplified by the 'new atheism' debate. What seems to fall between the chairs is an understanding of religion that sees it as a basis for both individual and collective public action. So, when a large majority of a 'secularised' Norwegian population takes part in religious rituals like baptism, confirmation and burial, this tends to be explained as 'tradition', not 'religion' because the personal (individual) faith is not seen to be prominent. Similarly, when the bishops in The Church of Norway issue statements about saving the earth from climate change, this is often seen as 'politics', and not as an expression of 'faith'. The same can be illustrated with debates about Islam; if Muslims have views on society they are often pictured as 'fundamentalists' or 'islamists', or alternatively, it is claimed that their position is not 'religious', it comes from the 'culture' they belong to or from the national or ethnic background.

Religion in Private Life

My argument is not in favour of essentialist definitions of religion, but I am in favour of being more open towards the continuous role of religion as a factor of public life, as a motivator for individuals and groups in their views on how to live their lives in society and how to move society in the direction of something they consider to be better. For religion and education research the conceptualisation of religion is vital for several reasons (Skeie, 2006c). Firstly, it matters a lot how a certain society justifies having religion as part of the curriculum and in which way this is done. This forms part of the educational context of the religious education subject and if no such subject exists, it shapes the context of dealing with religion in other school subjects as can be illustrated by comparing the situation in France and England. Secondly, the understanding of religion influences how we deal with the 'what' question both in curricula and also in classroom teaching and learning. This is well illustrated by Robert Jackson's discussion of 'representation' as a vital part of approaching religion in education (Jackson, 2004). Drawing further on Jackson, also the 'how' of teaching and learning is informed by conceptualisation if religion. He suggests involving students in the use of experience-near and experience-distant concepts as well as to reflect on one's own learning process in order to deconstruct and construct knowledge about religion. Text-book knowledge is not enough, even if it can be a useful reference point.

Religion in Education

The increasing preoccupation with the concept of religion within religious studies in later years can in many ways be seen as paralleling what religious educators have been experiencing in their classrooms discussing with students from a variety of backgrounds. I was reminded about this fact rereading Denise Cush' writing when I had the privilege to take part in her dissertation at the University of Warwick in 2012 (Cush, 2009). From another colleague, Hans Günter Heimbrock in Frankfurt University, I have learned that the understanding of religion has importance for how we deal with this in education. Günter has particularly emphasised the 'lived' religion, drawing on phenomenological perspectives

(Heimbrock, 1998). While Cush and Jackson criticise phenomenology in the understanding of religion, Heimbrock makes use of phenomenology in order to approach 'lived religion'. I see them as looking for similar 'objects', but they are philosophically not so easy to reconcile. In religious studies phenomenology is seen as a problematic example of essentialism and 'sui generis' view on religion, while Heimbrock grounds 'religion' in a cultural perspective allowing for a more general anthropological starting point while underlining the complexity and diversity related to 'culture'. This may serve as an illustration of a lack of consistence in my own thinking, since I prefer not to choose among conflicting perspectives, if I can avoid it, as long as both of them have proved to be fruitful. Perhaps is this a result of my early fascination with Paul Ricoeur, whose writing I first got seriously interested in through one of many ISREV friends, Wilna Meijer (Meijer, 1995). In Ricoeurs philosophy I find a will to mediate between oppositions without harmonising them, but also without seeing the two as irreconcilable opposites. I used this approach partly to deal with the issue of 'identity' in my PhD, suggesting a concept of 'transversal identity', which was an attempt to bridge between the postmodern deconstruction of identity and the modern search for identity, without conflating the two. Ricoeurs suggestion is to see the two opposing dimension of identity (ipse and idem) united in the narrative, and this still appeals to me, both theoretically and experientially. I do not feel comfortable when I am identified with a certain religious group or position since I am often in opposition and disagreement. On the other hand I like to have access to the meaning-making resources of the Christian tradition I still belong to. I therefore get provoked when somebody wants to dissociate me from this community of interpreters only because I do not fit in. Such an in-between position is sometimes comfortable and gives space to move, but at other times it feels narrow and under pressure. This may reflect the contrasting influences of my own biography.

PRAXIOLOGICAL EPILOGUE.

Are these reflections signs of an 'approach to religious education'? I do not know, but I have started to think that it might be possible to develop a critical, hermeneutical and practice-oriented approach to religious education research based on my own academic work. In addition to the stimulus of reflecting back on earlier writings there is also one particular dimension not yet mentioned, which is the recent years of engaging in practice development, cooperative research and the organising of religious education research communities in Norway and Sweden (Skeie, 2011). This has been strongly inspired by action research, a tradition which in many ways draws on the political and critical ethos of my younger years. My preoccupation with identity issues and pluralism going back to the 1990s I see as an act of solidarity with the life conditions and life world of children and young people in late modern societies (Skeie, 2002, 2006b). The cooperation with professional teachers has increased my respect for their challenges, but also been a great joy, contributing to the improvement of their practice. This collegiality across practices and contexts also includes the international community of researchers I was introduced to through ISREV, the European Network on Religious Education and Contextual Approaches (ENRECA), and not the least the REDCo project (Religion in Education – a contribution Dialogue or a factor of Conflict in transforming societies of European Countries) with Wolfram Weisse in the leading role, and where Siebren Miedema was always asking thought provoking questions. Is that not what research is about?

NOTES

[1] See the website of the Norwegian Humanist Association:
   http://www.human.no/Servicemeny/English/?index=3)
[2] See the website of the Norwegian government for the speech:
   http://www.regjeringen.no/nb/dep/smk/aktuelt/taler_og_artikler/statsministeren/statsminister_jens_st oltenberg/2011/tale-ved-statsminister-jens-stoltenberg-.html?id=651789

REFERENCES

Cush, D. (2009). Religious studies versus theology: Why I'm still glad that I converted from theology to religious studies. In D. L. Bird & S. G. Smith (eds.), *Theology and religious studies in higher education. Global perspectives* (pp. 15-30). London: Continuum.

Gullestad, M. (1992). *The art of social relations: Essays on culture, social action and everyday life in modern Norway*. Oslo: Scandinavian University Press.

Haakedal, E. (2009). School festivals, collective remembering and social cohesion: A case study of changes in Norwegian school culture. *Journal of Religious Education, 57*(3), 46-55.

Heimbrock, H.-G. (1998). *Gelebte Religion Wahrnehmen. Lebenswelt – Alltagskultur – Religionspraxis* Stuttgart: Kohlhammer.

Jackson, R. (2004). *Rethinking religious education and plurality. Issues in diversity and pedagogy*. London: RoutledgeFalmer.

Lied, S. (2009). The Norwegian *Christianity, Religion and Philosophy* subject KRL in Strasbourg. *British Journal of Religious Education, 31*(3), 263-276.

Meijer, W. (1995). The plural self. A hermeneutical view on identity and plurality. *British Journal of Religious Education, 17*(2), 92-99.

Skeie, G. (2001). Citizenship, identity politics and religious education. In H.-G. Heimbrock, C. T. Scheilke, & P. Schreiner (eds.), *Towards religious competence. Diversity as a challenge for education in Europe* (pp. 237-252). Münster: LIT Verlag.

Skeie, G. (2006a). Diversity and the political function of religious education. *British Journal of Religious Education, 28*(1), 19-32.

Skeie, G. (2006b). Is there a place for youth in religious education? In D. Bates, G. Durka, & S. Friedrich (eds.), *Education, religion and society. Essays in honour of John M Hull* (pp. 228-240). London/New York: Routledge.

Skeie, G. (2006c). What do we mean by "Religion" in Education? On disciplinary knowledge and knowledge in the classroom. In K. Tirri (ed.), *Religion, spirituality and identity* (pp. 85-100). Bern: Peter Lang.

Skeie, G. (2007). Religion and education in Norway. In R. Jackson, S. Miedema, W. Weisse, & J.-P. Willaime (eds.), *Religion and education in Europe: Developments, contexts and debates* (pp. 221-242). Münster: Waxmann.

Skeie, G. (2011). Teachers and researchers cooperating to develop new knowledge for religious education. *PANORAMA: International Journal of Comparative Religious Education and Values, 23*, 92-105.

AFFILIATIONS

Geir Skeie
Professor Religious Education
Stockholm University, Sweden
University of Stavanger, Norway

MARIAN DE SOUZA

RESPONDING TO PLURALISM AND GLOBALIZATION IN RELIGIOUS EDUCATION

Implications for Curriculum and Pedagogy

INTRODUCTION

Imprinted in my memory is
an experience of being a displaced person,
living within and, at the same time, outside the community

I grew up in North India in the early years of independence from colonial rule. In those early years of Independence, there were many Indian families that maintained the Anglo/European cultural trappings that their ancestors had so carefully cultivated over the previous 400 years. My family was one of them. Characteristics of this culture included belonging to a Christian faith tradition, having the English language as one's mother-tongue and being educated in private schools run by European Religious Orders. Most of these schools preserved the structure and traditions from that earlier era of colonial rule so that children grew up with a sound knowledge of western literature, music and the arts as well as with Christian principles which influenced how one viewed the world. This was the distinct cultural environment that contextualized the lives of Anglo-Indians and anglicized Indians so that they became displaced people, separated from the culture of their country.

I recall my first day at school when I went into a class filled with forty little girls who had long plaits down their backs and unpronounceable names. There were only a handful of girls with short hair like mine and whose names were ones I knew because they had names like Susan, Joan, Helen and other Christian names. These were names I knew because I had grown up reading the same books that British and Australian children read, all of which created another world for me, quite different from the reality of the Indian cultural context in which I lived. Music was another area where cultural difference became apparent so that I learnt classical piano and listened to popular western music. I knew nothing of Hindustani music and therefore, had no liking for it. Equally, I only ever went to see western movies at the one English cinema in town but never frequented the numerous Hindi cinemas.

I. ter Avest (ed.), On the Edge: (Auto)biography and Pedagogical Theories on Religious
Education, 199–210.

Family background

My ancestors on my father's side had converted to Catholicism in the 1500s in response to the action of the Portuguese who had colonized Goa and, as children, we heard stories of our grandparents who had travelled from their villages in Goa into British India to find more opportunities for work and ultimately, how they had succeeded. In particular, we heard stories of my own paternal grandfather who had established a highly successful business empire in the early decades of the last century. Part of the story spoke of the importance of his religion in his life since he had made significant donations to Catholic organizations including for buildings and renovations of the churches in his village in Goa as well as in Kanpur, the town in North India where the family had settled. Most importantly, it was stressed that he was a man of principle, known for his honest dealings with everyone. Thus, early in my life, there was this emphasis on our Catholic identity and to live by our principles which stressed the need to be fair and honest in our attitudes to and engagement with others. As well, there was the underlying element of pioneering, adventure and successful achievement. Certainly, the experiences of being a displaced person, living within and, at the same time, outside the community, prepared me well for the experiences of my later migration to Australia.

In the fifties and sixties, as I was growing up in Kanpur, the number of westernized Christians dwindled almost into insignificance as families and friends migrated to the UK, Australia and Canada. As a result, the Roman Catholic community became a relatively closely-knit group of people who gathered at the local, English speaking, Catholic Church each Sunday where the parishioners were mostly anglicized people of Indian and Anglo Indian origins. It was within the confines of this shrinking community that my parents, themselves, educated by the Belgian Jesuits and different European nuns respectively, were active in handing on the Catholic faith tradition to us, immersed as it was in a British Indian culture. Thus, we were brought up with an intense awareness that our Catholic heritage made us different from the wider society which was composed largely of Hindus, many Muslims and a few other much smaller religious groups like ourselves. In particular, with Christianity, the difference was more emphasized since it was perceived as a western religion by the rest of society. This was reinforced by the fact that most of us wore western clothes, spoke in English and could not speak very good Hindi. Through informal teaching and through the modelling of particular behaviours including religious practices, my parents' influence on my own religious and spiritual thinking and practice was much stronger in the formation of my spiritual beliefs and values. For instance, daily or weekly attendance at Mass, singing in the choir and becoming the church organist in my late teenage years were activities encouraged by my mother who was a deeply committed Catholic woman. From my father I learnt that when one was born into a privileged background, one had a responsibility to others, that is, one always treated others with respect and dignity and assisted those in need to the best of one's ability.

Moreover, my relationship with the Church was shaped by the learning and thinking of four generations in my family of tertiary educated people which meant that asking challenging questions about different issues and aspects of the Tradition was part of my experience. Therefore, I learnt to become discerning or even critical, about certain actions of the hierarchical Church that could not be aligned with my understanding of Christian teachings, to stand up for my principles and to speak out for the less privileged in order to right a wrong. It is, largely, such practices, generated by notions of justice and service, which have stayed with me as foundational to my way of being in the world. For instance, elemental aspects of my role as teacher and parent respectively, have been to help my students and my sons to believe in, value and think for themselves, to discover and use their strengths wisely, to accept and try to overcome their weaknesses, and to treat others with respect.

Educational Background

I arrived in Australia in 1969 as a new graduate and spent the next twenty-five years as a Music, Drama and English secondary school teacher, mostly in the Catholic education system which, today, is responsible for educating at least a fifth of the school going population. I found Australians to be a welcoming people. There were few Indian migrants and, since I shared with Australians a colonial culture, I found that I fitted into Anglo-Australian society very easily. In fact, I believe some found it almost a novelty that I was so different to their expectations because I did not fit the stereotypical images they had of Indians in terms of language and culture. In recent years, this kind of welcome and the relations between new migrants and other Australians has changed. Most Australians are 'tolerant' of the newcomers but their attitudes remain at that level. They rarely move on to engagement and acceptance in terms of including these people into their family and social circles. Arguably, the lack of social integration is one reason why the 'Living in Harmony' and the Diversity and Social Cohesion Program were introduced by the Australian Government where the main aims were to promote cohesion in Australian society.

Leadership in Catholic education. For myself, it was when I moved into senior leadership in Catholic schools in the nineties, that I began to identify a particular characteristic amongst Anglo Australian Catholics who were in leadership in Catholic education. They were people who were fourth and fifth generation Australian and whose ancestors had composed the fabric of early Australian society. Through an ongoing study of the situation, I discovered that the Catholic Church in Australia had its origins in 19th Century Irish Catholicism. Many of those early Irish had come to the country as convicts and later, they were people escaping the Great Famine and extreme poverty. At that time, since the British were the governing authorities, some of the divisions evident between the English and the Irish in their homelands, influenced the relationships between the British and Irish in the new country. With such attitudes being transported to the colonies, it is not surprising that Catholics became a marginalized people.

In their attempt to maintain their religious identity, the Catholic community founded their own schools and this only served to distance the Catholics even more from the rest of society. Most of them have spent their lives within Catholic education, first in schools, then in Teacher's College and finally, back into schools. Not surprisingly, this has led to a certain insularity implicit in the way they view the world which impacts on the way they engage with others. Leaders who had little engagement with the wider Australian community in their formative years, also had little understanding of how to engage with Catholics who came from multicultural backgrounds. A further factor was that the majority of leadership roles were held by males. So, for myself as a woman, a migrant from a non-European country working in a Catholic school system dominated by Anglo-Australian leadership, in a Catholic church dominated by a male hierarchical structure, I found myself, at this later stage of my career, once again experiencing a level of marginalization in the world of Catholic Education leadership.

Doctoral Studies. Another factor that influenced the direction I took in my professional life came about in 1991 when I embarked on part-time doctoral studies in Goan music. It was almost like a 'heavenly intervention'. I was awarded funds to travel to Goa, and, in the same week, we received a letter from a distant cousin who had returned to Goa and renovated the ancestral home . He extended to us an invitation to visit. I then spent three months in Goa, collecting my data, enjoying the incredible hospitality of my cousins and experiencing the simplicity of village life where the pace of life was leisurely, the sense of community was strong so that people knew and looked out for each other, and the fast, consumeristic life of a materialistic world was a long way away. It produced in me a sense of belonging and place. It was also the first time, I experienced India as a place where Hindus were accepting of Christianity, to the extent that some would actually pause and pay reverence to a statue of St Anthony or Our Lady that would be enshrined in the boundary wall or gate belonging to a Christian home. More importantly, I had time and space to become reflective and responsive to a world beyond the vicinity of fulltime work and the life of a single parent which had consumed me for so many years. I realized that my own religiosity and spirituality had become enmeshed in tiresome schedules and meaningless rituals, engaged in through force of habit rather than with thoughtful observance. My religious practice was on automatic pilot because, in my absolute state of weariness, the God I had come to know in my childhood as the Unseen Presence had also become an Unfelt Presence. My experience in Goa was one of spiritual renewal.

From Musicology to Religious Education. Returning to Australia, the rigorous demands of my professional life as the Curriculum Coordinator in a large Catholic secondary college, as well as the responsibilities of single-parenting my teenage sons, encouraged me to shift my doctoral focus from Musicology to Religious Education Curriculum since it was easier to research in a field that related to my professional work. My reasons for making this quite drastic change from my previous research areas was, both, a result of my Goan experience which had been like a spiritual awakening, and a response to the situation where the majority of Year 12 students displayed distinctly negative attitudes to Religious Education (de Souza, 2010).

Over the course of my doctoral studies, I became increasingly intrigued by a frequent mantra offered by the students: I am not religious, I am spiritual. It is this concept that has had a major impact on my subsequent teaching and research in Religious Education. It led me to articulating the need for religious educators to distinguish differences between religion and spirituality, as well as recognizing a spiritual dimension to all learning, including learning in religious education. The pluralistic, global context of many countries today requires that children should learn about other belief systems that exist in their societies. Accordingly, I have examined an interspiritual approach that will promote learning about different world views and belief systems. This approach seeks to enhance the relational dimension of the individual student and promote their sense of connectedness to themselves, to others, to the world and to a Transcendent Other.

CONTEMPORARY RELIGIOUS EDUCATION FOR PLURALISTIC
CLASSROOMS IN A GLOBAL WORLD

My initial research following my doctoral studies focused on understanding spirituality and what the relationship was between religion and spirituality. It soon became clear to me that explaining spirituality could no longer be restricted to theological and religious fields. In an effort to try and find answers to issues and problems, particularly with young people, other disciplines which were concerned with different aspects of human wellbeing and development were examining spirituality as one element that connected individuals to their communities and to the world. For instance, I discovered a significant body of literature that examined an understanding of spirituality as relational. From a neuroscientific perspective, others claimed that there was nothing magical about mystical experience since it was really an 'uplifting sense of genuine spiritual union with something larger than the self' (Newberg et al., 2001, p. 101). They concluded that 'humans are natural mystics blessed with an inborn genius for effortless self-transcendence' (p. 113) and that like all experiences, moods, and perceptions, these unitary states are made possible by neurological function.

Curriculum and pedagogical implications

My own early work was influenced by the notion of connectedness and initial findings from my early research supported the concept that spirituality was relational (de Souza, Cartwright, & McGilp, 2004). I concluded that humans pass along a relational continuum where, at one end, they are separate or even alienated from Other[1] but as they move along the continuum, the barriers between Self and Other disappear. Most people are moving somewhere along that continuum where they feel closely connected to people like themselves – family, community and so on. Some people reach a point where they experience a sense of connectedness to people different from themselves which could be expressed as a level of empathy for Other. Logically, the other end of the continuum moves past the point of relationality into a state where Self and Other merge into the whole (de Souza, 2011). I referred to this state as Ultimate Unity and aligned this state with being part of the whole, of returning to the centre, of becoming *one with Other*. Certainly, I believe that growing up in India which has, possibly, the oldest multicultural and multifaith society in the world may have something to do with my philosophy where accepting and learning from people who are different is an important facet of education, especially in the contemporary world where different faiths and cultures have become next door neighbours in so many parts of the world, and classrooms are filled with students who have different belief systems.

It is necessary to clarify what I mean by this state of Ultimate Unity. In my view this means that the Whole is made up of Difference where everyone and everything has a place/function/meaning. For instance the human body is composed of different parts but these parts have an essential place and function in order to form the whole. Similarly, *unity is composed of diverse elements*. This understanding, that spirituality is about human relationality and that humans are relational creatures, points to spirituality as an innate trait of Being. If we then consider the human person as a rational, emotional and spiritual being, it naturally follows that spirituality must have a role in the learning process. In fact, most western education programs in the past several decades have pursued cognitive learning through outcomes based education[2] with little attention being given to the affective and spiritual dimensions so that they have seriously denied the child an education that addresses the whole person.

Pedagogical strategies and aims. My research, has led to the development of a learning approach that recognizes the complementarity of the cognitive, affective and spiritual dimensions of learning and I have attempted to align these dimensions with rational, emotional and spiritual intelligences and with the processes of perceiving (or sensing), thinking (cognitive), feelings (affective) and intuiting/ imagining/creating (spiritual) (de Souza, 2004, 2005, 2006). In the end, it enables students to find value and meaning in their life experiences and helps them to know themselves and their place in the world.

In other words, when teaching religious education in school programs, it is important that teachers recognize these three dimensions of learning and articulate corresponding outcomes for these dimensions – cognitive, affective and spiritual.

For instance, a cognitive learning outcome may state:

By the end of this unit students will be able to: define, describe, recall, recognize, illustrate, interpret, explain, apply, relate, demonstrate, distinguish, analyse, compare, contrast, formulate, communicate, articulate, plan, evaluate, judge …

These verbs clearly identify knowledge and skills and are within the student's conscious control and physicality.

An affective learning outcome may state:

> By the end of this unit students will have had the opportunity to: show awareness of, experience –, accept, appreciate, participate, display interest, become involved, respond to, feel valued, reflect, show enjoyment of, show enthusiasm for, display an attitude of …

These verbs are linked to feelings, values and experiences that arise from below the surface of the conscious mind. They may be demonstrated through physical action such as movement, speech and/or facial and bodily expression.

Finally a spiritual learning outcome may state:

> By the end of this unit student will have had the opportunity to: develop a sensitivity to, empathize, develop compassion, reflect inwardly, experience –, accept responsibility, contemplate, meditate, develop self-knowledge, connect with, show a commitment to, dream, imagine, create, wonder, be peaceful, develop some resilience, change existing attitudes or behaviours …

These verbs suggest movement from the non-conscious mind, arising from the heart and soul of the student, usually something that is out of their immediate control and it may be reflected through speech, action, facial and bodily movement.

An Example: Applying the Learning Approach That Addresses the Cognitive, Affective and Spiritual Dimensions

An example of how this process may work is shown here in relation to teaching the topic – Kingdom of God – in a Middle Primary classroom, that is for children of 8-10 years.

The following learning outcomes may be stated:

Cognitive: By the end of the lesson students will
 – *Read the text of the Kingdom of God (this topic is from the religious education text book prescribed by the Catholic Education Office, Melbourne);*
 – *Demonstrate their understanding of what happens in the Kingdom of God;*
 – *Show what they understand by the terms 'peace and happiness'.*

Affective: By the end of the lesson students will have the opportunity to
 – *Share with others moments of 'peace and happiness' that they can recall in their own lives;*
 – *Appreciate that peace and happiness are important elements in families and in classrooms.*

Spiritual: By the end of the lesson students will have the opportunity to

MARIAN DE SOUZA

> – *Experience moments of peace and happiness;*
> – *Contemplate how they can contribute to peace and happiness in their families and classrooms.*

The activities employed to achieve these outcomes could be:

Activity 1:   Read and Discuss – Students to read Scriptural passage: Matthew 5:1-12

> – *What is peace and happiness (these terms are taken from the text)*
> – *What does it mean for them to live in peace and happiness in their families, with their friends.*
> – *What does it mean for the world to live in peace and happiness.*
> – *Why is it important for people to be peaceful and happy.*

Activity 2:   Musical activity

Each child will make up a sentence that explains what being peaceful and happy means to them (see below).

The sentence should go for 8 beats – Count in:

```
        1     2     3     4       5      6     7     8
        /     /     /   (rest),   /      /     /   (rest).
e.g. When I eat my tea    –    with my fami -  ly    –
```

Or

```
      1       2      3      4      5       6      7        8
      /       /      /      /      /       /      /     (rest).
  When the sky gets pink or red, it makes me feel so glad    –
```

Activity 3:   Drama activity

> *Blessed are the peacemakers for they will be called children of God (Matt 5:9)*

Students in groups can create freeze frames of people in their families, their communities or the world that show peacemakers. Each group gets into a particular space and then presents their frame one after the other Perhaps have one student announce at the end of each frame:

> *and they will be called children of God.*   Or

> *for this is the kingdom of God.*

206

Activity 4:   Group research work

Students may be asked to collect a variety of pictures or video clips of children who are 'peacemakers' from around the world. They could either make a collage of their own pictures or write a few sentences on the information they gather through their search which they can present to the rest of the class.

Activity 5:   Reflective activity

Students will respond to the question 'How can I contribute to peace and happiness in my family/classroom. They can write or draw their response in their books.

These learning activities involve thinking, feeling, intuiting, imagining and creating. Thus, they address cognitive, affective and spiritual learning and they directly relate to the learning outcomes articulated above.

As can be seen, for the affective and spiritual learning outcomes, opportunities have been provided through the different activities to encourage the achievement of this learning but it is important to recognize that both the affective and spiritual learning outcomes may be achieved beyond the time and space of the classroom lesson and no claims may be made about if or when they will be achieved. All that a teacher can do is plan to incorporate learning experiences that will allow this kind of learning (affective and spiritual) to happen.

It is useful to create unexpected, different and aesthetically pleasing learning environments. Learning environments should be chosen, both, within and outside the classroom, reaching out into the local and global community where possible *encouraging students to recognize that their individual gifts are not theirs alone but are there for them to use for the benefit of themselves and their communities.* Such learning requires time – time for thinking and reflecting, time for imagining and creating, time for intuiting and problem solving and time for just being still and silent.

THE IMPLICATIONS OF RELIGIOUS PLURALISM AND GLOBALIZATION FOR CONTEMPORARY RELIGIOUS EDUCATION FOR ALL STUDENTS

Australia, like many other western countries, has become a pluralistic society, contextualized by a globalized world and dominated by progressive communication technology. As such, educational programs, including religious education curriculum, now and in the future must be responsive to these factors if they are to be relevant and meaningful in preparing students for the societies in which they will live.

Religious education which restricts the content to the mainstream or traditional faith traditions is no longer appropriate in societies that are both multi-faith as well as secular. Instead, a study of religious and secular belief systems is more relevant because, at some stage in their lives, most of today's students are likely to encounter and engage with people who have a range of different beliefs and practices. It becomes imperative, therefore, that they have a sound understanding of the diversity of beliefs and practices that exist in their communities and that the barriers between different belief systems are removed or, certainly, made less significant.

This is where the spiritual dimension of religious education has a role. The foundational concept to this learning approach is that spirituality is innate, that is, it is about connectedness, the experience of transcendence, of being part of the whole, and about living as a relational Being. Accordingly, it is important that programs address this dimension of students' lives to help them realize that that they are not separate from Other, and that they may recognize something of themselves in Other and something of Other in themselves. As well, they may be encouraged to recognize the divine core at the heart and soul of every individual, and that it is that core that connects them to Other. They may even reach an understanding that Other's final destination could be the same as their own.

To this end, I propose an interspiritual approach to teaching and learning religious and secular belief systems as an appropriate one for today's students. It will focus on the connectedness between all individuals and have the potential to promote deeper knowledge and understanding amongst students which could lead to changed attitudes and levels of acceptance, thereby enhancing social cohesion and the wellbeing of communities. This idea of unity has also been supported more recently by Armstrong in her contention that the Ultimate Reality was not a personalized god (Armstrong, 2009, p. 19). Rather, it was a transcendent mystery, the depths of which could never be comprehended and that while different faith traditions have their own 'unique genius and distinctive vision: each its peculiar flaws' there are some fundamental principles common to most faith traditions: 'when one loses all sense of duality' (p. 31).

CONCLUDING THOUGHTS

On reflection, it is not difficult for me to see the connections between my own life experiences and the evolving philosophy that has generated and guided my educational research and practice in religious education and spirituality. Having a foot in both an Eastern and Western culture brought me different levels of understandings of the two. As well, growing up in an ancient pluralistic society like India and then moving to Australia as a young adult where I observed and participated in the development of a multicultural and multifaith society over a relatively short period of time, brought me into contact with different world views and religious practices. These experiences increased my awareness of how important it was to learn about other cultures and religions. Knowledge and understanding of different belief systems, potentially, promotes respect between people and removes the chance that some people may respond to others as if they were stereotypes rather than individuals.

Finally, the whole experience of being a marginalized person at the edges of a society or community provided me with some understanding of how marginalized people may think, feel and act. However, my background of privilege during my childhood which allowed my access to the upper stratas of society produced in me an interesting mix of knowing what it is to be a displaced person but at the same time having the confidence to wear this displacement quite comfortably! It is the combination of these experiences that directed my energies into finding ways to educate and enthuse children to learn about others and accept them as individuals.

Following the above discussion I proposed that an interspiritual approach to teaching and learning different belief systems is appropriate for contemporary society; we need to address the spiritual dimension of the student to promote understanding and appreciation of diversity as the first step towards acceptance and inclusion of Other. If students are to learn to live with and appreciate cultural otherness and religious diversity, they need to recognize that different belief systems are needed to complement each other in the human search for an Absolute Reality, or as I describe it, the state of Ultimate Unity.

NOTES

[1] I use a capital O for Other to collectively personify all others who are different from Self.
[2] Outcomes based learning in Australia focuses on the achievement of learning outcomes that identify particular knowledge and skills. See Donelly's (2007) article which provides a critical overview of the way Outcomes based education has been implemented and practised in Australia on: http://www.iier.org.au/iier17/donnelly.html.

REFERENCES

Armstrong, K. (2009). *The case for god.* Great Britain: The Bodley Head.

Culliford, L. (2011). *The psychology of spirituality. An introduction.* London, UK: Jessica Kingsley Publishers.

de Souza, M., (2004). Teaching for effective learning in religious education: A discussion of the perceiving, thinking, feeling and intuiting elements in the learning process. *Journal of Religious Education.*52:3, pp. 22-30.

de Souza, M. (2005). Engaging the mind, heart and soul of the student in religious education: Teaching for meaning and connection. *Journal of Religious Education, 53*(4), 40-47.

de Souza, M (2006). Rediscovering the spiritual dimension in education: promoting a sense of self and place, meaning and purpose in learning. In M. de Souza, K. Engebretson, G. Durka, R. Jackson, & A. McGrady (eds.), *International handbook of the religious, moral and spiritual dimensions of education,* 2 volumes (pp. 1127-1140). Dordrecht, The Netherlands: Springer Academic Publishers.

de Souza, M. (2010). *Year 12 students' perceptions of their religious education programs: Implications for curriculum development.* Germany: LAP Lambert Academic Publishing.

de Souza, M. (2011). Promoting inter-spiritual education in the classroom: Exploring the perennial philosophy as a useful strategy to encourage freedom of religious practice and belief. *Journal of Religious Education, 59*(1), 27-37.

de Souza, M., Cartwright, P., & McGilp, E. J. (2004). The perceptions of young people who live in a regional city in Australia of their spiritual wellbeing: Implications for education. *Journal of Youth Studies, 7*(2), 155-172.

Newberg, A., D'Aquili, E., & Rause, V. (2001). *Why God won't go away: Brain science and the biology of belief.* NewYork: Ballantine Books.

MARIAN DE SOUZA

AFFILIATIONS

Marian de Souza
School of Religious Education
Faculty of Education
Australian Catholic University, Ballarat Australia

WOLFRAM WEISSE

INTERRELIGIOUS DIALOGUE

Contextual and Mutual Learning

INTRODUCTION

*Sometimes you need to move to another place to understand what is
special about your own situation.*

I was born in Frankfurt am Main shortly after the Second World War. My parents
moved to Hamburg soon after my birth, so Hamburg is my home port – literally
and figuratively. My father would have liked me to go to Law School, but at the
time I was thinking more about studying Sinology – it had to be something
unusual. Theology became that unusual subject – a real surprise because I come
from a typical Hamburg family where 'we are religious without having to go to
church every Sunday'. My grandfather and I went to church, so we had something
in common, and after the service we walked home and my grandfather told me the
most interesting stories of his childhood and his life. Thus church and stories
combined into a special experience for both of us. As a teenager, openly critical
priests and pastors gave the youth group I belonged to enough space and
opportunity to experience new forms of religiosity in our parish. We introduced a
special form of service with strong elements of dialogue to create an alternative to
the usual monological and hierarchically structured sermon delivered by a pastor.
And we learned a new approach to the Bible, for example through the Sermon on
the Mount with its promise to the poor, the commandment to love your enemy and
the impossibility of serving two masters at once. That was a decisive experience
for my personal faith: to feel supported, safe and carried, but not to fall asleep. To
wake up, look at humanity and approach others. It also defined my choice to study
Theology, initially in Hamburg, later in Montpellier. Sometimes you need to move
to another place to understand what is special about your own situation.

From Another Perspective

At the 'Faculté Libre de Théologie Protestante' in Montpellier, where I graduated
in the academic year 1966/67, everything was different from what I had
experienced in Germany: Here, Protestantism was a minority religion with a
history of suppression in Catholic-dominated France and there was no church tax
or other form of public privilege, which meant the pastors had to be paid by the

*I. ter Avest (ed.), On the Edge: (Auto)biography and Pedagogical Theories on Religious
Education, 211–222.*

parishes – often earning lower wages than skilled labourers. Christians from all conceivable countries lived here. Some were from the former French colonies, many from Madagascar, and many brought with them completely unfamiliar practices and views of Christianity. I gained an impression of the many forms a Protestant Christianity in the reformed tradition could take, and an insight into Catholic devotion at the seminary in Montpellier – all that in the secular atmosphere of a Mediterranean university town. That experience has significantly strengthened my awareness of the diversity of Christianity and my interest in the connection between religion, context and culture.

Studying in Montpellier was idyllic: all the students lived on the first and second floor of a huge country house surrounded by a garden on the outskirts of town. The dining room was on the ground floor: breakfasts were frugal, but meals with several courses were always served for lunch and dinner. The activities took place on the ground floor; groups in the seminars and the lectures were small, and most lecturers invited the students for dinner at their home once every academic year.

But the idyll nonetheless showed cracks: the increasingly intense conflict in the former French colony of Vietnam was sharply criticised by some students, earlier than in other parts of Europe.

Back in Hamburg

When I returned to Hamburg in the summer of 1967, student protest was slowly starting there, too. I was actively involved in a group of theology students which was created in 1968 and worked on urgent issues neglected at university and in society in 'basic groups'. I belonged to a group that addressed Christianity and internationalism in the third world.

At the time, awareness of the existence of global structures which were useful to some, but for others represented repression, was slowly growing. Alongside seminars, we studied new literature on the third world and its dependence on the first world. At the same time, we became active, calling for a 'positive strike' for the last week of the winter term 1968/69. We went – with a queasy feeling, but convinced of our cause – to the seminars and lectures of all professors and called on the students to leave and instead come to our working groups to deal with the 'truly important' issues. Those groups were scheduled to meet not only in the last week of term, but for the whole semester break. And so we did, and prepared ourselves for the summer term with critical reading.

Our group on internationalism and Christianity in the third world registered for the post-graduate seminar of the then Professor in missionary and ecumenical sciences, Hans Jochen Margull. We only heard later that our 'block' registration was considered a possible threat to the peaceful conduct of the seminar, but it turned out differently. Hans Jochen Margull reacted to our identification with the subject with an offer that completely surprised us; whether we would not wish to obtain our doctorates with him in a special field of research that was already being developed? Of course we wanted to, and he offered us to analyse the 'self-conception and function of Christianity in communities overseas' in various countries in Africa, Asia and Latin America. From 1971-1974 I worked on a subject about which hardly any information was available in Germany then: issues of church, racism and anti-racism in South Africa.

I cannot discuss the results of my analyses here, but suffice it to say that I learned a lot during my stay in South Africa. As a theology student who – like many others – rejected traditional types of Christianity as obsolete in the years around 1968, my perspective broadened and changed. Not only the conservatives, but in particular those hoping for liberation were encouraged and supported through song and prayer, Bible studies and church services. Personal devotion, traditional church forms and public action for justice actually went together well and in effect were an elixir of life to many Christians who hoped for the abolition of apartheid in South Africa and took action to achieve that goal.

AWARENESS WORK

Journalism

In the research group working with Hans Jochen Margull, we considered it our main responsibility to also publicise our knowledge about the situation in the third world. For this, we saw a key possibility in a so-called 'peace march' some of us had organised in 1970. Participants pledged a set amount of money per kilometre to sponsors for projects in the Third World. We realised that this was good, but not enough on its own. At the time there was not enough reliable information about the third world and little to read in the press. We drew the consequences and daringly started our own magazine: EPK – Entwicklungs-Politische Korrespondenz (Writings on Political Developments).

Our magazine was the first in Germany to publish texts by Steve Biko and interviews with many exponents of South-African liberation theology, which I had brought back from South Africa. The black people – I learned in South Africa – read the Bible as explaining why they could not remain in the situation they were in. They had transferred the message of liberation to their lives. And I learned that the Bible can be directly applied to life when it gives people hope. That was a new perspective on my own religion for me. You sometimes need to move elsewhere to experience what is special in your individual situation.

We opened new perspectives with our analyses of the relationship between religion and politics in South Africa. To balance out the great expense of a self-funded and self-edited magazine, the work in the EPK had two great advantages: firstly, it enabled us to contribute to public debate on themes that were increasingly discussed. Alongside other professional groups, many teachers, magazines and TV editors were also EPK subscribers. I also had to write readable texts which were based on a long thought process and strong analysis work quickly and not only focus on finishing my thesis. My South African experiences brought me closer to the question I increasingly ask myself: whether and how dialogue between people of different faiths and different opinions can become possible.

We wanted to pursue 'normal' jobs after graduation, something we used to call 'basic level'. To me, that meant going to school as a teacher.

School and Teaching Materials

From 1975-1982 I taught at a Gymnasium in Hamburg-Barmbek, a traditional working class area which at the time was attended by a majority of pupils from the poorer social classes. I had to teach a lot there, but could also learn a lot. We could freely discuss problems and explore for new educational and thematic perspectives in the young teaching staff which at the start of my employment was still in its formative phase. That was a vital learning experience for me: working on project-centered lessons, interdisciplinary planning and teaching, holding conferences and organising and evaluating parents' days. This allowed for a cooperative approach in a profession that had previously been characterised by divides in the teachers' room and a focus on factual instruction. To me, the concrete insight into this world with its structural difficulties was helpful to understand and plan learning processes not only based on rational requirements, but also on social reality. Numerous pupils and their parents, too, looked to me for advice on questions of their daily life. At the time, I developed respect for the courage and scholastic performance of most of the pupils, considering the huge problems they were faced with in their home environment.

I also had good experiences with writing and testing out teaching units in my own classroom that I published later. After seven years in school, I wanted to return to university and accepted the offer of Fulbert Steffensky to work as research assistant. Some thought at the time that this was an exit, but I personally saw the opportunity to research freely while teaching only little as liberating. And it was.

BACK TO UNIVERSITY

Social Ethics and Education in the International Context: Ecumenical Learning and the Unity of the Churches

After my time as a teacher, I returned to university in 1982. My position was based in the Educational Studies department where religious education was valued and where a good, friendship-based co-operation soon started, e.g. with Reiner Lehberger, Ursula Neumann and Helmut Peukert. I also developed a friendship network in the Theology department, e.g. with Fulbert Steffensky, Matthias Kroeger and Dorothee Sölle.

Two subjects were central to my research; ecumenical learning and the social-ethical based precursor of the World Council of Churches, the movement called 'Life and Work'.

The concept of Ecumenical Learning had originated in the mid-70s and was developed in the 1980s. I felt it was natural to engage in this area, because Ecumenical Learning stood at the intersection of my current activities in the field of ecumenical theology, teaching and material development of international Christianity. It helped that Klaus Gossmann of the Comenius Institute invited me to a work group on Ecumenical Learning where all those working on the subject came together. I also considered for a while to write my 'Habilitation' on the subject, but I had the impression that the subject was less suitable and also, that I was more attracted by another question: the reconstruction of the movement Life and Work. I therefore focused on the latter while continuing to be active in the circle dealing with Ecumenical Learning, and also gave my 'Habilitation' presentation on the subject (Weisse, 1989).

I have never regretted that I focused on reconstructing the movement 'Life and Work'. My historical studies facilitated source work, which was required due to lack of previous research. The subject area also posed questions relating to education, but the main objective was inspiring the actors, after the collapse of the national Christian politics of the powers involved in the First World War, to work towards peace and justice on a theological and institutional basis and to help avert future wars with recourse to religion. Life and Work brought the Christians of the Western world together after WWI, and it led to a profound and controversial discussion about the understanding of the Kingdom of God – a resource that can be used today and that was the subject of my next publication (Weisse, 1997).

I submitted my 'Habilitation' on Life and Work (Weisse, 1991) at the University of Heidelberg. I had stayed in Hamburg the whole time, and there obtained the venia legendi both in ecumenical theology and religious education, with special reference to interreligious dialogue.

I will focus on two areas below: international research in relation to post-apartheid South Africa and religious education in Hamburg and at the international level.

Social Upheaval and Religion – South Africa from Apartheid to Democracy

When the South Africa committee of the Protestant Church in Germany asked me to carry out a study on the new developments in schools, religious communities and the society of South Africa in the early 1990s, it marked a return to research projects on South Africa continuing to the present, though with different focal points.

The analysis of the new thinking on Religious Education in South Africa was its starting point. After a national Christian education had prevailed for more than 50 years, there now were strong efforts to design and introduce a Religious Education in which the different religions represented in South Africa would be involved. An inter-disciplinary group at the University of Cape Town – including Gordon Mitchell and David Chidester – was busy establishing a new start for religious education in South Africa. In this – under different conditions than in Hamburg – ideas of dialogue and interreligiosity played a big part. This provided the foundation for a productive co-operation between religious education in Hamburg and Cape Town, which is still continuing today.

The participation in a 'Sonderforschungsbereich' (Centre of Collaborative Research) at the University of Hamburg titled 'Change in African societies and coping' which was funded from 1999 by the German Research Foundation was very important for me. I was in charge of research on South Africa as representative speaker and led two projects which addressed the role of the Dutch Reformed Church and of Muslim Communities in the transition from apartheid to democracy in South Africa (see Chidester, Tayob, & Weisse, 2004).

In the meantime, the Dutch Reformed Church in South Africa had undergone dramatic change. Its clinging to power had achieved the opposite of what had been hoped for: The close relationship between church and government had resulted in a marginalisation of the church with the end of the state power supporting it.

The previous national Christian education in schools was discredited and led to the abolition of religious education as a separate subject in South African state schools. Thus, the new plans came too late, but were still useful in the context of an overall subject called 'Life Orientation'.

RELIGIOUS EDUCATION FOR ALL

Parallel to my international research, focused on South Africa, I worked intensively on the development of a dialogical and interreligious 'Religion für Alle' ('Religious Education for All') in Hamburg. Conceptual studies were undertaken using empirical social science research methods which were new to me. In the early 1990s, doubt in other federal states of Germany grew whether the Hamburg model of religious education, where all pupils attended class together irrespective of their different religious and philosophical orientations, could actually work, whether the teachers would try to advocate and apply that concept, whether the pupils would not get confused, etc. The objective was to examine more thoroughly, using scientific methods, what pupils and teachers thought, wanted and practiced in the context of Religious Education. In co-operation with the sociologist Gerhard Kleining we carried out much research in Hamburg schools in the course of my research project 'Youth-Religion-Education in a multicultural society marked by social disparity' from 1993 (Weisse, 1999). It clearly demonstrated: teachers of different ages in different types of schools and stages in different areas of Hamburg stated that an alternative to 'Religious Education for All' was not an option for them. They did not want to divide the pupils by religion because the shared classes allowing an exchange of different religious views seemed appropriate at both a factual and didactic level (Knauth, Sandt, & Weisse 1994). However, they saw a deficiency in teacher training and in teaching materials, which did not – at the time – address such dialogue-based teaching sufficiently.

The pupils expressed more clearly than we expected that they found religious education in shared classes positive and more interesting than confessional segregation. In intensive teaching analyses, we found that the religiously and philosophically heterogeneous pupils were not confused at all, not even in the lower grades. Rather, they applied the various viewpoints with intensive interest in religious themes and intensive debates – also and especially amongst pupils of the same religion – on the practice, content and meaning of religion.

Conceptually I could follow on the experience and methods of dialogue analysis by Hans Jochen Margull in researching the question of an interreligious dialogue in religious education. During my doctoral research I knew about the dialogue activities of Margull only superficially – our group gained the impression that he moved away from our key theme of the self-conception and function of Christianity in the third world. This perception changed completely: In connection with religious education his premise has seemed very productive to me even until today because his starting point was not religious systems, but practiced religion and people in dialogue.

Over time, postgraduate researchers – Thorsten Knauth, Doerthe Vieregge and others – have produced a series of empirical analyses of Religious Education in Hamburg and the religiosity of youth with me. This has strengthened the dialogue-orientated 'Religious Education for all' approach in Hamburg and – fuelled by outside criticism – has made Religious Education in Hamburg more thoroughly researched than in any other federal state. The focus of the research was the religiosity of young people in Hamburg, aiming to come closer to those for whom education is designed.

The Hamburg 'Religious Education for all' could only withstand all outside storms and inner crises because many have critically and constructively supported and developed it further. Today, the experience with 'Religious Education for all' is so good that most Muslims, Jews, Buddhists, and Alevites actually do not want their children to receive separate Islamic Religious Education because the common experience and the exchange are more important to them.

The co-operation with professionals in religious education has had its permanent home since 1995 in the group 'interreligious education', which has retained its makeup throughout the discussion of complex and at times controversial subjects. Furthermore the adjustment of Religious Education was facilitated by the 'Religionspädagogische Sozietät' (Association for Religious Education), where all actors responsible for Religious Education in Hamburg are represented. This association was an innovation which I co-founded to discuss and align basic questions and problems of religious education from the perspective of all teacher training, continued and lifelong education, and the appointment of teachers through the involved institutions – university, teacher training institute, pedagogical-theological institute and school authority.

Finally, regarding the recognition of the Hamburg approach to religious education I should mention the public and political support it has received. One after another, all the parties of the federal state of Hamburg were convinced that Religious Education in Hamburg with its emphasis on inclusion and dialogue is appropriate for a cosmopolitan city because it can contribute to mutual understanding at school and in society (Weisse, 2003, 2008). The Hamburg model of Religious Education has also been explicitly praised several times by the 'Landesschulbeirat' (Federal School Advisory Board), in which all stakeholders in Hamburg are represented, for its dialogue orientation.

217

Furthermore, the opinions on Religious Education in other federal states began to change around the turn of the century. Whereas the Hamburg model was strongly criticised in the 1990s – which we in return did to confessional segregation – there is now a growing trend towards integrating matters of dialogue and interreligious understanding in teacher training at all German universities and schools.

RELIGION AND EDUCATION IN AN INTERNATIONAL CONTEXT

The start of the above-mentioned research project 'Youth – Religion – Education in a multicultural society marked by social disparities' already embraced international co-operation. When we started in 1993, we were the only ones in Germany trying to combine hermeneutical critical and empirical social science methods. We seized the opportunity to invite other interested academics to Hamburg on the occasion of a research symposium with South African colleagues, and the response was very positive. After we actively pursued Robert Jackson from Warwick/England, others also confirmed their participation, including Christo Lombard from Namibia, Trees Andree from the Netherlands and Geir Skeie from Norway. At the end of our conference it was suggested that we should establish a research forum for scientists from Europe and southern Africa which should meet every two to three years in our different countries under the name 'Interreligious and Intercultural Religious Education' (IRE). IRE now provides a forum for the exchange of European and South African experts who place great emphasis on empirical research.

This network also created support for concrete research projects we have carried out in the field of religious education. I will only name two projects here. The first one was about Islamic schools and the question whether these contribute to isolation or rather to stronger self-confidence and therefore openness to society and other religions. That research was part of a unified project in which I co-operated successfully with Abdulkader Tayob of the University of Cape Town and in which Inga Niehaus, a graduate of mine who studied the role of Islam in the transition to modern South Africa, in carrying out a comparative study of South African, Dutch and English Islamic schools (Tayob, Niehaus, & Weisse, 2011). Secondly, there was the REDCo project.

European Research: The REDCo Project

The large European research project REDCo should be mentioned here: 'Religion in Education. A Contribution to Dialogue or a Factor of Conflict in transforming societies of European countries'. It was very helpful here that I had established international contacts through the above-mentioned IRE as well as with other colleagues through conferences, etc.

The REDCo project was supported by the research department of the European Commission over a period of three years from March 2006 onwards. The project's main aim was to explore and compare the potentials and limitations of religion in the educational systems of selected European countries. Approaches that can contribute to making religion in education into a factor promoting dialogue in the context of European development were our main focus.

The wide religious and societal spectrum covered by our REDCo study is reflected in the range of countries involved in our research: Estonia, Russia, Norway, Germany, The Netherlands, England, France and Spain. The research group (consortium) was selected to include representatives from all these countries. All members had previously co-operated fruitfully. Their respective disciplines (theology, Islamic studies, education, religious education, sociology, political science and ethnology) complemented each other. In spite of a wide range of societal and pedagogical backgrounds, the research group held a common conviction: religion must be included in schools, as it is too important a factor in the social life and the coexistence of people with different cultural and religious backgrounds throughout Europe not to be addressed in the classroom. When studying religion, we did not focus on abstract belief systems or 'world religions' but concentrated on the religions and world-views as they are represented by their adherents themselves. With reference to E. Lévinas, we were studying 'neighbour religions' – the views of neighbours in classrooms, in the region, in the state, and throughout the continent. The world religions are, of course, present in the form of 'neighbour religions', and thus our approach permitted us to study them in their current forms and potentials for dialogue and conflict.

All our projects looked at religious education for school students in the 14-16-year age group in various countries. We combined analyses of concepts of Religious Education with the concrete views of pupils: We observed them, we interviewed them, we asked for written answers in questionnaires, and we analysed their interaction. With this combination, we were able to capture both the perspective from above and from below.

The REDCo project has considerably increased our knowledge about the willingness and possible reservations of youth in Europe to enter the interreligious and intercultural dialogue (see Knauth, Josza and Weisse 2009). We were surprised by the scope and the intensity of interest that young people openly showed for other religions and cultures in all the countries studied by us. And we were surprised and pleased that almost all young people – irrespective of the diversity of the countries involved in the project – spoke out in favour of the integration of religion in the tuition in public schools and, that where religious education is offered as a separate subject, thought it important to experience this and learn something about other religions with the opportunities given to them and thus promote the coexistence of people from different religions. Those results are a sound basis for further development (see Weisse, 2011).

Overall I can say that these three years of the REDCo project, including the preparatory phase and the processing phase until the present day, are among the most intense and best experiences of my professional life. The project managements in the participating countries were able to motivate 40 younger full or part-time researchers to build a network based on hard work and friendship. The combination of the experience of project leaders and the energy and creativity of younger scholars contributed greatly to the success of our research. For all the expected difficulties in personal interactions and factual debates between academics from eight different countries I can say: when problems occurred they proved manageable and could be productively resolved together.

In the REDCo period, my collegial friendship with Siebren Miedema was reinforced not least by the complementarity in our way of giving direction to such a large group of young researchers. Siebren Miedema and his colleagues contributed with excellence to both the REDCo project in general, and to the discussion of a 'Religious Education for All' (see ter Avest, Miedema, & Bakker, 2008).

The Academy of World Religions of the University of Hamburg

One of the issues addressed in the REDCo project, but not centrally studied, was the question of the necessary pluralisation of theologies at universities. We wish to contribute to this in Hamburg with the creation of the 'Akademie der Weltreligionen' (Academy of World Religions), an Academy that takes theories from the past seriously, questions the present practice and thus equips the new generation of teachers for creating a future of dialogue for all. This academy is supported by a group of scholars of Hamburg University, representing the subjects of sociology, economic sciences, political sciences, law, intercultural and interreligious education, the study of religion and ecumenical studies, Buddhist studies, Islamic studies and practical theology.

The Academy of World Religions – a department at the University of Hamburg – provides space for the anchoring and dialogical networking of theologies of the world religions in an academic context. Beyond Christianity, the Academy's research and courses develop theological resources for Islam, Judaism, Buddhism, Hinduism and Alevism, whereby the basis for a theology in the plural is created (see Weisse, 2009).

Reform-oriented theological approaches and the relation to living religiosity in Europe are the focus of research and teaching. Dialogue is central: the theologians at the Academy of World Religions are not independent from each other. Rather, they relate to each other in dialogue. The theological structures of the world religions are connected to each other to evaluate similarities and differences. This builds the basis for the scientific anchoring of interreligious dialogue. It also provides a prerequisite to further develop the teacher training for dialogical and inclusive religious education. Beyond this, the horizon on society is broadened at the Academy of World Religions: questions of interreligious dialogue are not only approached in their fundamental dimensions, but in relation to social issues in modern immigrant societies, to provide a practical contribution to coexistence in our multicultural and multireligious society.

Résumée: The Importance of Interreligious Dialogue

Talking to each other, starting the dialogue, is a prerequisite; dialogue in the sense of theory and practice being connected and faith and daily life related to each other. That is not the easiest road. It requires everyone not only to celebrate the similarities, but also – or rather, precisely – to cope with the differences. The road from the crusades to coexistence in Europe today is long. In our history we faced extremes where tolerance often was a foreign concept. Our aim now is to strengthen dialogue and understanding at both the academic and the societal level. There is no guarantee of success in dialogue: there are difficult and less difficult phases. Any religion, any faith contains a claim to absoluteness that excludes all others. But the proper distinction should be: my personal faith cannot be lived relatively; when I pray, I pray to the God I believe in without ifs or buts. But towards others, such absoluteness is inappropriate, as all religions have developed in connection with other religions: Christianity is unthinkable without Judaism, Islam without Christianity and Judaism. They share the story of their origins and many common themes. I wish I could turn talking about this into a culture, an interreligious culture, where the primary attention lies on what connects them whilst not losing sight of the differences. We would learn to continue the dialogue with the other also about the differences, to get to know the other and to understand ourselves better. You sometimes need to move elsewhere to experience what is special in your personal situation – I see that as an important task for the future of our subject of Religious Education.

REFERENCES

Avest, I. ter, Miedema, S., & Bakker, C. (2008). Getrennt oder zusammen leben in den Niederlanden oder: Die Bedeutung des interreligiösen Lebens. In W. Weisse (ed.), *Dialogischer Religionsunterricht in Hamburg: Positionen, Analysen und Perspektiven im Kontext Europas* (pp. 179-188). Muenster.

Chidester, D., Tayob, A., & Weisse, W. (eds.). (2004). *Religion, politics, and identity in a changing South Africa*. Religion and Society in Transition, Vol. 6. Muenster.

Knauth, T., Josza, D.-P., & Weisse, W. (eds.). (2009). *Religionsunterricht, Dialog und Konflikt: Analysen im Kontext Europas*. Muenster.

Knauth, T., Sandt, F.-O., & Weisse, W. (1994). Interkultureller Religionsunterricht in Hamburg: Erste empirische Erhebungen. In I. Lohmann & W. Weisse (eds.), *Dialog zwischen den Kulturen: Erziehungshistorische und religionspaedagogische Gesichtspunkte interkultureller Bildung* (pp. 217-232). Muenster.

Tayob, A., Niehaus, I., & Weisse, W. (eds.). (2011). *Muslim schools and education in South Africa and Europe*. Beitraege zu einer dialogischen Religionspaedagogik, Vol. 12. Muenster.

Weisse, W. (1989). Oekumenisches Lernen: Moeglichkeiten und Grenzen einer neueren paedagogischen Dimension. *Oekumenische Rundschau, 38*, 181-199.

Weisse, W. (1991). Praktisches Christentum und Reich Gottes: Die oekumenische Bewegung Life and Work 1919-1937. *Kirche und Konfession: Veroeffentlichungen des Konfessionskundlichen Instituts des Evangelischen Bundes*, 31. Goettingen.

Weisse, W. (1997). *Reich Gottes: Hoffnung gegen Hoffnungslosigkeit*. Goettingen.

Weisse, W. (ed.). (1999). *Vom Monolog zum Dialog. Ansaetze einer dialogischen Religionspaedagogik* (2nd revised edition of (1996) *Jugend – Religion – Unterricht, Beitraege zu einer dialogischen Religionspaedagogik*, 1). Muenster.

Weisse, W. (2003). Difference without discrimination: Religious education as a field of learning for social understanding? In R. Jackson (ed.), *International Perspectives on Citizenship, Education and Religious Diversity* (pp. 191-208). London: Routledge Falmer.

Weisse, W. (ed.). (2008). *Dialogischer Religionsunterricht in Hamburg: Positionen, Analysen und Perspektiven im Kontext Europas*. Muenster.

Weisse, W. (ed.). (2009). *Theologie im Plural: Eine akademische Herausforderung*. Religionen im Dialog, Vol. 1. Muenster.

Weisse, W. (2011). Reflections on the REDCo project. *British Journal of Religious Education, 33*(2), 1-15.

AFFILIATIONS

Wolfram Weisse
Director of the 'Academy of World Religions' of
Hamburg University, Germany